Unionizing the Armed Forces

Unionizing
the Armed Forces

Edited by
Ezra S. Krendel and Bernard Samoff

University of Pennsylvania Press / 1977

CI   b+T- BAP

Library of Congress Cataloging in Publication Data

Main entry under title:

Unionizing the Armed Forces.

    Includes bibliographical references and index.
    1. Military unions -- United States--Addresses,
essays, lectures. 2. Trade-unions--Government
employees--United States--Addresses, essays, lectures.
I. Krendal, Ezra S. II. Samoff, Bernard, 1914-
UH743.u54   331.88'11'35500973   77-75618
ISBN 0-8122-7727-9

Table of Contents

Foreword

This book had its origin in late 1972 in a conversation between Ezra Krendel and Wallace Sinaiko, Program Director, Manpower Research and Advisory Services, Office of Naval Research. In a discussion of manpower problems that an all-volunteer navy might meet in the coming decade, Ezra Krendel suggested military unionization, although insignificant at the moment, might have important implications for military planners in the future. A proposal was prepared by Ezra Krendel and submitted to the Office of Naval Research. Although the concept of a military union was greeted with apprehension by the reviewers, who were both uniformed and nonuniformed employees of the United States Navy, there was agreement that the Navy needed to know more about the issues. As a result, on 1 May 1973 the Office of Naval Research entered into Contract No. N00014-67-A-0216-0029 with the Wharton School of the University of Pennsylvania to study military unions. Dr. Martin A. Tolcott served as the Office of Naval Research scientific officer on the project. The principal investigator was Ezra S. Krendel; the coinvestigator was Dr. William Gomberg; Dr. Charles R. Perry and Messrs. Michael E. Sparrough, Roger Fradin, Jack L. Calkins, David R. Clarke and Mark Stevens were associates. Capt. Malvern E. Soper, USN, Professor of Naval Science at the University of Pennsylvania and Capt. William M. Braybrook, USN, (Ret.) both gave freely of their time and advice in helping the senior investigators during the study. This study was enjoined from examining United States military attitudes directly by either questionnaire or interview and consequently depended on other studies for such data on the United States Navy. Overseas site visits were made by Ezra Krendel and William Gomberg to obtain primary source information on the European military unions. The effectiveness of these visits was enhanced because of the cooperation and assistance of Mr. Daniel Goott, Special Assistant for Labor Affairs, Department of State and members of the staffs of United States embassies in the countries visited. We also thank Dr. Robert Strauz-Hupé, our ambassador to Sweden, for many courtesies and help during the visit to that country.

The result of this study was report No. NKG-10 entitled *The Implications of Industrial Democracy for the United States Navy* issued in January 1975. In the summer of 1975 a briefing on the report was held for the senior naval personnel of the Bureau of Naval Personnel (BuPers), following a similar briefing for the Office of Naval Research. In the ensuing months considerable interest in this report was expressed from many sources. By spring of 1976 the extension of public-sector collective bargaining to the United States Armed Forces was a possibility to be reckoned with.

The ongoing *process* by which we reached this state of affairs and the *implications* for the future provide a fascinating exercise for studying both collective bargaining in the public sector and the relation of a democratic society to its armed forces. We decided to augment, rewrite in part, and edit *The Implications of Industrial Democracy for the United States Navy* so that both the *process* and the *implications* could be presented to a larger readership.

We have produced a book which is meant to serve two purposes. The first is to inform our fellow citizens by clarifying the issues involved in military unions. The second is to serve an academic readership by providing an adequate number of references which lead deeper into the subject. Since the *process* continues, many of the sources we used were published within the last six months. The *implications,* on the other hand, draw upon historic precedent, and here we go back to the sixteenth century.

We thank Dr. Glenn L. Bryan, and Dr. Martin A. Tolcott of the Psychological Services Division, Office of Naval Research, and in particular Dr. H. Wallace Sinaiko of the Smithsonian Institution for supporting the study upon which this book is based. We hope that both you and they enjoy the result.

EZRA S. KRENDEL
BERNARD SAMOFF
The Wharton School
University of Pennsylvania

1

Trade Unions and the United States Armed Forces: The Issues and Precedents

EZRA S. KRENDEL

94TH CONGRESS
2D SESSION

S. 3079

A BILL

To amend chapter 49 of title 10. United States Code, to prohibit union organization in the armed forces, and for other purposes.

By

Mr. THURMOND, Mr. ALLEN, Mr. BARTLETT, Mr. BROCK, Mr. CHILES, Mr. CURTIS, Mr. DOMENICI, Mr. EASTLAND, Mr. FANNIN, Mr. GARN, Mr. GOLDWATER, Mr. HANSEN, Mr. HELMS, Mr. HRUSKA, Mr. LAXALT, Mr. MC-CLELLAN, Mr. MCCLURE, Mr. MORGAN, Mr. MOSS, Mr. NUNN, Mr. WILLIAM L. SCOTT, Mr. TAFT, Mr. TALMADGE, Mr. TOWER, and Mr. YOUNG

MARCH 4, 1976
Read twice and referred to the Committee on Armed Services

On 4 March 1976, bill S. 3079: "To amend chapter 49 of title 10, United States Code, to prohibit union organization in the armed forces, and for other purposes." was introduced in the Senate by Sen. Strom Thurmond and twenty-four cosponsors. On 15 March 1976 an identical bill, H.R. 12526, was introduced in the House by Rep. Floyd Spence. Hearings were not held on these and other similar bills and they died with the 94th Congress. On 4 January 1977 Rep. Richard Ichord introduced H.R. 51: "To amend title 10, United States Code, to prohibit collective bargaining with the Armed Forces, and for other purposes." Within a short period of time ten similar bills were submitted to the House. On 18 January 1977 Sen. Strom Thurmond and thirty-four cosponsors introduced S. 274, which was essentially similar to his previous submission, S. 3079.[1]

The purpose of this book is to explain the historical background which led to the introduction of these and similar bills and to equip the reader with the information necessary to understand the issues which they address.

In the late 1960s and early 1970s there was a minor effort, inspired by political activists, at creating a military union in the United States. The American Servicemen's Union (ASU), founded on Christmas 1967, had no connection with organized labor. Emerging from the Vietnam War protest movement, the ASU was a trade union in name only since its members were not and did not want to be stakeholders in a military career.[2] By July 1969 the ASU claimed 6,500 members but has long since faded away.

Military unions returned to public attention in this country beginning in the early 1970s when there was a spate of articles in the press on European military unions. On 1 October 1974, for example, *The Wall Street Journal* printed an article by Bowen Northrup entitled, "This Is An Army? Well, It Has Arms, Marches—Sort Of, But Thanks to Their Union, Dutch Soldiers Can Forget About Salutes and Reveille." This article in many ways was typical, in that it raised the specter of an undisciplined, disorganized mob of conscripts whose behavior was caused by what was alleged to be union representation.

One of the early surfacings of the issue of a United States military union in the committed trade-union sense is to be found in a report by the Defense Manpower Commission of a study of the attitudes of navy personnel in the San Diego area.

According to the report given to the commission by its Executive Director, Gen. Bruce Palmer, USA (Ret.), the dissatisfaction stems mostly

---

[1] S. 3079, 94th Congress 2nd Sess., H.R. 51 and S. 274, 95th Congress 1st Sess., Appendix A.

[2] Andy Stapp, *Up Against the Brass,* (New York: Simon and Schuster, 1970).

from constant changes in "people programs" and violations of enlistment contracts. . . .

Unrest over constant changes is running so high that the idea of unionization of military personnel came up frequently.[3]

On 27 June 1975 the issue of a United States military unionization surfaced in a credible manner with the appearance of a news item by Walter Mossberg and Richard J. Levine in *The Wall Street Journal* reporting that the American Federation of Government Employees (AFGE) was considering plans to unionize the military. *The Wall Street Journal* flamboyantly announced the news: "Union Plans '76 Drive to Represent Servicemen; Legalities are Explored, and Pentagon Shudders." Clyde M. Webber, late president of the AFGE, an AFL-CIO affiliate, which has about 300,000 members and represents about 700,000 employees in its contracts with government agencies, was quoted as saying, "Servicemen need somebody to represent them, that's for sure."

The Pro Union Position

On 18 August 1975 Clyde M. Webber gave testimony before the Defense Manpower Commission in which he summarized the essentially pragmatic goals which the AFGE had for military unions and emphasized that the AFGE was *studying* the possibility of taking members of the uniformed military service into membership. His position developed from the linking of the pay systems of uniformed military and civilian classified employees, administratively in 1968, and by statute in 1971. The white-collar pay system for civilians has been tied to comparable industrial jobs from 1962 to the present. The following, directly quoted from Webber's testimony, both expresses his position and describes the mechanics by which federal pay scales are determined:

> In 1970, the most recent Federal Comparability Act was passed by Congress and signed by the President. This Act mandates annual review of classified pay as well as linkage for uniformed military. The procedure for accomplishing this review calls for meetings of the President's Agent with the Federal Employee Pay Council, during which pay setting procedures are discussed and some agreements are reached. Following discussions carried on weekly over a period of several months the President's Agent, the Director of OMB, and the Chairman of the Civil Service Commission, prepare a report to the President reflecting agreements made, areas of controversy, and the unilateral decisions made by the agent regarding such controversies, together with a proposed salary schedule based on private sector pay data as interpreted by agent approved pro-

---

[3] Phil Stevens, "Navy People are 'disillusioned'—That's What Defense Manpower Panel Found in San Diego Study," *Navy Times,* 5 March 1975.

cedures. The Federal Pay Council also prepares a report which is attached for transmittal with the Agent's report.

The formal report of the President's Agent is transmitted to the President's Advisory Committee composed of three outstanding personnel authorities not employed by the Federal government in any other capacity, for purposes of review of the Agent's recommendations and for submission to the President of any recommendations they might have on the entire matter. According to the statute, the President must accept pay schedules submitted to him by his Agent, unless he decides to submit an alternate pay plan to Congress. If the President accepts the recommendations no action is required of Congress. If the President wants to adjust the amount of the pay increase, such a decision must be based on "national emergency or economic conditions affecting the general welfare," according to the provisions of Section 5305 of P.L.91-656. Under the terms of that law, the President must also submit his "alternate pay plan" to both the House and the Senate. If either of the two houses of Congress formally adopt a resolution of disapproval of the alternate plan, the original recommendations of the President's Agent become effective.

Since passage of the Comparability legislation there has never been a direct attempt to adjust the final amount, but on three occasions, the President has submitted an "alternate pay plan" deferring the effective date of the General Schedule pay increase due January 1, 1972, until July 1, 1972. Congress took no action to disapprove this plan and it became effective.

Following the 90-day freeze on wage and prices, which expired on November 14, 1971, pay guidelines were established which permitted pay increases up to 5.5 percent annually. The wage control authority of the President was scheduled to terminate in the early part of 1972. In the debate concerning the extension of controls, the equity of deferring pay increases for Federal and uniformed military personnel was questioned. Amendments were made to allow a 5.5 percent annual increase for Federal employees and uniformed military retroactive to January 1, 1972.

When it came time for the October 1972 pay increase, legal advisors to President Nixon informed him that he could defer the Comparability increase without an alternate pay plan because of the "annual" 5.5 percent limit established by the pay fixing authority.

This decision was tested in Federal court, and President Nixon lost. Employees were eventually granted retroactive pay increases for the three-month period. As you might guess, this caused considerable difficulty and administrative problems.

In 1973 President Nixon again proposed a three-month deferral of pay from October 1, 1973, until January 1, 1974, as an "alternate pay plan." This plan was soundly defeated by the 72–16 Senate vote.

You will recall that President Ford succeeded President Nixon on August 9 last year, and the decision to submit an "alternate pay plan" for the 1974 Comparability pay increase was one of his first major problems. Having served in office for less than three weeks, President Ford proposed to defer the pay increase for two months.

Considering the honeymoon climate that existed between President Ford and the Congress, his "alternate pay plan" became a major crisis for our union, our members, other Federal employees as well as the uniformed military personnel.

In considering the possibilities of overcoming the "alternate pay plan" the full impact of the effect it would have on the uniformed military was brought to my attention.

Since AFGE represents more than 392,000 employees of the Department of Defense, many of whom are employed at military installations where uniformed military personnel are quartered, we decided to try to bring the military into the pay increase fight.

I have attached a copy of the handbill which was distributed to members of the military. AFGE circulated several hundred thousand copies of this at that time.

In evaluating our position in 1974, AFGE expected a very close vote on the "alternate pay plan," even though we had the full support of all the AFL-CIO and affiliated union lobbyists located in Washington. To our surprise the vote was 64–35. Almost two-thirds of the Senate supported our position on equity in Comparability pay.

After the 1974 exercise was completed, I received reports of discussions which union lobbyists had with Senators before and after the vote. These conversations indicated a heavy letter-writing effort on the part of uniformed military people as well as the anticipated support from our members.

In January 1975, the President's State of the Union message and subsequent budget presentations to Congress indicated the President's plans for limiting the amount of the pay increases for civilian employees and the uniformed military to a five percent level. This notice came at a time when it was thought that the private sector survey data on which the pay increase would be based would indicate an increase of better than 8 percent. Since it appeared that AFGE and armed forces personnel would have a continuing mutual concern in pay adjustments in the future, I recommended to the AFGE National Executive Council—our policy board—that we consider offering membership within AFGE to members of the uniformed military.[4]

In September 1976 the delegates to the national convention of the AFGE amended its constitution by a voice vote so as to make military personnel of the armed forces eligible for membership in the union.[5]

An Example, Perhaps a Precedent

Clyde Webber's complete testimony referred not only to the linkage between civilian and military pay but also to the example of National Guard and Armed Forces Reserve civilian technicians, many of whom are presently represented by unions, and all of whom have a quasi-military

---

[4] Clyde M. Webber, *Testimony Before the Defense Manpower Commission: Organizing the Military Services into a Union,* American Federation of Government Employees, 18 August 1975, pp. 4–8.

[5] AFGE resolution, 23 September 1976, appendix B.

status in that they must be members of guard or reserve units to retain their civilian jobs.

Because of the broad implications and potential precedents inherent in such union activity so closely linked to the uniformed services, it will be useful to examine this development. The Air National Guard will be emphasized in what follows because of its high degree of combat readiness and its importance to the air defense of the nation.

Although the Air National Guard officially came into being on 26 July 1947 with the passage of the National Security Act, National Guard units had been important components of the Army Air Corps long before. National Guard units are a significant portion of our air-defense capability and were used in the Korean War, the war in Vietnam, the Berlin Airlift and the Cuban missile crisis. Almost three-fourths of the interceptor force currently available to protect the United States against air attack are Air National Guard units. Guard personnel are in two categories: part-time reservists and full-time civilian technicians who serve in dual civilian/ military roles. The reservists are full-time civilians who perform week-end and summer duty as military personnel. They comprise the bulk of Air National Guard personnel.

The civilian technicians, on the other hand, provide the stable core for the unit. Technicians are officers, airmen, instructor-pilots, weather forecasters, personnel specialists, typists, etc. As of 1 January 1976 there were about 51,000 technicians in both the Air and the Army National Guard. Even though these personnel were *paid* by the federal government, their status as state employees prevented the construction of a single uniform retirement-and-benefits package. It was this shortcoming which prompted the National Guard Association of the United States to lobby in the Congress for uniform retirement benefits. As a result of this pressure, Public Law 90-486, the National Guard Technician Act of 1968, came into being effective 1 January 1969. This act established the technicians as federal *employees* while retaining for the adjutant general of each state supervisory authority over these technicians. Membership in the National Guard was still required as a condition for employment in the noncompetitive civil service which covered about 95 percent of the technicians. The other 5 percent were primarily female employees, clerk-typists, and security guards.[6]

The Defense Manpower Commission, created by Act of Congress in November 1973, described these civilian technicians as follows:

[6] Francis W. A'Hearn, Capt., USAF, and Russell L. Weaver, Capt., USAF, "The Unionization of Air National Guard Technicians and its Impact on Labor Management Relations," (Masters thesis AD-785 954, Air Force Institute of Technology, Wright-Patterson Air Force Base, Ohio, August 1974).

The full-time technicians found in the National Guard and Reserve Forces of the Army and Air Force play an essential role, but their dual Civil Service–military status poses special problems. These individuals hold a large percentage of the field grade officer (major to colonel) and senior enlisted (E-7 to E-9) positions in the Reserve Components, and many are commanders. Large numbers of technicians already belong to unions. They earn their livelihood as full-time civilian technicians in their National Guard or Reserve unit, and the military part of their dual status is only a part-time avocation. It is not surprising that they are far more prone to seek union membership than their non-technician National Guard and Reserve associates and their active force counterparts. The implications of this situation are disturbing, particularly when viewed in the light of the possibility that public employee strikes may result in Reserve callups to handle civil disorders or to perform essential public health and safety functions.[7]

The immediate and presumably unexpected result of Public Law 90-486 was that the Army and Air National Guard technicians were covered by Executive Orders 10988, 11491, and 11616 which entitled federal employees to be collectively represented by labor unions. The result was that about 27 percent of the technicians were represented by unions in 1969, and this percentage rose rapidly with slight fluctuations to 72 percent by 1 January 1976. About 84 percent of the wage earning employees, or 20,100 persons, were represented and 62 percent of the general-schedule employees or 16,600 persons, were represented as a result of the 127 recognitions in Table 1–1 below.[8]

Thus, in effect, military units of the United States had been engaging in collective bargaining with little publicity and no apparent deterioration in military efficiency. In fact, Vincent J. Paterno, president of the ACT, has claimed, in interviews with the press, that its affiliate, the Association of Guard and Reserves (AGR) has been signing up reservists whose role is purely part-time military since February of 1976.[9] Noncommissioned officers appear to be the most interested candidates for membership from the pool of about 700,000 reservists.

The Defense Manpower Commission has totally rejected the concept of military unions and has addressed the guard technicians issue in the following straightforward manner:

> The objectives of the technician program can be accomplished at substantial savings by ultimately replacing the technicians with fulltime

---

[7] Defense Manpower Commission, *Defense Manpower: the Keystone of National Security,* report to the president and the Congress, April 1976, pp. 64–65.

[8] Personal communication from Scott Newton, Chief, Technician Management and Labor Relations Division, Office of Technical Personnel, Departments of the Army and Air Force, National Guard Bureau.

[9] Lee Ewing, "Guard Members Joining Unions," *Navy Times,* 17 May 1976.

Table 1-1. Army and Air National Guard Representation 1 January 1976

	Recognitions	Employees	Percentage	Agreements	Employees
National Association of Government Employees (NAGE)	50	11,861	23%	45	11,182
American Federation of Government Employees (AFGE)	30	7,750	15%	26	6,824
National Federation of Federal Employees (NFFE)	23	6,207	17%	23	6,207
Association of Civilian Technicians (ACT)	20	8,753	12%	15	5,931
National Air and Army Technicians Association (NAATA)	2	2,006	4%	2	2,006
American Federation of State, County and Municipal Employees (AFSCME)	1	100		1	100
Security Officers, Guards and Protective Employees Union (SOGPEU)	1	52			
Total	127	36,729	71%	112	32,250

active duty Guardsmen and reservists. The use of Guardsmen and reservists on active duty would protect the citizen-soldier concept which is
basic to this Nation's Guard and Reserve System. Implementation of this
change would eliminate dual pay and retirement for what in essence is
the same job.[10]

The Military Leadership's Position

The response of the senior military commanders and their civilian counterparts to the concept of military unions has been a more forceful echo of
the Defense Manpower Commission's rejection. Some representative remarks provide the flavor of these predictable responses.

A hard line on military unions was taken by the Joint Chiefs of Staff
chairman, Gen. George S. Brown, in testimony before the House Armed
Services Committee hearings on the Fiscal Year 1977 Defense Budget.
Brown's views on efforts to unionize the military were solicited by the
Committee:

> I think unionization and the operation of the military forces are
> totally incompatible. [He agreed with committee members who said some
> military people favor a union because they feel that the military benefits
> are diminishing.] I agree with you, I am not talking about a lot of things
> that people have come to think of as their "due," and, if they cannot be
> continued, we ought to take the time to explain why. This is leadership.
> We have a tough problem in the senior ranks in uniform, and I am not
> talking just generals. I am talking senior noncoms, too.[11]

In commenting before the Senate Armed Services Manpower and
Personnel Subcommittee on Military Unions, the position of the military
command was reiterated as follows:

> Air Force Maj. Gen. C. G. Cleveland: "Mr. Chairman, it would be detri-
> mental to good order and discipline."

> Army Maj. Gen. John Forrest: "I agree, Mr. Chairman. We want a team
> with high morale and that knows it can depend on its leaders for help."

> Rear Adm. C. N. Mitchell: "The Navy also agrees, Mr. Chairman. Look-
> ing at countries that have unions we can see no benefit."

> Marine Corps Brig. Gen. William Fleming: "It would be chaos, Mr.
> Chairman. You cannot run a combat unit by committee. It is up to the
> leadership to provide support and help."[12]

---

[10] *Defense Manpower*, p. 127.
[11] Lee Ewing, "JCS Head Hits *Navy Times* for Benefits Stories," *Navy Times,*
9 February 1976.
[12] "4 Service Officials Reject Union Idea," *Navy Times,* 5 April 1976.

The opposition of the armed forces hierarchy to military unions is echoed thunderously by the officers and organized members of the numerous military associations. The Fleet Reserve Association, the Reserve Officers Association, the Naval Reserve Association, and the National Association for Uniformed Services all have already gone on record as intending to fight military unionization. The organizations above are the tip of the iceberg. The number of United States military organizations of a professional nature are listed below:

The Association of the United States Army Air Force Association

Fleet Reserve Association (FRA)

Marine Corps Association

Navy League of United States

National Guard Association of the United States

Retired Officers Association

Naval Reserve Association

The American Legion

Veterans of Foreign Wars

Disabled American Veterans

American Veterans (AMVETS)

Marine Corps Reserve Officers Association

Non-Commissioned Officers Association of the United States of America

Armed Forces Benefit and Aid Association

Association of Regular Army Sergeants

Air Force Sergeants Association

Military Order of the World Wars

Society of American Military Engineers

Naval Enlisted Reserve Association

The Marine Corps League

National Association for Uniformed Services

United States Submarine Veterans

The American Legion, a powerful lobby in Congress with nearly three million members, at its national convention in 1975 in Minneapolis adopted a strong antiunion resolution. This resolution says in part, "Armed Forces personnel are adequately represented by senior Armed Forces personnel, their elected representatives . . . and by organizations of interested and influential U. S. Armed Forces veterans, such as the American Legion." The resolution went on to assert that "unionization of the Armed Forces runs contrary to the well-established and effective traditions of the military chain of command and military discipline."

Three hundred delegates to the Air Force Sergeants Association meeting in Las Vegas, Nevada, in early August of 1975 voted unanimously not only "to oppose any legislative or executive action which might permit any labor organization to be recognized as a collective bargaining agent for members of the Armed Forces," but also "to seek with special legislation and promulgation of Presidential Executive Orders to prohibit and prevent any such possibility." Thus, the Sergeants Association expressed precisely the sort of resistance to a union that might have been expected from foremen in industry or other first-line supervisors. On the other hand, the association itself has attributes of a trade union. It illustrated this as it passed resolutions denouncing the "erosion of promised enlistment benefits and the threat of further reductions in the retirement system." In a similar vein, 405 delegates to the FRA's forty-eighth National Convention in St. Louis, Missouri, in September 1975 unanimously adopted a strongly worded resolution opposing the unionization of military personnel. The delegates, representing more than 126,000 career enlisted personnel of the Navy, Marine Corps, and Coast Guard, appropriated a sum of $112,000 to finance their opposition to military unions. A special national committee of the FRA reported a series of findings related to this issue. One of these findings states that the FRA has in effect provided the benefits and services of a union to the armed forces without the threat of eroding our military command structure. Another finding claimed that the interests of the civilian and military federal employees are diametrically opposed and that hence no one servant can serve both masters! The delegates also instructed the association's national committee on legislative service to pursue all legislative goals and beneficial personnel policy with decisive action and extra vigor to demonstrate to all military personnel that there is no need for a military union.

It is difficult to read the protestations of the various special interest groups which have grown up among veterans without sensing the strong smell of sour grapes. In the statements of both the Sergeants Association and the FRA, it is clear that they view a potential military union as encroaching upon their territory. In a sense, they view the union as a rebuke and possible threat to their own power and continued existence. This is not at all surprising, and the behavior of the many professional military organizations may be compared with that of professional or technical interest groups in other fields such as education or engineering.

For example, in the teaching profession the National Education Association (NEA), a nationwide organization of teachers, principals and administrators, concentrated in its early years on professional and technical matters. As economic and other conditions changed, the NEA was prodded into a union stance by the American Federation of Teachers (AFT), an avowed teacher's union from its inception. Modifying its internal structure and excluding from membership supervisory and non-teaching administrative educational employees, the NEA embarked on an aggressive drive of union activity among teachers in competition with AFT. Just as the NEA evolved into a union, although still retaining many characteristics of a professional organization, the Air Force Sergeants Association and other associations of military professionals could be forced into the posture of military unions, if only to remain viable to their members. However, these associations would have to change their internal structure and membership criteria to serve as exclusive bargaining agents under our national labor laws and executive orders. Such transformation is quite feasible in view of the experience of NEA and other professional organizations, such as the American Association of University Professors (AAUP).

Constitutional Issues

The positions of a union and of the senior military and the military association have been presented and the existing precedent in the guard has been described. Let us now examine the scattered legal precedents which derive from the relevant portions of the United States Constitution.

The courts have already held that public employees enjoy a protected constitutional right to join unions.[13] The basis for this right resides in the italicized portions of the First Amendment, which follows:

> Congress shall make no law respecting an establishment of religion, or prohibiting the free exercise thereof; or abridging the freedom of speech or of the press; *or the right of the people peaceably to assemble, and to petition the Government for a redress of grievances.* [Italics added.][14]

The armed forces were compelled to address the First Amendment issue because of the protest demonstrations which began in the mid-1960s. As a consequence, in 1969 the Department of Defense issued guidelines to assist commanders in dealing with dissident groups and protest activities. These guidelines affirm the right of soldiers to freedom of association as guaranteed by the First Amendment and hence can not and do not

---

[13] *Atkins* v. *City of Charlotte*, 296, F. Supp. 1068 (D.C.N.C., 1969).
[14] U.S. Constitution, Amendment 1.

prohibit "servicemen's union" membership. Commanders are, however, enjoined from recognizing or bargaining with so-called "servicemen's unions."[15]

Should S. 274, H.R. 51, or a similar antimilitary union bill become law, litigation as to the law's constitutionality would presumably ensue. The Supreme Court would have to balance its support of the First Amendment with a reluctance to invade the constitutional mandate of the Congress to regulate the armed forces.

> The Congress shall have Power To . . . make rules for the Government and Regulation of the land and naval forces; To provide for calling forth the Militia to execute the Laws of the Union, suppress Insurrections and repel Invasions; To provide for organizing, arming, and disciplining the Militia, and for governing such Part of them as may be employed in the Service of the United States.[16]

It is clear that the issue will turn on the extent to which the uniformed military enjoy First Amendment rights and the interpretation of article I section 8 above. Efforts to regulate free speech for military personnel provide precedents for interpretations of First Amendment rights in both military and civilian courts. These precedents arise from litigation over several broadly written and vague articles in the Uniform Code of Military Justice, for example:

> *Article 88:* Any commissioned officer who uses contemptuous words against the President, Congress, the Secretary of Defense, the Secretary of a military department, the Secretary of the Treasury, or the Governor or legislature of any State, Territory, Commonwealth or possession in which he is on duty or present shall be punished as a court-martial may direct.[17]

> *Article 133:* Any commissioned officer, cadet, or midshipman who is convicted of conduct unbecoming an officer and a gentleman shall be punished as a court-martial may direct.[18]

> *Article 134:* Though not specifically mentioned in this chapter, all disorders and neglects to the prejudice of good order and discipline in the armed forces, all conduct of a nature to bring discredit upon the armed forces, and crimes and offenses not capital, of which persons subject to this chapter may be guilty, shall be taken cognizance of by a general, special, or summary court-martial, according to the nature and degree of the offense, and shall be punished at the discretion of that court.[19]

---

[15] Department of Defense Directive 1325.6, 12 September 1969, appendix C.
[16] U.S. Constitution, article 1, section 8.
[17] Uniform Code of Military Justice, 10 U.S.C., section 888.
[18] Ibid., section 933.
[19] Ibid., section 934.

The constitutionality of article 88, however broadly written, has been sustained by the United States Court of Military Appeals (USCMA) in *United States* v. *Howe*.[20] The USCMA findings are at variance, however, with the past United States Supreme Court decisions which required a strong demonstration of clear and present danger to discipline and good order within the military before allowing restrictions of First Amendment rights. A large number of USCMA decisions bearing on this issue have been reviewed by Ronald Boyce, and there is reason to believe that if put to the test of constitutionality, the Supreme Court would require that article 88 be more specific.[21] Daniel Sullivan extends the First Amendment argument to defend the actual formation of soldiers' unions, provided that the proper bounds on the union relationship be established.[22] One such obvious bound is a restriction on strikes; another is a curtailment of the areas where union activities might take place. Combat zones are one such example. In wartime, union activities, if allowed at all, would be restricted to those areas where no impairment of the wartime mission would occur.

A recent United States Supreme Court ruling in the case of *Parker, Warden, et al.* v. *Levy*, decided on 19 June 1974, provides direct opinion on the issue of constitutional rights for military personnel.[23] Captain Levy had appealed his conviction for violating article 133 and article 134 of the Uniform Code of Military Justice on the grounds that they are "void for vagueness" under the due process clause of the Fifth Amendment and overbroad in violation of the First Amendment. The Supreme Court rejected this contention and in so doing made the following comments:

> This court has long recognized that the military is, by necessity, a specialized society. We have also recognized that the military has, again by necessity, developed laws and traditions of its own during its long history. The differences between the military and civilian communities result from the fact that "it is the primary business of armies and navies to fight or be ready to fight wars should the occasion arise." [*United States ex re. Toth* v. *Quarles,* 350 U.S. 11, 17 (1955)][24]

> More recently we noted that "(t)he military constitutes a specialized community governed by a separate discipline from that of the civilian," *Orloff* v. *Willoughby,* 345 U.S. 83, 94 (1953), and that "the rights of men in the armed forces must perforce be conditioned to meet certain overriding demands of discipline and duty." [*Burns* v. *Wilson,* 346 U.S. 137, 140 (1953, plurality opinion)][25]

---

[20] *United States* v. *Howe,* 17 U.S.C.M.A. 165, 37 C.M.R. 429 (1967).
[21] Ronald N. Boyce, "Freedom of Speech and the Military," *Utah Law Review* 13 (May 1968): 240–66.
[22] Daniel P. Sullivan, "Soldiers in Unions—Protected First Amendment Right?", *Labor Law Journal* 20 (September 1969): 581–90.
[23] 417 *U.S. Reports,* p. 733.
[24] Ibid., p. 743.
[25] Ibid., p. 744.

Finally, dealing directly with the First Amendment, the court held:

> While the members of the military are not excluded from the protection granted by the First Amendment, the different character of the military community and of the military mission requires a different application of those protections. The fundamental necessity for obedience, and the consequent necessity for imposition of discipline, may render permissible within the military that which would be constitutionally impermissible outside it. Doctrines of First Amendment overbreadth asserted in support of challenges to imprecise language like that contained in Arts. 133 and 134 are not exempt from the operation of these principles.[26]

The above opinion indicates that the First Amendment rights of members of the armed forces might well be restrained if a deterioration in discipline leading to the compromise of a higher public interest could be demonstrated. Whether it could be shown that a military union would cause such a deterioration in discipline is, of course, an entirely separate issue.

Analogies and Trends

The pressures for trade unionism in this country arose in a context which had much in common with that of European industrial countries. There are, however, significant differences which arise because of the higher degree of politicization of European trade unions.[27] Countries such as Sweden, Holland and Germany, have often led the way for us in a variety of social innovations such as social security and health insurance, much of which was the result of the political participation and strength of the labor movements. The American Federation of Labor under Presidents Samuel Gompers and William Green, however, opposed governmental programs of social security, unemployment compensation and health insurance until the late 1930s. Unlike the western European unions evolving from a Marxist tradition which pressed their governments and obtained many social welfare benefits, the anti-Marxist American unions insisted upon a clear separation between the federal government and their private organizations and wanted to secure social benefits through collective bargaining and their own power.

Despite the foregoing differences, the aspirations and goals of American and European industrial labor have much in common. Hence, by observing the content of western European industrial labor negotiations,

---

[26] Ibid., p. 758.

[27] Adolph Sturmthal, *Comparative Labor Movements, Ideological Roots and Institutional Development* (Belmont, California: Wadsworth Publishing Company, 1972) pp. 129–37.

one may detect issues which have implications for subsequent collective bargaining negotiations in the United States. An example of one such goal, which has emerged in western Europe, is variously called industrial democracy or participative management; a movement to enable labor to share certain managerial prerogatives. Although trends toward this generally described goal have resulted more in rhetoric than in substantive change, and although both here and abroad, the vigor of the movement wanes during periods of economic recession, the pressures remain and reappear in different forms and under different names.

The European collective bargaining experience is not limited to the civilian context. Collective bargaining units exist in the armed forces of the Federal Republic of Germany, Sweden, Norway, Denmark, and Austria. In fact, the oldest labor union in Norway, founded in 1835, is a union of naval officers! These European military unions are primarily officers' unions which have arisen in response to professional and economic needs which have been satisfied up to now in our country by a variety of formal and informal lobbies influencing Congress and the executive branch.

American decision makers in government, both in and out of the military, might well examine these foreign trends. The culture and values of the military personnel in these European countries are sufficiently similar to those of United States military personnel so that, as with civilian trade unions, the content of the negotiations between these unions and their governments may reveal issues which, though quiescent at present, will later become active in the United States armed forces. There are, of course, many important differences between the European and American strategic and political positions as there are between the values and cultures of our respective peoples. The United States has a unique role in the defense of the western democracies. The United States has entered into an All-Volunteer Force (AVF) military posture. The European forces consist of cadres and conscripts. These differences require that we evaluate the European military union experience against a political, historical and socio-cultural background before interpreting their activities as early indicators of future issues in the United States.

Values and social forces in the United States will have a more immediate bearing on trends toward military unions in this country. The AVF comes from a broadly defined American middle class. Neither the very rich nor the very poor provide a large proportion of accessions to this force. (Blacks comprised about 16 percent of the enlisted personnel and 3.0 percent of the officers in 1974.)[28] These figures vary widely among

---

[28] Defense Manpower Commission, *Defense Manpower,* pp. 161–67.

the services and among units within the services. There is no evidence that the AVF personnel in aggregate differ widely in the values they hold from the general American workforce—in particular, from policemen, firemen, municipal employees and teachers. In subsequent chapters we describe the recent inclination of public sector employees (such as teachers, for whom a service role model once prevailed) towards an occupational role and union militancy. In fact, the sociologist, Prof. Charles C. Moskos, Jr. has pointed out that a similar change in self-concept of role among the AVF personnel from service and "calling" to a vocational model can be expected to make the concept of military collective bargaining more acceptable to these personnel.[29] This change has been viewed with alarm by many who fear not only that good order and discipline will be compromised, but that the *esprit de corps* of the military units would suffer.[30]

In the following chapters we describe the history and traditions of American unionism, the philosophical underpinnings of the federal relations systems for nonuniformed employees, their benefits and pay structure, rights systems and appeals processes, and the development of grievance arbitration in the federal service. Next, we review due process and bargaining rights in public education. A substantial chapter is devoted to collective bargaining in the police and fire-fighter services because of the obvious relevance to military unionism. Final chapters describe the historical background and current status of military unions in the Federal Republic of Germany, Sweden, and Norway, discuss the conscript organization of the Netherlands, examine the implications which the emergence of military unions in western Europe have for the United States, and conclude by presenting some American alternatives.

---

[29] Charles C. Moskos, Jr., *Trends in Military Social Organization* (Paper presented at the conference, The Consequences and Limits of Military Intervention, University of Chicago, 17–19 June 1976), pp. 2–5.

[30] e.g. William J. Taylor, Jr., Col. U.S.A., *Military Unions for the United States: Justice Versus Constitutionality* (Paper presented at the 1976 Annual Meeting of the American Political Science Association, Chicago, 3 September 1976).

2

History and Traditions of Trade Unionism

WILLIAM GOMBERG

Introduction

In what follows the cultural history of trade unionism is presented from a broad philosophical point of view. This is in keeping with the approach of this book which examines trends and social forces in western industrial societies in order to determine their possible effect on their military establishments. In particular, of course, our interest is in the implications for the United States military. Although the relationship of the military to general American society has been changing rapidly over the past two generations, there is reason to believe that the emerging American military tradition will simultaneously display organizational trends which are both civilianized and traditionally military.[1] It is because of our belief that the armed forces will continue to be influenced by the changes and attitudes of civilian society—albeit with time lags and modifications—that we present a discussion of unionism and its implications.

The institution of unionism is rooted in our concept of democracy, the multiethnic and multiracial character of our population, the unique physical resources of the country and the character and style of our management and union leaders and the interaction of these influences. The principal distinctions that separate American and British democracies from autocracies may be subsumed into two basic concepts: first, the participation of the governed in the formulation of the laws and regulations which accommodate individual freedom to group needs; and, second, the concept of due process or a set of procedures instituted to resolve differences between the governed and the governors with the added protection of a

---

[1] Charles C. Moskos, Jr., "The Emergent Military," *Pacific Sociological Review* 16 (April 1973).

culminating decision vested in a judiciary that should be completely independent of any pressure exercised by either group.

These concepts have been basic to our political life since 1776 when the thirteen colonies declared their independence from the British crown. They were institutionalized in the form of our national constitution in the last decade of the eighteenth century and in the various state constitutions of later dates. The Senate and the House of Representatives, the national legislative arms of our government, embody the participation of our citizenry in the legislative process.

The judiciary resolves conflicts between citizens and their institutions and the executive branch of our political government in the event of conflict between individual citizens and the various areas of that government.

Paradoxically, the political citizen in the 1970s who was beginning to enjoy due process and participative decision making, albeit of an incomplete and rudimentary sort, in his political life, was subjected to complete autocracy in his occupational role as an employee. If his employer was benevolent, he enjoyed benevolent despotism. If his employer was harsh, then he suffered harsh despotism.

From the very beginning of the republic, some men revolted against this schizoid duality in their role as political citizen and economic subject if their labor was for hire. Their status as employee derived from the ancient law of master and servant. The contradiction between their political role and economic role led to the ultimate rejection of this status as servant. The vehicles which embodied the efforts at participation in deciding their fate which these workingmen created became known as unions. They were industrial analogs of the legislature in the political domain.

Because the economic demands which unions voiced were so much easier for the public to understand, the reporting of their revolts was generally expressed as a demand for a raise in wages. The demand for changes in rule making, so that the workingmen could participate in the rules governing the work place, received attention largely from specialized scholars. Nevertheless, this second demand was present from the start as one of the twin pillars of the labor movement.

The first record of an American strike goes back to 1786 when the Philadelphia printers struck for a minimum income of six dollars a week and indirectly for future participation in the determination of conditions of employment. They lost on both grounds.

Following this inauspicious beginning, the labor movement waxed and waned throughout the years and assumed its modern form in 1881 with the formation of the Organized Trades and Labor Unions, later renamed the American Federation of Labor (AFL) in 1886.

Collective Bargaining Emerges

In 1890 the United Mine Workers of America pioneered the concept of the collective agreement, an instrument achieved through collective bargaining with the employer, and which represented a focusing of hitherto diffuse union tactics into an effective means for addressing their problems. Surprising as it may seem, many of the notions of a collective agreement, however "natural" it seems to contemporary Americans, represented a new departure in labor/management relations.

The process of collective bargaining has been defined as follows by the leading scholar in the field, Professor Sumner Slichter, late, of Harvard. He divides collective bargaining into two basic functions.

> Collective bargaining, as carried on by labor unions with employers, has two principal aspects. In the first place, it is a method of pricemaking— making the price of labor. In the second place, it is a method of introducing civil rights into industry, that is, of requiring that management be conducted by rule rather than by arbitrary decision. In this latter aspect, collective bargaining becomes a method of building up a system of industrial jurisprudence. Through the institution of the state, men devise schemes of positive law, construct administrative procedures for carrying them out, and complement both statute law and administrative rule with a system of judicial review. Similarly, laboring men, through unions, formulate policies to which they give expression in the form of shop rules and practices which are embodied in agreements with employers or are accorded less formal recognition and assent by management; shop committees, grievance procedures, and other means are evolved for applying these rules and policies; and rights and duties are claimed and recognized. When labor and management deal with labor relations analytically and systematically after such a fashion, it is proper to refer to the system as "industrial jurisprudence."[2]

The rise of the labor movement antedates the emergence of the institution of collective bargaining. The unions as a group within the labor movement *evolved collective bargaining after a long period of experimentation with other techniques.*

The unions first arose as a blind protest imbued with a purely adversary attitude. The progression from independent craftsman, owning and working with his own tools, to that of hired man to faceless capital was stormy and had few precedents. It was only after a long period of experimentation with other devices and tactics that the institution of collective bargaining evolved. Earlier programs were predicated upon an anti–private enterprise program. The unions opposed the wage system as an institution

---

[2] Sumner H. Slichter, *Union Policies and Industrial Management* (Menasha, Wisc.: George Banta Publishing Co., 1942), p. 1.

and promoted producer cooperatives to escape the thralldom of the wage system. They rapidly became disenchanted with these cooperatives when they discovered that most of them failed because of lack of managerial competence. Those that succeeded presented an even more troublesome problem. Those who had pioneered the venture were loath to take on additional cooperators with the same ownership privileges enjoyed by the pioneers. Within a short time there was little to distinguish the enterprise that started as a producers cooperative from any other private enterprise. For all purposes the producers cooperative had become a private partnership of the pioneers who then employed latecomers to the institution on the same basis as any other private enterprise. This classic progression has been repeated in some of the manufacturing-oriented kibbutzim in Israel in the last decade.

Similarly, attempts to solve problems via the political route by alliance with farmers and small businessmen led them to discover that, when the coalition succeeded, small business resented organization even more bitterly than did big business because the former operated at so close a margin to survival.

Finally, the adoption of collective bargaining was predicated upon the frank acceptance of capitalism as an institution and the desire to improve the workers' status under that economic system.

This meant an abandonment of any class-war doctrine and the adoption of a creed that acknowledged the simultaneous presence of both a bounded conflict of interest with the employer and an identity of interest with him in the prosperity of the enterprise. In addition, it raised fundamental problems about the governance of the enterprise and the extent to which the employers participated in that governance. Management was acknowledged the industrial ruler, but this ruler was obliged to rule under law or "working rules," as they were called in industry. Conflicts over the interpretation of these laws or rules had to be resolved in accordance with the principle of due process.

This industrial law now is widespread but not characteristic of all industrial management. Among the ideas are entrance to the trade, the method of production, and the terms of the introduction of technological change. Each industry constitutes a local culture of its own and reflects the wide diversity of practices that fall under the rubric of industrial rights.

What led to the revival of labor organizations, many of which were left moribund by the depression of the early thirties? The enactment of the Norris-LaGuardia Act of 1932 had set the stage for this revival by sharply restricting the terms under which federal courts could issue labor injunctions which had previously been capricious devices whereby management hobbled labor. President Franklin D. Roosevelt's election, section

7(a) of the National Industrial Recovery Act of 1934 and the National Labor Relations Act of 1935 (Wagner Act) set the climate in which unions could and did revive and flourish.

Arbitrable and Negotiable Issues

From the very beginning of collective bargaining, management generally has stood for a containing strategy designed to restrict the subjects about which it is willing to talk in collective bargaining. It has sought to restrict the area of collective bargaining to wages and hours, arguing that all remaining areas constitute management prerogative. The labor movement, on the other hand, has argued that management is obliged to negotiate in any area that exercises an impact on worker welfare.

Some years ago these points of view received formal expression in a controversy between Mr. Phelps, at the time a Bethlehem Steel executive, and Mr. Goldberg, at the time the attorney for the United Steel Workers of America, later secretary of labor under President Kennedy, and still later Justice Goldberg of the United States Supreme Court. Mr. Phelps claimed that in the beginning all rights belonged to management and management was therefore obligated to discuss only those areas which labor had managed to tear away and insert in the collective agreement.

Mr. Goldberg dissented, stating that in the beginning management was able to impose an absolute dictatorship on its workers; that collective bargaining broke this usurpation and that equity had become the criterion for determining the area of collective bargaining upon which management was compelled to engage in joint decision-making with the union.

The conflict over the permissible areas of collective bargaining has had a stormy history in the saga of United States industrial relations. Following World War I, President Wilson called an industrial-relations conference in 1919 to head off a threatened outbreak of nationwide strikes. Management acknowledged the right of any individual worker to join a union but insisted that it remained management's right to deal with or refuse to deal with the union. After a series of bloody recognition strikes over the issue of whether management should or should not deal with the union, the United States Government took this issue out of controversy with the passage of the National Labor Relations Act of 1935 (Wagner Act). The act imposed upon management the obligation to bargain collectively with representatives of the workers who had been certified in an election procedure.

Now the controversy was transferred to the areas over which management was obligated to bargain. Almost every arbitration procedure over working conditions was bedeviled by management's claim that the dispute before the arbitrator was nonarbitrable because the areas were not specifically treated in the collective agreement.

A conference similar to the Wilson Industrial Relations Conference of 1919 was called by President Truman in 1945 to avert anticipated post–World War II strikes. The conference foundered on the issue of management's insistence that labor must carefully restrict the collective-bargaining subject area and recognize all other areas as management prerogatives. Labor demurred, insisting that such a move was impractical in a time when a rapidly changing economy disclosed that areas hitherto reserved by management had developed a powerful impact on working conditions.

Arbitrator Harry Shulman, late dean of the Yale law school, was called upon to resolve a strike called by the United Automobile Workers (UAW) against the Ford Motor Company over an alleged speedup of the assembly line in 1947. Shulman resolved this problem by drawing a distinction between absolute management rights and conditional management rights. He defined the setting of production standards as a conditional management right, and management's right was restricted to initially proposing a standard over which the union could present grievances. As an example of an absolute management right, he listed the location of a plant.

Yet even this apparently compelling management right was subject to question. The garment-workers union had a restriction in their agreement with the garment employers that was of ancient vintage even in 1947. It imposed upon the management the obligation not to move its plant outside the five-cent-fare zone of New York City. This provision had been prompted by the predilection of garment employers to sign an agreement on Friday and then escape the union by moving their plant out of town over the weekend.

The auto workers, who thought nothing of plant location in 1947, were concerned with it by 1958. This came about because, as a result of the decline in auto sales, the primary layoffs were in the older areas like Detroit where older plants were located. What work was being performed was in plants distant from Detroit of a much more modern vintage. Plant location, a matter of no interest in the UAW in 1947 had become a major concern in the late fifties. Thus, the nature and definition of what constitutes a management prerogative is clearly changeable.

The matter of what areas are relevant to collective bargaining is generally linked to what is arbitrable under a collective agreement. The United States Supreme Court, in three decisions known as the Steelworkers Trilogy, struck down the strict construction that arbitrators are confined to those issues specified in the contract.[3] They defined the industrial relationship as a form of constitutional government in which the scope of arbitration is expanded to include contract implications as well as specific agreement subject areas.

The system of industrial governance in United States collective bargaining is rooted in the shop or factory in which the worker participated in industrial government by means of the individual grievance. European unions, where organization does not reach into the shops, do not enjoy the same kind of rank and file participation in the everyday affairs of the union. For example, in Holland, as in Sweden, Norway, The Federal Republic of Germany and the United Kingdom, the labor unions play a much more publicly significant role in governmental political matters than in the United States. Yet Professor Jack Barbash, after observing the Dutch system of industrial relations, concluded that in the shop the sovereignty of management is absolute.[4] European unions have been attempting to overcome some of these problems by voicing a demand for codetermination or participative management. By and large, United States labor has eschewed that approach, settling instead for participation in shop governance via the grievance procedure.

The Public Sector

Labor organizations in the United States developed later in the public sector. As early as 1912 the International Association of Machinists among others struck the Watertown Arsenal in the wake of efforts by the local management to introduce work measurements by time study into the plant. The result was that from that time to the 1940s all military appropriation bills carried a rider forbidding the expenditure of funds for any work measurement purpose. However, the few unions that confined themselves to the governmental sector were relatively weak and ineffective with the possible exception of the postal employees.

While all governmental unions eschewed the right to strike, the ubiquitous distribution of the postal employees throughout every hamlet in the land gave them a lobbying clout in Congress that was more effective than any strike.

The fundamental attitude towards labor unions in the public sector

---

[3] *United Steelworkers of America* v. *American Mfg. Co.*, 303 U.S. 564 (1960); *United Steelworkers of America* v. *Warrior & Gulf Navigation Co.*, 363 U.S. 574 (1960); and *United Steelworkers of America* v. *Enterprise Wheel & Car Corp.*, 363 U.S. 593 (1960).

[4] Jack Barbash, *Trade Unions and National Economic Policy* (Baltimore: Johns Hopkins University Press, 1972), p. 67.

was laid down in 1919 by the then Governor of Massachusetts, later President Calvin Coolidge, who broke the Boston police strike, declaring that "There is no right to strike against the public safety by anybody, anywhere, any time."

President Roosevelt, largely responsible for the revival of unionism in the private sector, did not believe that collective bargaining could be transplanted to the public sector. There were various arguments extant during the 1930s supporting the view that government could not bargain collectively with its employees. The nature and purposes of government, its representation of the whole society and the policies, procedures, and rules in personnel matters, precluded the establishment of a bargaining process wherein management and labor could negotiate and enter into binding commitments. And finally, opposition to public sector collective bargaining was linked with the strike. No one at that time could support threats to strike, picketing, and strikes or militant tactics. What was good for the private sector was inapplicable to the public sector.

Yet some thirty years later a Republican administration in Pennsylvania, led by Governor Schaeffer, put into effect Act 195 which granted to state employees the statutory right to collective bargaining, including the right to strike. The only exceptions to inclusion in Act 195 were the police, firemen, and guards at prisons and mental hospitals. They were covered by Act 111 that eschewed strikes but invoked joint fact-finding and binding arbitration over issues which the parties could not resolve in collective negotiations.

President Kennedy issued Executive Order 10988 in 1962, which set forth the procedures to facilitate union recognition and negotiation in the federal service. It directly stimulated employee organization and negotiations, not only in the federal service, but also indirectly at the state and local levels as well. The order provided somewhat the same impetus for public-sector labor relations that the National Labor Relations Act of 1935 did in the 1930s for labor relations in the private sector. Executive Order 10988 was superseded by President Nixon's Executive Order 11491 in 1969, which revised some procedures and amplified others. This in turn was followed by Executive Order 11616 in 1971.

At the present time, local governments are increasingly becoming accustomed to dealing with their employees on the basis of the customs and procedures of collective bargaining. A number of individual states have passed legislation granting collective bargaining to state or local employees.

Public workers (who had not been expected to be able to make use of such an instrument) are today engaged in collective bargaining. For example, the federal government has adapted collective bargaining to the very special circumstances of the government employee. Quite obviously, wages for civil-service employees are set by the Congress. The participation which the government employee has in the setting of the government wages is the same as every other citizen who acts through his Congressional representative. At the worksite, collective bargaining has been used to lend more reality to the appeals procedure which, formerly, the civil service furnished exclusively as a due-process means of avoiding arbitrary, unreasonable behavior by the supervisory force. Although the civil service had long ago created an appeals procedure for individual federal workers, virtually all agree that the procedure was so weighted on the supervisor's side that the procedure left much to be desired in terms of a due process criterion.

What is unique about collective bargaining in the public sector is that the civil-service worker is represented by a person independent of the civil service against whom the employee's supervisor can exercise no power. In this respect, the federal-civil-service problem with collective bargaining is very similar to those of any manager who must cope with the problem of due process enjoyed by his employees. In the last decade or so, collective bargaining has become a regular tool increasingly available to the public employee. Local government representatives as a matter of course today meet with the Policemen's Benevolent Association, the Fraternal Order of Police, and the AFL-CIO International Association of Fire Fighters to determine the terms and conditions of employment for these uniformed protective services.

With the spread of collective bargaining throughout the entire economic culture of the United States, it is natural to expect that its influence be felt among the military much as collective bargaining presented itself as a problem between police commissioners and the rank-and-file police and fire chiefs and rank-and-file firemen.

Since World War II, the military forces of the free world have been subjected to one shock after another because of the changing international culture. It is not uncommon among European democracies for members of the military to be organized into unions in much the same manner that other government employees are organized into unions.

It is significant that many organizations created for self-protection, mutual welfare, or because of shared technical interests, sooner or later found themselves reshaped by the logic of events into adversary roles demanding rights that ultimately led to the rejection of the master-servant and rigid hierarchical role and the development of a code of rights for the employee that were appropriate to the role of economic citizen.

The railroad-operating unions, the engineers and conductors, started mutual societies for insurance purposes. The hazard of their occupations banned them from ordinary commercial insurance at the time of organization. In a short time, their preoccupation with safety led them to demand certain working rules from railroad management as a part of working conditions.

The letter carriers' union likewise started as a mutual-welfare organization for insurance and recreation. The organization of letter carriers' musical bands were undertaken for this purpose. At their recent convention in Seattle, the letter-carrier unions were reminded of their origin by the large number of letter-carrier bands entertaining the local citizenry and the delegates.

Professional Organizations, the Military, and Future Trends

At times, professional organizations organized for professional development, began by avoiding collective bargaining as subprofessional activity, only to develop all of the union functions under the pressure of the logic of events. The NEA, originally made up of teachers, principals, and administrators, was challenged by the American Federation of Teachers. The NEA found itself participating in election contests against the AFT for collective-bargaining representation, an activity to which the association was allegedly opposed. Then they won the election and, before long, any differences between them and the AFT was reduced to a matter of rhetoric. In fact, the organizations have been discussing merger; the Los Angeles and New York State organizations have already merged. The administrators and principals excluded from NEA as supervisory employees have organized their own organization, which is assuming on their behalf very much the same functions as the NEA continues to perform on behalf of the teachers. The AAUP is having a similar experience.

Engineering organizations, shaken by the vulnerability of their constituents in the labor market of late, have moved to imitate certain aspects of unionism while at the same time avoiding unionization as being subprofessional. The world's largest professional organization of engineers, the Institute of Electrical and Electronic Engineers, has been compelled by the economic decline of many of its members that followed from the curtailment of aerospace and defense research and development spending to concern itself with its members' economic well-being. This is in striking contrast with the traditional technical and professional interests of past years. In fact, position statements made in 1976 by each of the three candidates for the presidency of the institute are concerned with portable pensions, patent rights for engineers, the technical obsolescence of engineers, and controlling access to the labor market by controlling entry to the profession.[5] The engineers' need for economic security and due process asserts itself despite the reiteration of symbolic ideological pretension. Middle management, a euphemism for a whole host of technicians and subalterns, has begun to wonder at this selfsame vulnerability, and their discussion about due process must sound positively subversive to the old line manager.

Gunnar Myrdal, the Swedish social scientist, has observed that we are moving closer and closer to a completely organizational society in which each group will bargain with the greater collective to define the condition and limitation governing its contribution of goods and services to the commonweal. The problems raised by the recent general strike of professionals in Gunnar Myrdal's Sweden are discussed in Chapter 8. In essence, professionals in status-conscious Sweden struck to preserve their traditional "superior status."

The significance of this organizational society, to which we seem to be moving, is quite apparent for our military. The navy, army, air-force, and marine officers have created a variety of organizations, none of which looks upon itself as a union, but each of which is keenly aware of the interests it represents and seeks to promote.

Many of these interests have been met, by and large, by a Congress which is sensitive to the needs of our military personnel. Our society is more fluid than the Sweden which Myrdal described. The forces in Sweden which created professional classes of well-defined self-interests do not exist as powerfully in our country. There is much overlap of interests, and there are many routes to the sources of power and to the decision points. Thus the Congress represents the military man as effectively or more so than could a special-interest organization. The American military man is first and foremost a citizen with a citizen's right, duties, and aspirations. Subsequent chapters indicate where similar aspirations have led public-sector workers in our country and the military personnel of the Federal Republic of Germany, Sweden, and Norway, and what implications can be seen for the armed forces of the United States.

---

[5] Robert M. Saunders, Irwin Feerst and Robert A. Rivers, "Election Statements", *IEEE Spectrum* 13 (August, 1976): 54–55.

3

Historical and Philosophical Underpinnings of the Federal Labor Relations Systems for Nonuniformed Employees

MICHAEL E. SPARROUGH

Historical Perspectives

Unionization of civilian federal employees began at the Philadelphia navy yard in the early 1800s. In 1835 these employees participated in the first full-fledged labor dispute with the United States government. The issue was working conditions. Today, almost 140 years later, not only is the succeeding federal agency, the Department of Defense, searching for meaningful approaches to labor relations, but it is also grappling with remarkably similar issues. The main difference is that the cast of characters has changed with the passage of time. A century-and-a-half ago, civilian naval personnel were forced to deal with an unresponsive and insulated power structure. Today, certain uniformed military personnel perceive that they are in a similar position. With such a series of parallels, perhaps, a study of the evolving system of due process for civilian federal employees can provide valuable insights into and approaches to the labor-relations problems which may confront the leadership of the armed forces in its dealings with uniformed personnel. Furthermore, the employer-employee relationship which exists between the armed forces hierarchy and its civilian federal employees provides an extremely close parallel, from a managerial perspective, to the military command structure and its uniformed personnel. In both cases, management is confronted with the same set of administrative and fiscal constraints. For example, both must exist in the federal bureaucratic environment, and both must have congressional approval of their budgets to operate.

From the beginning, federal employees found it more fruitful to lobby before Congress than to attempt to negotiate with the agencies involved. In fact, many agencies refused either to recognize or consider the demands of employee organizations.[1] The Philadelphia navy yard dispute of 1835–36, the first in the history of the federal service, illustrates this point rather cogently.

The Ten-hour Day in the Philadelphia Navy Yard

The workday for mechanics at the Philadelphia navy yard was officially set from sunrise to sunset with forty-five minutes for breakfast at 7:00 A.M. and an hour for dinner at 1:00 P.M. The effect of this pronouncement, officially approved in 1819, was to unilaterally set a variable length work schedule for civilian-federal craft employees. Agitation for a change began in 1834 when mechanics at private shipyards in the Philadelphia area succeeded in winning a workday running from sunrise to 6:00 P.M. with an hour for breakfast at 8:00 A.M. and two hours for dinner at noon. This gain created an obvious disparity of prevailing work schedules in the area. When uniformity with the private sector was sought by the workers in 1835, commandment of the Philadelphia navy yard, James Barron, refused to employ ship riggers and others who were unwilling to accept the existing schedule of work hours but had expressed willingness to work at the schedule obtaining in private yards in the same metropolitan area. After Barron informed the Board of Navy Commissioners of his actions, the chairman of the board, John Rodgers, gave his approval but suggested that some relaxation allowing perhaps an hour for breakfast and up to 1½ to 2 hours for dinner on the long, hot days of summer might be granted. This would be carried out, of course, at the discretion of Barron.

On the spot in the midst of the agitation, Barron then suggested the advantages of instituting a workday of 6:00 A.M. to 6:00 P.M., arguing that these hours already existed at some private yards and would more than likely become the standard at some time in the future anyway. Rodgers scuttled that approach because there were many reasons why it would be inexpedient to adopt them in the public service. Up to this point, the evidence of any form of dialogue with employees is conspicuously absent. It seems quite apparent that the employer-employee relationship fostered by the navy in 1835 was analogous to that of a ship captain on the high seas.

With the workers up against a brick wall with both Rodgers and Barron, the National Trades' Union stepped into the picture and petitioned

---

[1] Clyde L. Schuiten and Bruce M. Garnett, *Labor Relations in the Federal Service—A Changing Environment for Managers* (Air Force Institute of Technology, 1973), p. 10.

the secretary of the navy directly for some action. Acting Secretary John Boyle (in the absence of Secretary Dickerson) replied to the correspondence expressing sympathy with the union and agreeing that the work schedule should indeed be modified. After receiving the letter, the mechanics took it to Barron, who refused to act on it until he had been instructed officially. When Secretary Dickerson returned to his office, he wrote to John F. Stump of the mechanics committee, concurring with Boyle's opinion. Nine days later, on 26 August 1835, Chairman Rodgers issued a circular to all navy yards which modified the existing work schedule but fell short of parity with the standard in effect at the private yards. Still short of its goal, the National Trades' Union decided to escalate its battle to the highest levels of government, namely, to petition Congress and the President. The fruits of this endeavor were realized in August 1836, when Secretary Dickerson wrote to Rodgers to instruct Barron to adopt the hours prevailing in private yards in the city and county of Philadelphia. Rodgers transmitted the instructions to Barron on 1 September, and they were posted on 3 September 1836. The work schedule corresponded in all essentials with the demands earlier propounded by the mechanics.[2] Thus, organized civilian federal employees got what they wanted, but not through any form of bargaining. The gains realized were the product of working *around* management rather than negotiating *with* management.

The Next Seventy-five Years

Similarly, union petitions to Congress over the next twenty-year period were directly responsible for the enactment of the first prevailing wage-rate law in the history of the country. The protagonists of this bill were again the civilian employees of naval shipyards, and the predominant issue was again working conditions. This piece of legislation became the cornerstone of the federal-wage-board pay system which exists today.

Federal employee craft unions continued to exert their influence on Congress and by 1868 had succeeded in persuading Congress to enact legislation establishing an eight-hour workday for all laborers, workmen, and mechanics employed by the government of the United States. Thus, the federal government had become the first employer on record to recognize eight hours as a day's work. As in the past, these pace setting advancements in working conditions were not achieved through labor-

---

[2] O. L. Harvey, "The 10-Hour Day in the Philadelphia Navy Yard 1835–36," *Monthly Labor Review* 85 (Washington, D.C.: Government Printing Office, March 1962): p. 258.

management cooperation. They were achieved by going around the various agency power structures.

Although the 1868 legislation marked a victory for labor, the secretaries of the navy and the War Department were still able to frustrate its implementation through bureaucratic techniques. They reacted by reducing the pay of employees in their departments by 20 percent, an amount equivalent to the reduction in working hours. Although this action was in flagrant disregard of the intent of the act, it was not until four years later that Congress enacted a joint resolution to force the agencies to pay the same wage for eight hours as they had previously paid for ten hours of work.

The next significant event in the history of federal personnel relations occurred in 1883 when the Pendleton Act was passed. The act established the United States Civil Service Commission, and simultaneously eliminated the executive patronage, or so-called "spoils system." Under the previous system, the federal civil-service employee enjoyed a very limited degree of job security, in that, upon the inauguration of a new president *all* employee positions were available to the new administration for the satisfaction of campaign promises. With the advent of the Civil Service Commission also came a federal agency which was to unilaterally shape federal labor relations through its policy decisions for the next eighty-one years.

As the nineteenth century drew to a close, agency management moved decisively to curb union lobbying efforts. In 1895 Postmaster General Wilson issued the first in a series of "gag orders" which stated that any employee of the postal service who went to Washington with the purpose of influencing Congress would be subject to removal. In 1902, President Theodore Roosevelt issued an executive order imposing the "gag order" principle to all federal employees. In 1906 this principle was continued by him in another executive order. Specifically, these orders said:

> All officers and employees of the United States, of every description. . . . are hereby forbidden, either directly or indirectly, individually or through associations, to solicit an increase in their pay or influence or attempt to influence in their own interests any other legislation whatever, either before Congress or its committees, or in any way save through the departments. . . . in or under which they serve, on penalty or dismissal from the Government service.[3]

In 1909 President William Howard Taft elaborated on the Roosevelt "gag orders" by issuing another executive order adding, "Nor may any such person respond to any request for information from either House of Congress, or any committee from either House of Congress, or any

---

[3] Executive orders of 31 January 1902 and 25 January 1906.

Member of Congress, except through or as authorized by the head of his department."[4]

Incensed by what they felt was an infringement of their rights, federal employee unions and a sympathetic Congress pushed for legislation to repeal the "gag order."

The Lloyd-Lafollette Act of 1912

As the result of a prolonged campaign of protest against the "gag orders," the Lloyd-LaFollette Act was passed in 1912. It provides:

> that membership in any society, association, club, or other form of organization of postal employees not affiliated with any outside organization imposing an obligation or duty upon them to engage in any strike, or proposing to assist them in any strike, against the United States, having for its object, among other things, improvements in the conditions of labor of its members, including hours or labor and compensation therefore and leave of absence, by any person or group of persons in said postal service, or the presenting by any such person or group of persons of any grievance or grievances to the Congress of any member thereof shall not constitute or be cause for reduction in rank or compensation or removal of such person or groups of persons from said service. The right of persons employed in the civil service of the United States, either individually or collectively, to petition Congress, or any member thereof, or to furnish information to either house of Congress, or to any committee or member thereof, shall not be denied or interfered with.[5]

It is interesting to note that this section of the act which guarantees the right of government to petition Congress applies to federal employees generally. On the other hand, the proviso which prohibits the removal or demotion of employees for union membership applies only to postal employees. Probably this distinction is attributable to the fact that in 1912 there were no federal employees' unions per se other than postal unions. The National Federation of Federal Employees was not founded until 1917, and the American Federation of Federal Employees did not come into existence until 1932. Even a literal interpretation would therefore have excluded all non–postal union members from the protection of the act. However, it has generally been assumed that the spirit of the act provides all federal-employee union members equal protection. No administration has ever proceeded against a non–postal employee for union membership on the theory that the act was inapplicable.[6]

---

[4] Executive order of 26 November 1909.

[5] 37 Statute 555.

[6] Wilson R. Hart, *Collective Bargaining in the Federal Civil Service: A Study of Management Relations in United States Government Employment* (New York: Harper and Bros., 1961), p. 19.

As is frequently the case with reform legislation, the final effects of the Lloyd-LaFollette Act, after undergoing judicial interpretation, were somewhat disappointing to the union people who had fought for its enactment. First, the act did not encourage union organization but rather tolerated such organization.[7] Although federal employees had the right to organize and join unions, there was no obligation on the part of management to negotiate, bargain collectively or even consult with the unions. Any success reached in developing mutually satisfactory labor-management agreements seemed to result from the benevolent attitude of particular administrators. Second, labor leaders had assumed that the act would entitle any union member who was removed or reduced in grade or pay to obtain a court order directing his restoration to his prior job-status upon a successful showing that, regardless of what may be contained in the official statement of charges, the real motivating reason for the adverse action was his union membership or his activities in behalf of the union cause. The courts, however, refused to look beyond the official record. They reasoned that this action would constitute an unwarranted interference with management authority. Despite labor's disappointment with some aspects of the bill and its judicial interpretation, the Lloyd-LaFollette Act still represents a major piece of legislation in steering the course of the government's internal labor relations program.

The Next Fifty Years

For the next fifty years, federal-employee unions continued to grow in membership and power, but continually fell short of their objective of achieving a form of collective bargaining. During the 1920s and 1930s a dramatic change occurred in public policy toward employee unionism and collective bargaining in the private sector. Public sentiment shifted toward a position that public welfare would be advanced by encouraging strong independent unions to negotiate and bargain collectively with management. However, public sentiment for public-employee rights to collective bargaining was not included in this philosophical shift. In 1928, while campaigning for the presidency, Herbert Hoover is reported to have said:

> The government by stringent civil service rules must debar its employees from their full political rights as free men. It must limit them in the liberty to bargain for their own wages, for no government employee can strike against his government and thus against the whole people. It makes a legislative body, with all its political currents, their final employer

---

[7] Richard G. Deane, *The Managerial Role of the Installation Commander in Labor Relations* (Carlisle Barracks, Pa.: U.S. Army War College, Dec. 1972), p. 3.

and master. Their bargaining does not rest upon economic need or economic strength but on political potence.[8]

The Norris-LaGuardia Act was passed in 1932 and the National Labor Relations Act was passed in 1935. Both excluded public employees from their purview. In 1937, President Franklin Delano Roosevelt made probably the most-often quoted pronouncement about employee rights in government service. In a letter to the president of the National Federation of Federal Employees he is reported to have stated:

> All government employees should realize that the process of collective bargaining, as usually understood, cannot be transplanted into the public service. It has its distinct and insurmountable limitations when applied to public personnel management. The very nature and purposes of government make it impossible for administrative officials to represent fully or to bind the employer in mutual discussions with government employee organizations. The employer is the whole people, who speak by means of laws enacted by their representatives in Congress. Accordingly, administrative officials and employees alike are governed and guided, and in many cases restricted, by laws which establish policies, procedures or rules in personnel matters.[9]

The extraordinary impact of this statement is attributable much more to the source than to the content. Roosevelt was generally considered to be a "friend of labor," and his words therefore received widespread publicity. To get an accurate picture of the situation, though, one must examine the environment in which it was written. The letter was not written by Roosevelt to record his theoretical views for posterity. Instead, the letter was written to head off a group of congressmen who were alarmed by the sensational successes which were then being chalked up by the recently formed CIO in organizing many industries never previously unionized. Much of this success was attributable to militant tactics such as the sit-down strike. When the CIO announced plans to organize public employees they unintentionally generated support in Congress for a movement to enact legislation outlawing all forms of collective bargaining in the public service.[10] Thus, the letter appears to have been written to pacify Congress that the administration had no intention of engaging in collective bargaining with government unions, and, therefore, the proposed legislation was not needed. In addition, it can also be reasoned that Roosevelt simply wanted to let it be known that he opposed strikes by government employees. This becomes clearer in the second paragraph of the same letter.

---

[8] Sterling D. Spero, *Government as Employer,* (New York: Chemical Publishing Co., 1948), p. 4.

[9] Franklin D. Roosevelt, *The Public Papers and Addresses of Franklin D. Roosevelt,* 1937 Volume, ed. Samuel I. Rosenman (New York: The Macmillan Co., 1941), p. 325.

[10] S. 95 H.R. 6, 86th Congress, 1st Session (1959).

Particularly, I want to emphasize my conviction that militant tactics have no place in the functions of any organization of Government employees. Upon employees in the Federal service rests the obligation to serve the whole people, whose interests and welfare require orderliness and continuity in the conduct of Government activities. This obligation is paramount. Since their own services have to do with the functioning of the Government, a strike of public employees manifests nothing less than an intent on their part to prevent or obstruct the operations of the Government until their demands are satisfied. Such action, looking toward the paralysis of Government by those who have sworn to support it, is unthinkable and intolerable.[11]

This governmental policy still exists today although the system of employee rights has undergone significant change.

In the 1940s and 1950s a trend towards better labor-management relations in the civilian federal service began to emerge, and the United States navy appears to have been one of the leaders. One authority on labor relations in the federal service has stated:

The Navy Department has long prided itself for being more liberal than most government agencies in the field of labor relations. For years it has been the only military department which employs a full-time labor-relations advisor in its headquarters. The preamble to Department of the Navy regulations exudes a higher degree of official warmth towards labor organization than is typical in conventional policy pronouncements . . . in the same period. Specifically, the preamble states: "This policy recognizes that effective communication between employees and management develops respect and creates good will; that employees express themselves more freely through an organization than individually; and that frequent discussion of mutual problems is generally to the advantage of both employees and management. It is the policy of the Navy that management officials should deal with the representative of employee organizations, and should, as a matter of good labor relations, encourage them to express themselves concerning the development and administration of personnel policies, new programs, work methods, and working conditions.[12]

Thus, as the 1950s drew to a close, we find the employee-management relationship in the United States navy to be far more advanced than in many other federal agencies. Reminiscing back to the 1835 Philadelphia navy yard dispute, it seems evident that the navy's civilian labor relations policies had progressed considerably. Therefore, one can assume that the same potential exists for the navy with respect to its uniformed personnel. Unfortunately, the navy does not have 125 years to complete this transformation; a significant abbreviation of the time span is mandatory.

---

[11] George Meany, in hearings on S. 3593 before the Senate Committee on Post Office and Civil Service, 84th Congress, 2nd Session, (1956), p. 281.

[12] Hart, *Collective Bargaining*, p. 34.

Executive Orders 10988, 11491, and 11616

Despite studies by some federal agencies towards meaningful employer-employee relations in the 1940s and 1950s, Representative George M. Rhodes of Pennsylvania introduced a bill in every session of Congress between 1949 and 1961 which would have provided statutory recognition of organizations of postal and federal employees. In the latter part of the 1950s, companion bills were offered in the Senate by Senator Olin D. Johnston of South Carolina. Although the wording of the bills varied from year to year, they were essentially the same. Some of the essential provisions of the bill offered in 1959 (H.R. 3745 and Sen. Con. Res. 76) were:

(e) (1) The right of officers of national employee organizations representing employees of a department or agency to present grievances in behalf of their members without restraint, coercion, interference, intimidation, or reprisal is recognized.

(2) (A) Within six months after the effective date of this Act, the head of each department and agency shall promulgate regulations specifying that administrative officers shall at the request of officers or representatives of the employee's organizations confer with such officers or representatives on matters of policy affecting working conditions, safety, in-service training, labor-management cooperation, methods of adjusting grievances, transfers, appeals, granting of leave, promotions, demotions, rates of pay, and reduction in force. Such regulations shall recognize the right of such officers or representatives to carry on any lawful activity, without intimidation, coercion, interference, or reprisal.

(B) Disputes resulting from unresolved grievances or from disagreement between employee organizations and departments or agencies on the policies enumerated in subsection (e) (2) (A) shall be referred to an impartial board of arbitration to be composed of one representative of the department or agency, one representative of the employee organization, and one representative appointed by the Secretary of Labor who shall serve as chairman. The findings of the board of arbitration shall be final and conclusive.

(3) Charges involving a violation of this subsection shall be referred to the Civil Service Commission, which shall be charged with making certain that effective grievance machinery is established within each agency, and that unresolved differences are referred promptly to the impartial arbitration board established in subsection (e) (2) (B). The head of the department or agency involved shall take such action as may be necessary to cause the suspension, demotion, or removal of any administrative official found by the board of arbitration to have violated this subsection.

During the 1950s extensive hearings were held on the Rhodes-Johnston bills, and unions unanimously endorsed them. They gave repeated assurances that they were demanding nothing that had not already been guaranteed by the government to their brethren in private industry and that the bills provided nothing so radical as the right to strike, collective bargaining, or representation procedures of the type prescribed in the Wagner Act. In the 1956 hearings, George Meany testified: "Federal employee organizations are asking for the assurance that they will enjoy the benefits of a program for cooperating with management. They are not seeking the same kind of collective bargaining in which unions engage in private industry, the objective of which is a bilateral agreement with respect to specific working conditions. In sum, opponents of the various bills made the following points:

The legislation is unnecessary;

the provisions of the bills granting union officers the right to carry on any lawful activity constitute such a broad delegation of power to unions that it could paralyze the government; and

the compulsory arbitration feature of the bills would divorce executive authority from executive responsibility in a manner severely hampering governmental operations.[13]

When the ballots had been counted in the 1960 presidential election, one of the closest in the country's history, it was clear that the Kennedy administration owed its victory to labor. However, President Kennedy was in a peculiar position. He had supported the Rhodes-Johnston Bills (possibly because it would have been political suicide for him to oppose them), but he never was very strongly in favor of them. Knowing that labor expected him to produce some type of strong labor bill for them, President Kennedy, on 22 June 1961, established a task force of some of the most influential executives in his administration. The list included:

Arthur J. Goldberg, Secretary of Labor, Chairman;

Robert F. McNamara, Secretary of Defense;

J. Edward Day, Postmaster General;

David E. Bell, Director, Bureau of the Budget;

John W. Macy, Jr., Chairman of the United States Civil Service Commission; and,

Theodore C. Sorenson, Special Counsel to the President.[14]

The task force was a new approach to an old problem of attempting

---

[13] John W. Macy, Jr., "The Role of Bargaining in the Public Service," in *Public Workers and Public Unions,* ed. Sam Zagoria, (Englewood Cliffs, N.J.: Prentice–Hall, 1972), pp. 5–19.

[14] John W. Macy, Jr., "The Federal Employee-Management Cooperation Program," *Industrial and Labor Relations Review* 19 (1966): 549–61, 549.

to produce sweeping changes in a bureaucratic environment. First, the work was assigned to top-level political appointees in the federal service who were not experts in the field of federal personnel policies and regulations. Therefore, there were no preexisting civil services prejudices to cloud the view of task force staffers in analyzing the situation. Second, for the first time, the Department of Labor assumed the leadership in the field of internal personnel management in the federal government. Previously, this had been an endeavor reserved strictly for the Civil Service Commission.

The result of the task force's labors was Executive Order 10988, issued 17 January 1962. The timing and the content of the order proved to be a political coup for the Kennedy administration. The Rhodes-Johnston Union Recognition Bill, which might have been passed, was much stronger and less desirable to the administration than was Executive Order 10988. Executive Order 10988 gave labor what it *said* it wanted but *denied* labor the windfall victories it would have gained had the Congressional bill been passed. Thus, labor was put in the position of having to praise the order even though it fell short of the congressional bill.

Even though Executive Order 10988 fell short of certain union expectations, it has been hailed by some observers as "one of the most far-reaching and significant advances in the federal personnel system in recent times."[15] Basically, the order grants:

>   1. The right to organize and present views collectively to executive officials, Congress or other appropriate authority;
>   2. The right of an employee organization to informal, formal, or exclusive recognition;
>   3. The right of formally and exclusively recognized organizations to be consulted and to raise for joint discussion matters of concern to their members; and,
>   4. The right of exclusive representation to negotiate written agreements applying to all units within a unit.

Executive Order 10988 was greeted initially with enthusiasm and optimism by labor, but this mood quickly shifted to disenchantment as several major problems surfaced in the order's implementation. Foremost, among labor's complaints was their contention that, lacking a formal national policy-making organization which would oversee labor-management relations in the federal service, the program was not being implemented uniformly throughout the government. Accordingly, decisions on what constituted an appropriate bargaining unit were being made by local managers. The labor position was that this constituted a *unilateral* decision by management. Additionally, without a central agency having been estab-

---
[15] B. V. H. Schneider, "Collective Bargaining in the Federal Civil Service," Reprint no. 235 (Berkeley, Calif.: Institute of Industrial Relations, 1964), pp. 101–2.

lished, the executive order had provided that impasses in negotiation should be resolved at the local level by means other than arbitration. Once again, labor felt that management held excessive power when negotiating agreements. Labor's proposed solution to the problem was the establishment of an impartial agency or board like the National Labor Relations Board.

A second major dissatisfaction by labor became evident when the procedures for establishing exclusive recognition of a union were promulgated by the Civil Service Commission. First, the responsibility for administering elections was left at the local level without a measure for impartial review. This, in turn, led to a wide range in methods by which elections were held. Secondly, the "sixty-percent rule" in elections was a major union complaint. For a union to be designated as an exclusive bargaining agent, sixty percent of all employees eligible to vote had to *cast* ballots and the union had to *receive* fifty-one percent of the vote. If *less* than sixty percent of the eligible voters actually voted, the union then needed to receive fifty-one percent of *all* the eligible votes. This rule made the gaining of exclusive recognition extremely difficult for unions and understandably was a source of disenchantment.

Experience-Growth in Membership

In 1967, President Johnson established a committee to evaluate the performance of Executive Order 10988 in its first five years and to recommend adjustments. In 1969, under President Nixon, the committee issued its recommendations and indicated that the need for change centered in six areas.

1. A central body to administer the program and make final decisions on policy questions and disputed matter;
2. Revision in the multiple forms of recognition authorized, and improved criteria for appropriate units and consultation and negotiation rights;
3. Clarification and improvements in the status of supervisors;
4. An enlarged scope of negotiation and better rules for insuring that it is not arbitrarily or erroneously limited by management representatives:
5. Third party processes for resolving disputes on unit and election questions for investigation and resolution of complaints under the "Standard Conduct for Employee Organizations" and "Code of Fair Practices," and for assistance in resolving negotiation impasse problems and grievances; and,
6. Union financial reporting and disclosure.[16]

[16] U.S. Civil Service Commission, *Labor-Management Relations in the Federal Service: Report and Recommendations,* (Washington, D.C.: Government Printing Office 1969), pp. 35–36.

President Nixon incorporated these recommendations in Executive Order 11491 which was issued on 29 October 1969. Section 4 of this order established a Federal Labor Relations Council with designated members and additional ones the President could appoint. The Civil Service Commission was to provide administrative support and services to the Council, and the latter was given the following authority and duties:

> (b) The Council shall administer and interpret this Order, decide major policy issues, prescribe regulations, and from time to time, report and make recommendations to the President.

> (c) The Council may consider, subject to its regulations—

>> (1) appeals from decisions of the Assistant Secretary issued pursuant to section 6 of this Order;
>> (2) appeals on negotiability issues as provided in section 11 (c) of this Order;
>> (3) exceptions to arbitration awards; and
>> (4) other matters it deems appropriate to assure the effectuation of the purposes of this Order.[17]

The Federal Services Impasses Panel was also created and empowered to consider negotiation impasses as provided in the order and to take any action it considers necessary to settle an impasse and prescribe regulations needed to administer its function under the order. In addition, under Section 6 the assistant secretary of labor for labor-management relations was instructed to:

> (1) decide questions as to the appropriate unit for the purpose of exclusive recognition and related issues submitted for his consideration;

> (2) supervise elections to determine whether a labor organization is the choice of a majority of the employees in an appropriate unit as their exclusive representative, and certify the results;

> (3) decide questions as to the eligibility of labor organizations for national consultation rights under criteria prescribed by the Council; and,

> (4) decide unfair labor practice complaints and alleged violations of the standards of conduct for labor organizations; and

> (5) decide questions as to whether a grievance is subject to a negotiated grievance procedure or subject to arbitration under an agreement."[18]

Thus, many of the problem areas which existed in Executive Order 10988 were adjusted, and, in the context of the public-sector collective-bargaining model, federal employee organizations enjoyed essentially the

---

[17] Ibid., p. 9.
[18] Ibid.

same protections provided in the Taft-Hartley Act. Executive Order 11491 stands today essentially intact. It was, however, revised somewhat by Executive Order 11616, issued 26 August 1971. The three most significant areas of revision included clarifications of the use of official time for union business, the methods of collecting and allotting union dues, and grievances and arbitration procedures.

Other Labor Relations Systems in the Federal Service

Labor relations in the current federal environment are covered over-whelmingly by Executive Orders 11491 and 11616. However, other systems do exist in somewhat of an adjunct form. Among these systems, different degrees of collective bargaining exist as usually envisioned in the private-sector model. Probably, the closest parallel to this private-sector model is the postal system. For all practical purposes, the Postal Reorganization Act of 1970 transformed labor relations from the public-sector to the private-sector model. Collective bargaining at the Tennessee Valley Authority has existed since the late 1930s but has more economic restraints than the current postal service system. The State Department has developed its own labor relations system very much along the same lines as Executive Orders 11491 and 11616 and exists in a more constrained environment than the two previously mentioned systems.

Conclusions

This chapter has shown that since the early 1800s labor relations of civilian federal employees have matured almost exponentially. The system of due process for civilian federal-service employees started slowly and developed at a somewhat constant rate until 1962 when Executive Order 10988 was issued. Since then, gains have been substantial. Undoubtedly, the federal system of due process will become more sophisticated and responsive in the future.

We have also demonstrated in this chapter that civilian federal employees have traditionally found it more advantageous to lobby before Congress than to meet and confer with their employers. This undoubtedly was a response by workers to an unreceptive and insulated power structure in the federal service. To some extent, the system of due process for uniformed personnel is similar to that which existed in the Philadelphia navy yard in 1835. In the civilian sector, Executive Orders 10988, 11491, and 11616 have sought to alleviate these conditions by fostering bilateralism. Whether this bilateralism is feasible for uniformed personnel is a question for the future.

4

The Benefits and Pay Structure for Nonuniformed Federal Employees

Introduction

Collective bargaining in the federal service is most often viewed as a system through which grievances are processed and certain working conditions are negotiated. There is, however, a significant amount of consultation and bargaining over economic issues. At present, there are approximately 2.8 million civilian and about 2.4 million uniformed personnel in the federal government. The compensation of these 5.2 million persons is either the direct or indirect result of union activity. Since 1970, postal employees, numbering more than 600,000 have bargained directly for their wages and fringe benefits. Thus, they can be characterized as having achieved "full collective bargaining," which is viewed as having all the rights and protections of private-sector bargaining except the legal right to strike. Excluding uniformed personnel and postal employees the remaining 2.2 million federal employees are essentially comprised of "general-schedule" and "wage-board" employees. These persons more popularly are referred to as the "white-collar" and the "blue-collar" segments of the federal civilian workforce. Both can be characterized as having achieved "quasi-collective bargaining." "Quasi-collective bargaining" in this context can be viewed as having many but not all the rights and protections of private-sector bargaining. Federal civilian employees under section 305 of the Taft-Hartley Act do not have the right to strike. In addition, wages and virtually all fringe benefits are not negotiable. However, consultation rights over these items is provided. Finally, the 2.4 million armed forces personnel must be examined as participants in an inchoate and semistructured labor-relations system which does not yet approximate collective bargaining. Because both the paths and problems encountered by white- and blue-collar workers in the federal service are likely to face uniformed personnel, our discussion will focus on these two civilian components of the federal service.

Federal Pay/Benefit System

Since unionization of federal employees began with blue-collar employees, perhaps this pay/benefit system should be examined first. The term "wage board" was coined by the United States Navy in 1861 when it set up boards to collect wage data, hear employees, and set rates of pay subject to revision by the secretary of the navy, because it was engaged in shipbuilding, repair and maintenance. Other government agencies quickly copied this concept of setting pay, and, not surprisingly, a lack of uniformity of wage rates soon developed. After many years of nonuniform wage rates among wage-board employees, the Personnel Classification Board, in 1931, conducted a study of the various procedures and methods used by agencies and concluded that under the circumstances it was not likely that any degree of uniformity was being maintained in pay levels for work under like conditions. In 1943 the Civil Service Commission requested that it be given authority to coordinate pay schedules for wage-board positions, citing the lack of coordination among the various agencies in a direct interference with the government's war program. The various agencies rejected this approach believing that the great diversity in agency purposes and characteristics required more flexibility than could be achieved operating under a central board.[1]

The Classification Act of 1949 inaugurated a new method of setting blue-collar pay which exists essentially intact today. The act introduced the "prevailing wage rate" concept into the determination of pay scales. Unfortunately, the three main government agencies who set blue-collar wages chose to define it in their own unique way. The army-air force wage board used the "unadjusted-prevailing-rate system," the navy wage board used the "prevailing-rate-adjusted-by-the-evaluation system," and the Bureau of Labor Statistics utilized the "prevailing-rate-adjusted-by-averages system." In addition, the two Defense Department wage board systems used some additional criteria in determining the prevailing wage rate in the area. In 1965, a survey of the disparate rates was conducted at the request of Congress with the following results from the "Wage Board Pay Rates"— Report No.187, House of Representatives, 89th Congress, 1st Session— Union Calendar No.79, March 1965:

---

[1] Kenneth J. Mulligan, "The Federal Wage Board Program," *Public Personnel Review* 19 (Chicago: Public Personnel Association, 1958): 40.

Location	Army Air Force	Navy	GSA	VA	Range of Rates
New York	$2.37	$2.45	$2.06	$2.06	$.39
Philadelphia	2.32	2.40	1.91	1.95	.49
Washington, D.C.	2.10	2.23	1.54	1.67	.69
Norfolk	1.94	1.92	1.52	1.51	.43
Chicago	2.35	2.49	2.07	2.05	.44
San Francisco	2.57	2.62	2.49	2.48	.14

As the above chart shows, there was up to a $.69/hour disparity of rates for the same job in the same city. This dichotomy of pay scales spurred labor unions to pressure Congress for legislation which would correct the nonuniformity of wage rates. On 1 December 1967 the Civil Service Commission submitted regulations to Congress calling for far-reaching changes that were to be effective 1 July 1968. This new program, which was passed by Congress, was called the Coordinated Federal Wage System (CFWS).

The CFWS replaced the separate wage boards maintained by various departments and agencies. The true significance of this in the context of emerging collective bargaining is that employee organizations were to be represented under the new system. This was a breakthrough for federal unions because, heretofore, employee organizations were not represented on wage-survey teams. Also, the data were not subject to review by any agency other than the governmental agency. The statistical data were analyzed and interpreted only by authorized agency personnel. The CFWS is divided into six parts:

1. the Civil Service Commission;
2. the National Wage Policy Commission;
3. lead agencies;
4. agency wage-committees;
5. local wage-survey committees; and,
6. a host installation.[2]

The chairman of the Civil Service Commission is responsible for giving leadership in establishing and operating the Coordinated Federal Wage System, for consulting with appropriate employee organizations, and for keeping the president currently informed of significant developments. With the advice of federal departments and agencies and of interested employee organizations, the chairman determines the basic policies, practices, and procedures for the system.

[2] William J. Lange, "The Federal Wage Board System of the United States Government," *Public Personnel Review* 32 (Chicago: Public Personnel Association, 1971): 241.

The Civil Service Commission carries out the staff and operating functions involved in:

Developing and issuing basic policies and procedures for the system;

Defining the boundaries of individual local wage areas;

Designating the lead agency for each local wage area;

Prescribing requirements for the statistical design and accomplishment of wage surveys and for the establishment of pay schedules;

Establishing occupational grouping and titling;

Establishing a job grading system;

Developing and issuing job grading standards;

Providing a system for and making final decisions on employee job grading appeals;

Establishing rules governing the administration of pay for individual employees, for example, upon appointment, transfer, promotion, and demotion, including retention of pay rates as appropriate;

Authorizing additional pay as appropriate for work performed under unusually hazardous or severe working conditions;

Determining need for and authorizing use of special schedules as appropriate;

Performing necessary audits and inspections of agency wage board programs to insure compliance with overall system requirements; and,

Otherwise providing for a continuing program of systems maintenance and improvement designed to keep the wage system fully abreast of changing conditions, practices, and techniques both in and out of government.

The chairman of the Civil Service Commission establishes a National Wage Policy Committee consisting of eleven members. Five members are designated by the chairman of the Civil Service Commission from among federal departments and agencies employing wage-board employees. Four members are designated by the president of the AFL-CIO. One member is designated by the head of an independent labor organization selected on a rotating basis by the chairman of the Civil Service Commission. These ten members serve at the discretion of their respective designating authorities. The chairman of the National Wage Policy Committee is designated by the chairman of the Civil Service Commission. The salaries of the chairman and members are established and paid by their respective employers. The functions and responsibilities of the National Wage Policy Committee are:

Consideration of new or revised basic policies and procedures of the Coordinated Federal Wage System and makes its recommendations to the chairman of the Civil Service Commission;

meeting from time to time at the call of its chairman. Additionally, a member may request at any time that a meeting be called to consider policy matters within the concern of the committee; and

deciding by majority vote, but a member of the minority may file a report with the committee's recommendation.[3]

The *lead agency* is responsible for planning and executing wage surveys, analyzing the survey results, and developing wage schedules for the designated areas based on its surveys and determinations. This agency is the most important element in the CFWS. The lead agency collaborates with the Bureau of Labor Statistics where the bureau conducts surveys in order to eliminate dual-employer contracts. Other departments and agencies having wage-board employees in the local wage area are provided schedules of wage rates established by the lead agency and establish and administer these rates for wage-board employees of their organizations.

Each federal agency designated as a lead agency establishes an *agency wage-committee* consisting of five members. Two members are designated by the head of the labor organization having the largest number of wage-board employees covered by exclusive recognition in the lead agency. These four members serve at the discretion of their respective designating authorities. The authority to designate labor organization members remains with the same organization, at a minimum for a two-year period. The chairman of the agency wage-committee is designated by the head of the lead agency. The designating authorities may provide for alternates to the chairman and members. The salaries of the chairman and members are established and paid by their respective employers.[4]

The tasks and responsibilities include the following:

The agency wage-committee determines and recommends to the head of the agency those local wage areas having local wage-survey committees for which the agency wage-committee desires to participate in planning and reviewing full scale wage surveys and recommending wage schedules.

For such local wage areas the agency wage-committee considers and makes recommendations to the lead agency on any matter involved in developing the specifications for a full scale local wage-survey on which the lead agency proposes not to accept the recommendations of a local wage-survey committee and any matters on which a minority report has been filed by the labor representative on the local wage-survey committee.

Upon completion of a full scale wage-survey, the agency wage-committee considers the survey data, the local wage-survey committee's report

[3] U.S. Civil Service Commission, *Federal Personnel Manual,* chap. 532 subchap. 3, sec. 3–1, (Washington, D.C.: Government Printing Office, 1967), p. 532–37.
[4] Harry A. Donoian, "Setting Blue Collar Pay," *Monthly Labor Review* 92 (Washington, D.C.: Government Printing Office April 1969): 31.

and recommendations, and the statistical analyses and proposed pay-schedules derived therefrom as well as any other data or recommendations pertinent to the survey and recommends wage schedules to the pay-fixing authority.

A majority vote of the agency wage-committee constitutes the decision and recommendations of the committee, but a member of the minority may file a report with the committee's recommendation.

The *local wage-survey committee* conducts hearings and makes recommendations to the lead agency on local option features of the survey specifications. It determines the number of data collectors needed for the survey and provides for their training, makes preliminary contacts with establishments to be surveyed, decides on any differences between data collectors on job, matches any differences in policy and procedures, insures the confidentiality of all data obtained, and forwards such data to the lead agency.

The *host installation,* designated by the lead agency, serves as the focal point for the local wage-survey committee. It provides technical and clerical resources to the committee and obtains data on the number of such workers covered by exclusive recognition.

Thus, the basic philosophy behind the CFWS is that all employees in the same wage grade will receive the same basic pay rate, regardless of the job held. The actual method of determining the wage rate is found by using the "least-squares method" of regression analysis. Also, by using further mathematical analysis a "payline" is indicated, and this "payline" is used as a benchmark to determine the three steps for each respective grade.

The CFWS can, therefore, be characterized as a system with extensive union consultation rights through which the size of pay boosts is determined. At virtually every level of wage determination, labor organizations provide some input into the decision-making process. Be it the statistical design of the survey, the areas and/or jobs to be studied, or the method of analysis to be used in determining the size of the wage adjustment once the data have been collected, the labor union is always directly involved.

It should be rather evident at this point therefore that a very real form of collective bargaining does exist in the federal service, particularly for its blue-collar employees. The Federal Personnel Manual states: "Nothing in the Coordinated Federal Wage System restricts any independent agency or agency subdivision within a governmental department which engages in collective bargaining in connection with wage fixing from continuing such practices until an opportunity is presented to the National Wage Policy Committee for consideration and recommendation." As one concrete example of the extent of collective bargaining in the federal service over wage rates, the manual states: "Each grade of a regular wage board schedule has three rates of pay, with the first and third rates 4 percent below and above the second, respectively." In essence, this clause means that a blue-collar employee is hired at 96 percent of the "prevailing wage rate in the area"; after twenty-six weeks his rate of pay moves to 100 percent and after seventy-eight weeks, his wage rate is 104 percent of the "prevailing wage rate in the area." Thus, the majority wage-board employees are paid at rates 4 percent above the average in the area. A bill has just been passed by Congress which adds two more steps into the progression schedule. After stipulated periods of time, the employees are now to receive 108 and 112 percent respectively of the "prevailing wage rate in the area." One may or may not choose to call this collective bargaining over economic issues, but the practical implications of such legislation are the same as if management and labor had sat down at the bargaining table and agreed over two 4 percent pay boosts.

The overwhelming majority of remaining federal civilian employees are covered by the Federal Pay Comparability Act (FPCA) of 1970. This act is an outgrowth of the Federal Salary Act of 1962 which put forth the philosophy that federal salary rates should be comparable with those of private industry for the same level of work. Although the 1962 act established the comparability feature of federal pay, it still required specific future legislation to change the salaries. The FPCA of 1970 was intended to eliminate this necessity. The FPCA is applicable to general-schedule employees, foreign-service employees, doctors, dentists, and nurses in the Department of Medicine and Surgery of the veterans administration. Like the CFWS, there is extensive consultation with employee organizations over pay scales. In fact, one might argue that this consultation process is really a form of "softened bargaining."

The two main features of the FPCA are extensive consultation by management and labor and semiautomatic pay increases. Once the amount of the pay adjustment for civilian federal employees has been determined, it will automatically be put into effect on 1 October of each year. That is, unless the president sends an alternative plan to Congress. The president can take this action if he finds it inappropriate in any year to make the comparability adjustment because of a national emergency or economic conditions affecting the general welfare.[5] If the president so chooses to take this action, Congress must disapprove his plan within thirty calendar days of continuous session if the original pay adjustments are to be made.

The actual process of determining the exact amount of pay increases

---

[5] U.S. Civil Service Commission, *Questions and Answers Regarding the Federal Pay and Comparability Act of 1970* (Washington, D.C.: U.S. Civil Service Commission, 8 Jan. 1971), p. 3.

to be paid is rather interesting. The Bureau of Labor Statistics sets them originally through its National Survey of Professional Administrative, Technical and Clerical Pay (PAT Survey) and submits them to the president via the president's agent. The PAT Survey pegs general-schedule salaries to salaries of comparable occupations in private industry. At this point, the Advisory Committee on Federal Pay (ACFP), and the Federal Employees Pay Council (FEPC) enter the act. The ACFP is a three-member panel of persons generally recognized for their impartiality, knowledge, and experience in the field of labor relations and pay policy. The Committee reviews the annual report of the President's agent and considers such views and recommendations with respect to the analysis and pay proposals contained in that report as may be presented to it in writing by employee organizations, the president's agent, other officials of the government, experts, etc. The committee then reports its findings and recommendations to the president. Thus, federal employee unions have a direct say in the process of determining federal civilian pay.

Even more important than their rights to present views to the ACFP, federal employee organizations serve on the FEPC. The FEPC has five members who represent substantial numbers of employees under the statutory pay systems. They are appointed by the president's agent, and no more than three members at any one time are from a single employee organization, council, federation alliance association or affiliation of employee organizations. The role of the FEPC is pervasive and has the potential for significant impact on federal pay scales. The FEPC makes recommendations concerning such matters as:

> the coverage of the annual Bureau of Labor Statistics survey;

> the process of comparing current rates of pay of the statutory pay system with rates for the same levels of work in private industry; and,

> the adjustments that should be made to achieve comparability between them.

Thus, the FEPC indirectly affects the size of the pay adjustment by affecting the data base from which the size of the increase is determined. In effect, federal employee organizations bargain with management over who is to be included in the PAT Survey, over the methodology of setting pay, and ultimately over the magnitude of the increase. The bargaining of federal general-schedule employees, although not quite as overt as under the CFWS, is still substantial when one considers what goes on behind the scenes. All of these actions, when combined with the Congressional appeal, still open to federal labor unions, make their bargaining power credible and potent.

Summary and Conclusions

The determination of wages and fringe benefits of white- and blue-collar federal employees reflects the interaction of the following four forces: the economic environment in the private sector; the political accommodation among various groups; the influence of unions and collective bargaining; and the rational bureaucratic structure managed by the Civil Service Commission.

Examination of the history and development of the pay/benefit system for blue-collar workers reveals the impact of the above-noted factors. Based upon administrative and statutory authority, we see how "wage boards" functioned and evolved in fixing wages and benefits. We see also how the Civil Service Commission (CSC) achieved more and more authority to coordinate pay schedules for wage board positions. Introducing the notion of the "prevailing wage rate," not uniformly interpreted and implemented by the three principal federal agencies setting blue-collar wages and benefits, the Classification Act of 1949, is the basic statute today for determining pay and benefits.

As we review operations under the act we see the continuing interaction of the above forces. The establishment of the coordinated federal wage system, the representation of employee organization on the board and the authoritative role of the chairman of the CSC coupled with the concept of prevailing wages demonstrate the way in which blue-collar pay and benefits are determined. This process illustrates the importance of accommodating plural interests in our society. The membership of the National Wage Committee reveals the necessity of establishing a structure which gives representation to the affected parties.

Particularly noteworthy is the significant impact of unions in setting pay/benefits for blue-collar workers. At every level unions provide input into the decision-making process. In effect, there is collective bargaining in this aspect of the federal service. To resolve any questions, the Federal Personnel Manual requires agencies to involve their unions and to integrate the pay/benefit process with collective bargaining.

Turning to federal white-collar workers, we find that their pay benefits are governed by the Federal Pay Comparability Act of 1970 and congressional legislation. Again the structure and process illustrate the four forces mentioned earlier. Here, however, the intent is provide for objective and automatic increases using private-sector pay standards as the determinant. Federal managers consult with unions and politics influences the actions of Congress. Indeed, the recent elimination by Congress of the 1 percent "kicker" in pay scales to compensate for the delay in the automatic operation of the system illustrates the strength of partisan politics. Finally, the Advisory Committee on Federal Pay and the Federal Employees Pay Council suggest how input on fixing wages for white-collar workers is obtained from both neutral and representative organizations.

What does the experience of having set pay and benefits for both blue- and white-collar workers indicate for the armed forces? *First,* there are the laws, administrative rulings and structures known and implemented by the United States army, navy and air force in handling pay and benefits; *second,* there is their familiarity and established relationship with unions and employee organizations; *third,* there is their extensive experience with collective bargaining; *fourth,* there is the existence of rational structures and processes probably adaptable for handling similar problems in the armed forces; *fifth,* there is a trained and knowledgeable cadre of managers capable of dealing with the problems arising when and if uniformed personnel engage in collective action; and, *sixth,* there is the capability of the managers to work constructively with various interest groups and Congress.

In short, adding uniformed personnel to the blue- and white-collar workers as another group with whom collective relationships will be established is not a huge leap into the unknown. As indicated in this and earlier chapters, there are established patterns clearly identified for expanding collective bargaining to uniformed personnel. The tools, techniques, and knowledge suggest that the shift will be incremental, not gigantic, and that the working stability of American society will facilitate the collective determination of pay and benefits for uniformed personnel.

5

Rights Systems, Appeals Processes, and Grievance Arbitration for Nonuniformed Federal Employees

MICHAEL E. SPARROUGH

Introduction

Any discussion of labor relations in the federal service must begin with a review of the complex web of employee rights, appeals procedures, and grievance arbitration. These systems were created by statute and/or administrative action, both of which predate and, in most cases, take precedence over those rights accorded by Executive Order 11616. Broadly speaking, the most basic rights of an employee are his constitutional rights. These rights, while important, have had only limited relevance in the federal labor-relations system until recently. The most elaborate and dominant force of employee rights in the federal environment is the Civil Service System. The government operates from day-to-day on the basis of the civil-service regulations and guidance. Until Executive Order 10988 was issued in 1962, virtually all federal employee-management relations were governed by CSC regulations. Executive Orders 10988, 11491 and, presently, 11616 have successively diminished the role of the CSC in the protection of employee rights, substituting instead a form of collective bargaining and bilateral determination of working conditions. However, Executive Order 11616 still represents only a minor part of the total employee rights system in the federal service. As the movement toward full collective bargaining has progressed, existing tensions among the various systems have been accentuated. This chapter will examine some of them.

Statutory Rights

The Federal Labor Relations Council, in its first annual review of Executive Order 11491 discussed the following twelve types of appeals which are outside the scope of negotiated grievance procedures.

1. *Adverse action appeals.* Initial adverse action appeals are either processed at the agency level or at a civil service first-level appellate office. The employee has the right to a hearing regardless of the route taken. If the initial appeal be to the agency, further appeals are processed through the CSC (with the right of hearing) and then to the Civil Service Board of Appeals Review (BAR). However, if the agency have two appellate levels, the employee must choose between going to the agency second level. If the initial appeal were to the CSC first-level office, further appeals are taken directly to the BAR. Adverse action appeals are governed by section 7701, 5 U.S. Code (for veterans) and by section 22 of Executive Order 11491 (for nonveterans). The right of appeal is contained in part 752 of the Federal Personnel Manual (FPM); appeals to agencies are covered in FPM part 771; and appeals to the CSC are contained in FPM part 772.

2. *General schedule classification appeals.* Initial appeals of this nature are handled at the agency or CSC first-level office. If the initial appeal be to the agency, further appeals are directed to the CSC first-level office. If the initial appeal be to the CSC first-level office, there is no further appeal. This type of classification appeal is governed by section 5112, 5 U.S. Code and FPM part 511.

3. *Wage-board classification appeals.* Initial appeals of this type are processed through the agency, and further appeals are received at the CSC first-level offices. These types of appeals are governed by section 5345, 5 U.S. Code and FPM part 532.

4. *Appeals concerning discrimination.* These types of appeals include discrimination on the basis of race, sex, color, religion, or national origin. Initial appeals are processed at the agency level and there is a right to a hearing. Further appeals are directed to the CSC and then to the BAR. Discrimination appeals are governed by section 104 of Executive Order 11246 and FPM part 713.

5. *Level of competence.* Initial appeals are processed at the agency level where the individual has the right to make a personal presentation. Further appeals are then directed to the CSC and then to the BAR. Level-of-competence appeals are governed by section 5335, 5 U.S. Code and FPM part 531.

6. *Performance ratings.* Initial appeals are processed at the agency level or directly by the BAR (with the right to a hearing). If the rating appealed be "unsatisfactory" and if the initial appeal be to the agency, further appeal is to the BAR (with the right to a hearing). If the rating appealed be "satisfactory" or better, there is no further appeal regardless of whether the initial appeal was to the agency or to the BAR. These types of appeals are governed by section 4305, 5 U.S. Code and FPM part 430.

7. *Reduction in force.* Initial appeals of a reduction in force are handled at the CSC first-level office. Only veterans have the right to a hearing. Further appeals are referred to the BAR. Reduction-in-force appeals are governed indirectly by section 3502, 5 U.S. Code and directly by the FPM part 351.

8. *Salary retention.* Initial appeals are referred to the CSC first-level office, and there is no procedure for further appeal. Salary retention appeals are governed indirectly by sections 5377 and 5388, 5 U.S. Code and directly by FPM part 531.

9. *Separation of probationers (for unsatisfactory performance or conduct).* There is no right of appeal unless the employee alleges discrimination, in which case the appeal is to the CSC first-level office. Further appeals are then taken to the BAR. These types of appeals are covered exclusively by the FPM part 315.

10. *Separation of probationers (for conditions existing before appointment).* These types of appeal are referred to the CSC first-level office for procedural review only (unless discrimination is alleged). Further appeals are referred to the BAR. These types of appeal are covered exclusively in the FPM part 315.

11. *Suspension for thirty-days or less.* Initial appeals of this type are referred to the CSC first-level office for procedural review only (unless discrimination is alleged). Further appeals are directed to the BAR. These types of appeals are governed indirectly by section 7501, 5 U.S. Code and directly by the FPM part 752.

12. *Working conditions and other grievances.* Initial appeals are processed at the agency level with no further appeals procedure. These types of appeals are covered exclusively by the FPM part 771.[1]

In addition to these twelve types of appeals, a subsequent report after the issuance of Executive Order 11616, listed some additional avenues of appeal which are available to federal employees. They included many of those stipulated by the Civil Service Commission and added:

1. *reemployment priority rights* (FPM, chapter 330; 5 U.S. Code 3502);
2. *reemployment or reinstatement rights* (FPM, chapter 352, 5 U.S. Code 2193 (d), 2835 (b);
3. *military restoration* (FPM, chapter 353, 5 U.S. Code 3551);
4. *level of competence (pay)* (FPM, chapter 531, U.S. Code 5304,5338);
5. *job granting* (FPM, chapter 532, 5 U.S. Code 5338);
6. *national security* (FPM, chapter 732, 5 U.S. Code, Executive Order 10430);
7. *political activity* (FPM, chapter 733, 5 U.S. Code 1504–6, 1508);
8. *fitness-for-duty examination* (FPM, chapter 890, 5 U.S. Code 8337);
9. *health benefits* (FPM, chapter 890, 5 U.S. Code 8912); and,
10. *injury compensation* (FPM, chapter 890, 5 U.S. Code 8121–22).[2]

A second item to be considered is that the federal government is the epitome of a highly bureaucratic structure and contains a plethora of subordinated levels of authority. One only need look at the organizational structure of the Department of Defense to appreciate this statement. Agency regulations are promulgated at each echelon of authority so that the farther down the hierarchical structure one goes, the larger the "web of rules" becomes. When one considers this second aspect along with the

---

[1] *Federal Labor Relations Council 1970 Annual Review,* Staff Paper no. 12.

[2] William Kilberg, Thomas Angelo, and Lawrence Lorber, "Grievance Arbitration Patterns in the Federal Service," *Monthly Labor Review* 95 (Washington, D.C.: Government Printing Office, November 1972): 30.

intricate system of appeals previously mentioned, it becomes quite evident that federal labor relations exist in a particularly constrained environment. These aspects should be remembered while reading the remainder of this chapter.

The full impact of the various rights, appeals systems and grievance arbitration on management's ability to control and direct its environment has not yet been determined nor is it likely to be in the near future. However, many persons assert that it has been substantial. Regardless of how substantial the impact of these rights, appeals and arbitration systems has been in the past, there is suggestive evidence that it has recently become more dramatic. For example, employee activism has brought constitutional questions increasingly into play. The case of *Arnette, et al.* v. *Kennedy, et al.* is illustrative.[3] This case involves the constitutional rights of an individual, Wayne Kennedy, a nonprobationary federal employee, who was discharged from his position as a field representative with the Chicago branch of the Office of Economic Opportunity (OEO) in March 1972.

Against the wishes of his superiors, Kennedy participated in a press conference at which representatives of Indian groups protested the policies of several governmental agencies, including OEO. Federal law (5 U.S. Code 7501 [a]) authorizes the removal of federal employees "for such cause as will promote the efficiency of the service." This was the basis upon which Kennedy was discharged. Instead of utilizing appeals procedures within the federal service for redress, Kennedy sought relief from the courts. He claimed that both his first and fifth amendment rights were denied by his superiors.

First, Kennedy's lawyers claimed, "that the procedure by which Kennedy's employment was terminated deprives him . . . of due process under the fifth amendment by its failure to provide a full evidentiary hearing *prior* to termination, with the right to be heard by an impartial hearing officer; the right to present witnesses, the right to confront and cross-examine adverse witnesses, and the right to a written decision indicating the reasons for discharge or suspension and the evidence relied upon."

The United States District Court for the Northern District of Illinois agreed with this contention and ordered OEO, "to reinstate Kennedy to his former position with back pay. If further removal proceedings are initiated, the agency shall afford him the opportunity for a hearing consistent with this opinion within a reasonable time prior to any subsequent removal."

Kennedy's lawyers also alleged that both the statute and the related OEO regulations used as a basis for discharge "are unconstitutional on their face inasmuch as they chill the first amendment rights of freedom of speech of OEO employees due to their vagueness and overbreadth."

---

[3] 416 U.S.134 (16 April 1974).

The court agreed with these contentions also, and stated: "Accordingly, we hold that [5 U.S. Code 7501] and the related rules are unconstitutional on their face insofar as they are construed to regulate the speech of competitive service employees and enjoin their further enforcement as so construed. This decision does not, of course, affect the validity of agency regulations which, unlike those challenged here, define the conduct proscribed in unambiguous terms."[4]

The decision of the district court was appealed by the government, and in April 1974 the Supreme Court sustained OEO on the main points but remanded to the district court for further hearings. Thus, dismissal "for such cause as will promote the efficiency of the service" has been sustained.

Executive Order Rights

Executive Orders 10988, 11491, and 11616 added two additional sets of rights and procedures in the federal service. Specifically, they included the right of workers to organize and be recognized and the right of employee organizations to bargain with management. This second right involves participation in both rule formulation and rule implementation. As attempts were made to integrate these additional rights into the totality of the rights system which exist in the federal service, certain problems developed. This conflict between agency regulations and executive-order and statutory rights will be addressed in this section.

The Right to Organize

Since the issuance of Executive Order 10988, the United States Government has officially recognized the rights of workers to organize and bargain with management over working conditions.

Executive Order 11616 sets down unfair labor practices paralleling those found in the Labor Management Relations Act of 1947 for both management and employee organizations in section 19. Section 19(d) is an actual amendment to Executive Order 11491 and is an attempt to alleviate the "double-bite" problem (previously stated). The section states:

> Issues which can properly be raised under an appeals procedure may not be raised under this Section. Issues which can be raised under a grievance procedure may, in the discretion of the aggrieved party, be raised under that procedure or the complaint procedure under this Section, but not under both procedures. Appeals or grievance decisions shall not be con-

---

[4] Decision of United States District Court for the Northern District of Illinois, *Government Employee Relations Report,* (Washington, D.C.: Bureau of National Affairs, 1972), p. F-11; 349 F. Supp. 863 (N. O. Ill., 1972).

strued as unfair labor practice decisions under this Order nor as precedent for such decisions. All complaints under this Section that cannot be resolved by the parties shall be filed with the Assistant Secretary.

A case involving the conflict between an unfair labor practice under Executive Order 11616 and existing regulations of the Texas Air National Guard (TANG) occurred in 1973. The aspect of this case that makes it intriguing is that, as a condition of employment, a civilian employee of TANG must also be a uniformed member of TANG. James E. Burgamy was just such an employee, but was refused reenlistment in TANG, allegedly for failure to complete a "career development course" designed to improve guard members' proficiency in their military specialties. The refusal of reenlistment was, of course, tantamount to a dismissal from his civilian job. Burgamy, who had been an active union member, filed an unfair labor practice charge with the assistant secretary of labor for labor-management relations. He claimed that the real reason he was rejected reenlistment stemmed not from his failure to complete the "career development course," but because of his union activity.

Previous to his appeal to the assistant secretary of labor, however, Burgamy had appealed his case through the negotiated grievance procedure up to the Adjutant General's office of TANG. His commanding officer was sustained at every level. When Burgamy took his complaint to the assistant secretary of labor, "the agency argued that since Burgamy had protested the refusal to reenlist him to the Adjutant General of Texas, he was barred from filing an unfair labor charge covering the same ground." The rationale for the TANG argument was that provisions of the Texas Code of Military Justice provided an adequate forum for Burgamy to appeal his refused reenlistment.

Labor Department administrative law judge, Samuel A. Chaitovitz, in his decision found "no reason to believe that this Section . . . permitted Burgamy to seek consideration of whether he was denied reenlistment because he engaged in protected union activity." Therefore he decided "that the Section does not operate as a bar to the processing of a complaint as an unfair labor practice charge under the Order as contemplated by Section 19(d) of the Order."[5]

Chaitovitz, therefore, recommended that the assistant secretary of labor order Burgamy's reinstatement to his civilian job with TANG along with full back pay plus 6-percent interest. Chaitovitz did not recommend that the assistant secretary of labor order TANG to reenlist Burgamy, suggesting that such an order is outside the assistant secretary's authority. However, he did state that, "reinstatement to the civilian job could be

_____

[5] Bureau of National Affairs, *Government Employee Relations Report*, no. 515, (Washington, D.C.: Bureau of National Affairs, 6 August 1973), p. a-5.

expected to prompt the guard to accept him back into its ranks in view of the dual status of civilian technicians." This case illustrates that even though there have been attempts to eliminate the "double-bite" problem in federal civilian labor relations, the problem still persists. In this case, Burgamy complained through the TANG appeals procedure, and when this avenue did not produce a favorable outcome, he then took the path of appeal to the assistant secretary of labor for a violation of Executive Order 11616.[6]

The Right to Negotiate

In addition to the right to organize, the right to negotiate is also guaranteed by the executive orders. Executive Order 11616, section 11, outlines the ground rule for the negotiation of collective bargaining agreements; section 12 describes the boundaries within which bargaining may occur and identifies the rights of management. It also forbids compulsory union membership but permits a voluntary checkoff of union dues. Finally, section 13 sets forth the grievance and arbitration procedures. The reasons for this section, which substantially revises and replaces sections 13 and 14 in Executive Order 11491, are set forth as follows by the Federal Labor Relations Council:

> The root of the persistent dissatisfaction with grievance and arbitration procedures in the Federal program appears to be the confusing, inter-mixture of individual employee rights established by law and regulation with the collective rights of employees established by negotiated agreements. This intermixture has resulted in overlap and duplication of rights and remedies, and in requirements with respect to negotiated grievance procedures which are less in some respects and greater in others than are suitable for effective grievance handling in a labor relations system.

Section 13, which resulted, states:

> (a) An agreement between an agency and a labor organization shall provide a procedure, applicable only to the unit, for the consideration of grievances over the interpretation or application of the agreement. A negotiated grievance procedure may not cover any other matters for which statutory appeals procedures exist, and shall be the exclusive procedure available to the parties and the employees in the unit for resolving such grievances. However, any employee or group of employees in the unit may present such grievances to the agency and have them adjusted, without the intervention of the exclusive representative as long as the adjustment is not inconsistent with the terms of the agreement and the exclusive representative has been given opportunity to be present at the adjustment.
>
> (b) A negotiated procedure may provide for the arbitration of grievances over the interpretation or application of the agreement, but not over

---

[6] Ibid.

any other matters. Arbitration may be invoked only by the agency or the exclusive representative. Either party may file exceptions to an arbitrator's award with the Council under regulations prescribed by the Council.

(c) Grievances initiated by an employee or group of employees in the unit on matters other than the interpretation or application of an existing agreement may be presented under any procedure available for the purpose.

(d) Questions that cannot be resolved by the parties as to whether or not a grievance is on a matter subject to the grievance procedure in an existing agreement, or is subject to arbitration under that agreement, may be referred to the Assistant Secretary for decision.

(e) No agreement may be established, extended or renewed after the effective date of this Order which does not conform to this Section. However, this Section is not applicable to agreements entered into before the effective date of this Order.[7]

Issues Involving the Scope of Bargaining

Prior to the issuance of Executive Order 10988, personnel relations in the federal service were guided exclusively by the system of statutory rights and agency regulations previously described. There was an *informal* system of employee consultation rights, but all decisions were strictly a unilateral management function. Executive Order 10988 formalized these consultation rights of employees and employee organizations, but did little more. Unions were afforded the rights of recognition, etc., but, in a very real sense, there were "empty rights." Management at the agency level could, for example, reverse unilaterally specific terms of any agreement negotiated at a lower level of the hierarchy. Thus, labor agreements negotiated in the federal service were in fact not enforceable unless the agency paternalistically and unilaterally deemed that they would be. It is not surprising, therefore, that management tended to show less than normal resistance to "negotiating" over a wide range of items.

In an attempt to eliminate this situation, Executive Order 11491 was passed in 1969. The order brought a degree of maturity and true bilateralism to the federal labor-relations framework by instituting a system of third-party review. The Federal Labor Relations Council (FLRC), and the Federal Service Impasse Panel were established, and the assistant secretary of labor for labor-management relations was empowered to rule on unfair labor practices under the order. Until that time, statutory appeals procedures and agency regulations were able to coexist with negotiated labor agreements without controversy. The reason for this was that both

---

[7] United States Federal Labor Relations Council, *Labor-Management Relations in the Federal Service* (Washington, D.C.: Government Printing Office, 1971), p. 28, 13.

agency regulations and negotiated labor agreements were unilaterally controlled by management, and thus there was little chance for conflict.

However, with the advent of Executive Order 11491, there also came an emerging conflict between agency regulations and the terms of negotiated agreements. Those managements who under Executive Order 10988 were willing to negotiate over a wide range of issues, were now willing to negotiate over very few. They viewed third-party review as a vehicle which would be utilized by unions to break down barriers to issues traditionally considered to be "management prerogatives."

With such an attitude on the part of management, the natural union response was to appeal to the FLRC. Negotiability appeals by unions increased drastically, as management resisted union efforts to expand the areas of negotiability. The FLRC, in response to this phenomenon, collaborated with the Civil Service Commission in a campaign to "deregulate." Through this process it was hoped that new areas would be opened for negotiation and that genuine strides toward bilateral determination of working conditions would be made. Briefly, the process of "deregulation" involved the perusing of CSC regulations and the elimination of unnecessary sections. Put more succinctly, the CSC attempted to "trim the fat" from its rules and regulations and to encourage agencies at lower levels to do the same.

Despite the good intentions of the FLRC and the CSC, unilateral trimming of lower-echelon regulations in the spirit of Executive Order 11616 was not forthcoming. In fact, a reverse situation occurred. When higher-level agencies "deregulated," lower-level agencies, attempting to maintain the status quo, tended to "reregulate." Those rules and regulations eliminated from parent organizations were reincorporated by lower-level agencies into their regulations.

The FLRC has not been disposed to look too favorably upon these tactics of management. In fact, when it has been shown that attempts were deliberately made to circumvent the intent of Executive Order 11491 and 11616, the FLRC has been inclined to find in favor of unions. One of the more recent cases of this nature which has been appealed to the FLRC involves the International Association of Machinists (IAM) and two "tenant" activities at the Aberdeen Proving Ground (APG) in Maryland. The case was entitled *Kirk Army Hospital and Aberdeen Research and Development* vs. *IAM*. It covered a number of negotiability issues, one of which was nonsupervisory wage-grade promotions. "The broadcast, touching all but a few of the disputed provisions in the union proposals, concerns whether, under section 11(a) of the order, the servicing host installation's merit-promotion regulation, as interpreted by the agency head, may properly limit the scope of negotiation on the matters covered by that directive at the serviced "tenant" activities. Both the Kirk Army Hospital (KAH) and the Aberdeen Research and Development Center (ARDC) were Department of the Army "tenant" activities located at the APG, an army host installation.

The important aspect to be recognized in this case is the way management tried to restrict the negotiability of issues. Regulations at the level at which negotiations are conducted are negotiable. But, regulations at the next higher level and beyond are not.

> The commanding officers of the KAH and ARDC . . . *delegated* . . . [their] personnel management authority, including the authority to issue personnel policy directives, to the commanding officer of APG. The latter, exercising the authority so delegated to him, issued the regulation promulgating the installation-wide promotion plan here at issue. . . . However, as already indicated, the commanding officers of ARDC and KAH could not properly limit their own obligation to bargain with the union on otherwise negotiable matters under section 11(a) merely by issuing a regulation.

The FLRC saw this tactic for what it was, and on 17 September 1973, declared:

> In our opinion, the APG merit promotion regulation delegated by the activity commanding officer in connection with a servicing arrangement, must constitute an equally improper limitation on the scope of bargaining at the activities. In other words, the delegations, by the activity of commanding officers, of their personnel management authority in no way modifies the operation of Section 11(a) with regard to actions taken pursuant to such authority.[8]

Other Union Responses to Issues of Negotiability

There are at least two other interesting ways in which unions can respond to attempts by management to avoid meaningful collective bargaining because of a conflict with higher echelon regulations. First, unions can attempt to change the structure of bargaining. They can accomplish this by enlarging the bargaining unit. A second approach is to attempt a wholesale transference of higher-level agency regulations into their collective bargaining agreements.

Federal civilian employees unions can circumvent the issue of negotiability over higher-level regulations by effecting their wholesale transference into negotiated agreements. Thus, whole sections of upper echelon regulations might be incorporated unchanged into federal service

---

[8] U.S. Federal Labor Relations Council, "Report of Case Decisions," (Washington, D.C.: Government Printing Office, 1973), p. 3.

labor agreements. This may become the first step to make all agency regulations negotiable. Incidentally, this tactic has been used extensively in other public sector agreements (police, firemen, and teachers), although the layering of regulations was in no way as extensive as in the federal service. Management must be alert to this proposal by unions, lest it seriously jeopardize its future "right to manage." The second step, once higher-level regulations are part of the labor agreement, is to seek changes in the next round of negotiations. The effects of this might be staggering when taken in the context of third-party review over negotiation issues and impasses. At this point, unions begin to "call the shots" and management's decision-making capacity becomes seriously impaired.

The Grievance Problem

One of the foremost reasons for management's desire to limit the scope of negotiability has been its fear of enlarging the scope of the negotiated grievance procedure. A brief historical sketch of the development of the negotiated grievance procedure in the federal service will explain this situation. Executive Order 10988 allowed the negotiation of grievance procedures, and, in addition, permitted grievance arbitration. However, the order stipulated that arbitration provisions could only be "advisory." Thus, an agency was put in the enviable position of being able to agree to a grievance procedure with arbitration, and, in actuality, agree to nothing. The agency could negotiate when it wanted to do so over a grievance and defer to arbitration when pressed for a settlement. If the award was not what was desired, it was simply rejected by the agency. Ultimately, the final disposition of a grievance was left to the discretion of the agency head. This was essentially the same situation which predated Executive Order 10988.

Executive Order 11491, with its system of third-party review also "permitted the negotiated grievance procedure to be the exclusive method for resolving dispute during the life of the contract. . . . it was soon discovered . . . that the conflict between employee rights by law or regulation and rights created by the collective agreement was not resolved by allowing the grievance procedure to be the sole route open to employees."

In an attempt to alleviate this situation, Executive Order 11616 was issued in 1971. The order amended Executive Order 11491, "substantively in the areas of grievance and arbitration procedures. The new Order provides that negotiated grievance procedures and arbitration can deal only with the interpretation or application of a negotiated agreement, and cannot deal with matters outside the agreement, including those for which statutory appeals procedures exist. These changes are codified as Section

13 of the amended Order and are applicable to all agreements established, extended, or renewed beginning November 24, 1971." Section 13 of Executive Order 11616 excludes "from coverage in the negotiated grievance procedure matters which are subject to statutory appeals procedures."

Thus, Executive Order 11616 clearly delineated the scope of the negotiated grievance procedure. It further amended the duties of the assistant secretary of labor for labor-management relations stating that he shall "decide questions as to whether a grievance is subject to a negotiated grievance procedure or subject to arbitration under an agreement." Taken by themselves, these actions would seem to circumvent the whole negotiated grievance framework in the federal service. In the maze of statutes and regulations, which again are not negotiable, it would appear that few issues would ever be resolved by the negotiated grievance procedure. This is another reason why FLRC and CSC chose to urge "deregulation." Statutes were taken as "given" and thus there was little chance of wholesale changes. Regulations, however, were easily amendable, and the FLRC, as previously described, chose this route. The FLRC encouraged agencies to "deregulate" so that the scope of negotiations could be evidenced. This, in turn, would widen the scope of negotiated grievance procedures. As already described, managerial resistance was widespread, and caseloads at both the agency and FLRC level have included a significant number of attempts by management to reduce the effectiveness of the negotiated grievance procedure.

One interesting case concerns an attempt by management to limit the scope of the negotiated grievance procedure through "reregulation." The parties in the dispute were the AFGE local 1668, and Elmendorf AFB in Alaska. The Department of Defense (DOD) in this case had attempted to circumvent negotiated grievance procedures by DOD Directive 1426.I VII B, 2.e. (5) and VII B. C. issued 9 December 1971. This directive was issued about three months after Executive Order 11616 was issued and states:

> Any agreement negotiated with a labor organization accorded exclusive recognition will contain, as a minimum: . . . . A statement that questions as to interpretation of published agency policies or regulations, provisions of law, or regulations of appropriate authorities outside the agency shall not be subject to the negotiated grievance procedure regardless of whether such policies, laws or regulations are quoted, cited, or otherwise incorporated or referenced in the agreement.

In a recent round of negotiations, an agreement was reached by the parties and submitted to the Department of the Air Force for approval. The air force refused to approve the agreement, alleging that it violated the above-listed regulations. The union then filed with the DOD a negotiability appeal, which was rejected. The AFGE then appealed to the FLRC. Without delving into the legalism of the case, the FLRC found in favor of the AFGE, declaring that the DOD regulation was a violation of section 13 of Executive Order 11616 (this section covers grievance and arbitration procedures in negotiated agreements). By requiring that the negotiated labor agreements contain a clause which specifically states, "that questions as to interpretation of published agency policies or regulations, provisions of law, or regulations of appropriate authorities outside DOD shall not be subject to the negotiated [grievance] procedure," the Department of the Air Force was, in fact, attempting to limit the scope of the negotiated grievance procedure.

Thus, on 15 May 1973, the FLRC ruled decisively that it will not tolerate "reregulation" by agencies which threatens to destroy the intent of Executive Order 11616 with respect to issues of negotiability and the scope of negotiated grievance procedures.

Implications for Management

At present, labor relations in the federal service is in a developmental stage. The FLRC, the Federal Service Impasses Panel, and the assistant secretary of labor for labor-management relations are attempting to provide guidance to an emerging federal labor relations system, but sometimes the issues confronting them have been difficult to answer. As such, these tribunals of third-party review, which are not infallible, can make decisions which might seriously impair "management's right to manage." In a very real sense many of the ultimate decisions which affect an agency's long-run efficient operations are presently being decided neither by management nor by unions, but by third parties. The Federal Service Impasses Panel is exercising its powers to break impasses in negotiations. The FLRC is deciding what is negotiable and subject to grievance, and the assistant secretary of labor for labor-management relations is deciding what is arbitrable. In addition, the courts are becoming increasingly involved in labor-management disputes. Why, then, are there so many issues being decided by third-party review? The answer, as previously described, is management's resistance to meaningful collective bargaining and the traditional federal union response of "going around management" to achieve its goals. The lesson to be learned is that by negotiating with unions in the short run, many potential problems in the long run can be solved.

As discussed in this chapter, management has chosen to let the courts and third-party review boards make decisions for them with obvious results.

By using an excess of unilateral decision-making powers in the TANG case, the plaintiff was provided with excellent grounds for third-party review by the assistant secretary of labor.

By trying to limit the scope of negotiations, the KAH forced the FLRC to hand down a decision which now serves as a valuable precedent for unions in the conflict of agency regulations and terms of negotiated agreements.

By a general resistance to collective bargaining, employee organizations are now attempting to form a Veterans Administration (VA)-wide bargaining unit.

Therefore, we see the conduct of federal labor relations has sustained significant changes. Management's right to promulgate rules on a unilateral basis has been lessened by the introduction of a system of third-party review. In addition, management's right to interpret and apply rules has been limited. Grievance and arbitration procedures are now a fact of life in federal-service labor relations. These procedures have supplanted the so-called "doctrine of administrative initiative," prevalent in the federal service before Executive Order 10988 was issued. In conclusion, it should be stated that, with the mere stroke of a pen, the president could one day extend just such a system to the armed forces. If this situation does occur, the experiences of federal managers in the civilian sector should provide a cogent set of examples of how not to resist collective bargaining and how not to approach it on a mature basis.

Grievance Arbitration

We turn to discuss in more detail the development of grievance arbitration for nonuniformed federal employees. A trend toward binding arbitration of grievances in the federal service began in the early 1960s. In 1970 the United States Department of Labor reported that, "contracts in eighteen Federal agencies contained arbitration provisions in 1967 compared with 10 in 1964.[9] In April 1973 the Department of Labor reported that a study of federal collective bargaining agreements in effect before November 1971 (date of Executive Order 11616 amended Executive Order 11491), found that, "binding arbitration was employed in two fifths of the agreements with grievance procedures."[10] Of course, a larger number of agreements provided for advisory arbitration.

---

[9] U.S. Department of Labor, Bureau of Labor Statistics, *Negotiations, Impasse, Grievance, and Arbitration in Federal Agreements,* Bulletin 1661, (Washington, D.C.: 1970), p. 25.

[10] U.S. Department of Labor, Bureau of Labor Statistics, *Summary Report: Collective Bargaining Agreements in the Federal Service,* 1971, (Washington, D.C.: Department of Labor, April 1973), p. 3.

Thus, when third-party review was only advisory, federal employee organizations showed a tendency of favoring it over agency procedures as a vehicle for the settlement of grievances. When Executive Order 11491 established the possibility of binding arbitration of employee grievances, the attractiveness of third-party review increased even more. Like workers in the private sector, civil service employees have demonstrated a preference for binding arbitration of grievances over the unilateral determinations of management. Unions and their members feel that their chances of winning are improved by opting for the impartiality of third-party review. Management in the federal service has characteristically viewed unionization, the expanding areas of negotiability, and the increasing role of the negotiated grievance procedure in the dispute resolution process as potential restraints on its "right to manage." With such partisan views, it is hardly surprising that unions and workers alike in both the private and public sectors should prefer binding arbitration of grievances.

Experience Under Executive Order 11616

At present, no major study dealing exclusively with the experience under Executive Order 11616 has been completed. It seems logical, however, that the trend toward the inclusion of more binding arbitration provisions in federal service agreements will continue. In a *Monthly Labor Review* article, it was stated: "We conclude that grievance arbitration procedures in the Federal sector have made many advances since its inception. The refinements in Federal labor relations made by Executive Order 11616 strongly indicate that Federal labor-management relations should continue to evolve into a fair and effective means of dispute resolution."[11]

To gain an understanding of how this trend has affected the Department of Defense, a more current but limited, sample of navy contracts was selected. Particular emphasis was placed on the analysis of specific grievances and arbitration provisions contained in these navy contracts.

Sample Selection

There are some 2,400 current labor agreements on file at the United States Civil Service Commission that cover civilian federal employees. Of these, about 400 cover navy employees. It was from this universe that a sample of agreements was drawn. Three broad criteria were utilized in selecting a representative sample: the contracts selected should cover large numbers of employees, preferably more than 1,000; the agreements selected should include a cross section of navy installations on both coasts; and, the agree-

---

[11] Kilberg, Angelo and Lorben, "Grievance and Arbitration Patterns," p. 30.

ments selected should include a cross section of the major unions in the federal service.

Using these three criteria, a sample of twenty agreements covering 61,020 employees was selected (see Table 5–1). All but three contracts covered at least 1,000 workers, and five agreements covered more than 4,000 employees. Both, in terms of the numbers of agreements and workers covered, naval shipyards dominated the sample with eight contracts and 38,251 workers, respectively. There were eight different types of navy installations included in the sample. Geographically, the sample was rather evenly distributed with nine agreements on each coast and two contracts in the central states. The most heavily represented union in the sample was the Metal Trades Council (MTC) in nine agreements covering 37,039 employees. Fourteen of the twenty contracts expired in 1973 or 1974.

Agreement Analysis

Although no two labor agreements in the federal service are exactly alike, a surprising number contain similar sections. The table of contents from the Hunters Point naval shipyard is typical of the provisions which are included in navy labor agreements. Grievance and arbitration provisions are the core of virtually all agreements in the federal sector. Yet in a typical contract, they appear toward the end. A glance at Table 5–2 reveals the main reason. There are various types of appeals procedures which are outside the scope of the negotiated grievance procedure. The typical federal labor contract explains them, and, in so doing, clearly delineates the scope of the negotiated grievance procedures. So precise are the descriptions of appeals procedures for civilian naval employees that fourteen of the twenty agreements sampled contained either a specific section or appendix which listed those appeals procedures that are excluded from the negotiated grievance procedure. The remaining six contracts described them generally. An example of these listed exclusions, which were extracted from the Navy Supply Center agreement at Norfolk, Virginia, is presented in Table 5–3. In addition, all the navy contracts sampled contained clauses describing an alternative approach of grievance resolution, the navy grievance procedure. The last sentence of Table 5–3 is an example of this type of clause. Another example of this type of clause is presented later in the negotiated grievance procedure of the same contract. The provision states:

> If no satisfactory settlement is reached . . . it is agreed by both parties to this Agreement that at this point the aggrieved employee shall indicate in writing on a form mutually agreed to by the Employer and the Union the choice of either the Union grievance procedure, a part of this Agreement, or the Navy grievance procedure under CMMI, and such grievance will be processed accordingly. THE CHOICE SHALL BE IRREVOCABLE.

Table 5-1. Agreement covering civilian employees at selected navy installations

Installation and location	Union(s)	Types of employees covered	Number of employees covered	Expiration Date
Boston Naval Shipyard, Boston, Mass.	NAGE	blue-collar	3,379	8/24/73
U.S. Naval Academy, Annapolis, Md.	AFGE	blue-collar	793	5/16/75
Naval Air Rework Facility, Norfolk, Va.	IAM	blue-collar	3,436	7/9/76
Navy Public Works Center, Norfolk, Va.	MTC	blue-collar	1,268	9/26/74
Norfolk Naval Shipyard, Portsmouth, Va.	MTC	blue-collar	6,500	Indefinite
Navy Regional Finance Center, Norfolk, Va.	AFGE	blue- and white-collar	1,250	5/6/75
Navy Supply Center, Norfolk, Va.	IAM	blue-collar	1,534	12/6/73
Charleston Naval Shipyard, Charleston, S.C.	MTC	blue-collar	4,123	12/21/75
Naval Air Rework Facility, Jacksonville, Fla.	NAGE	blue-collar	1,890	7/9/74
Naval Ammunition Depot, Crane, Ind.	AFGE	blue- and white-collar	4,778	7/18/74
U.S. Naval Ammunition Depot, McAlister, Okla.	AFGE	blue- and white-collar	2,731	10/29/74
Puget Sound Naval Shipyard, Bremerton, Wash.	MTC	blue- and white-collar	5,967	6/23/74
Hunters Point Naval Shipyard, San Francisco, Calif.	MTC	blue-collar	3,910	11/11/73
Navy Supply Center, Oakland, Calif.	AFGE	blue- and white-collar	1,897	11/15/74
Mare Island Naval Shipyard, Vallejo, Calif.	MTC	blue-collar	5,112	1/30/73
Naval Weapons Center, China Lake, Calif.	MTC	blue-collar	899	7/7/74
Naval Weapons Station, Concord, Calif.	AFGE	blue- and white-collar	1,585	11/16/73
Long Beach Naval Shipyard, Long Beach, Calif.	MTC	blue-collar	5,150	10/31/73
Naval Supply Center, San Diego, Calif.	AFGE	blue- and white-collar	708	1/3/74
Pearl Harbor Naval Shipyard, Honolulu, Hawaii	MTC	blue- and white-collar	4,110	5/3/75

Table 5-2. Table of contents of Hunters Point naval shipyard labor contract

Article no.	Preamble	Page no.
I	recognition and unit determination	1
II	support of common goals	3
III	rights of employer	4
IV	rights of council	8
V	rights of employees	13
VI	provisions of law and regulations	17
VII	council representation	18
VIII	hours of work	26
IX	overtime	34
X	holidays	39
XI	environmental differential pay	42
XII	sea trials	61
XIII	travel and temporary duty	65
XIV	wage surveys	71
XV	job descriptions and ratings	72
XVI	details	74
XVII	trade jurisdiction	77
XIX	annual leave	83
XX	leaves of absence and excused absence	86
XXI	civic responsibilities	90
XXII	merit promotion program	92
XXIII	demotions and repromotions	106
XXIV	reduction-in-force and reemployment	108
XXV	apprenticeships and training programs for job ratings	112
XXVI	safety and health	114
XXVII	adverse action appeals	121
XXVIII	disciplinary action appeals	128
XXIX	grievance procedure for employees	133
XXX	arbitration	145
XXXI	equal employment opportunity	148
XXXII	general working conditions	151
XXXIII	general provisions	153
XXXIV	duration and changes	157

In obvious attempts to reduce the incidence of grievances submitted to third-party review, some installations have succeeded in negotiating provisions which still allow the Commanding Officer to be the final word even though binding arbitration is provided. Three examples illustrate this point. First, at the Mare Island shipyard, an aggrieved employee can make an irrevocable decision, after step 1 of the grievance procedure, whether to process his grievance through the various department heads, around the shipyard commander, and directly to binding arbitration, or to process it directly to the shipyard commander for a final decision. If the worker chooses the former path, the final decision is made either by the arbitrator or the FLRC; if he chooses the latter path, his fate rests with the shipyard commander.

Table 5-3. Typical items excluded from negotiated grievance procedures in navy contracts

---

a violation of reemployment priority rights

a reduction-in-force action

a violation of reemployment or reinstatement rights

a violation of military restoration rights

a performance rating

a job-grading decision

a salary-retention decision

an allegation or complaint of discrimination

an adverse action for political activity

an adverse action appealable under subpart B of part 752, CSC regulations

a fitness-for-duty examination decision

a health benefits decision

actions taken at the direction of the CSC

adverse actions under USC 7532, Executive Order 10450, and failure to be cleared for sensitive duties

action taken under any statute which authorizes any agency to take suspension or separation action without regard to 5 USC or the provisions of any other law

separation for failure to satisfactorily complete a trial probationary period

decisions by an official of another activity

questions concerning the interpretation of any regulation or policy of the Department of the Navy or a higher authority

a matter which is subject to final administrative review outside the agency under law or the regulations of the commission

the content of published agency policy

nonselection for promotion from a group of properly ranked and certified candidates

In grievances and complaints arising out of matters personal to the employees, or appeals from letters of reprimand, suspensions, demotions and removals, the employee may elect to use either the Navy grievance procedure or the procedure set forth in this article.

A second example is at the Pearl Harbor Naval Shipyard where the worker has essentially the same situation as at the Mare Island Naval Shipyard. The main difference is that the worker can process his grievance through three steps of the grievance procedure instead of only one before making an irrevocable decision. It seems that the employee has a better chance of picking the most advantageous path in this second example than

Table 5-4. Grievance and arbitration procedures in selected navy agreements

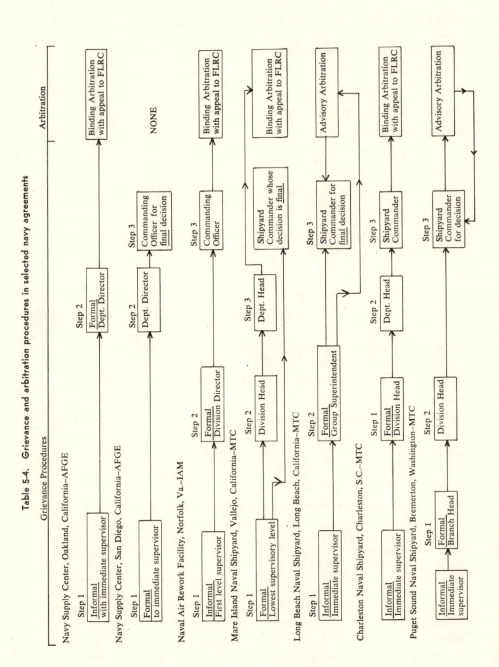

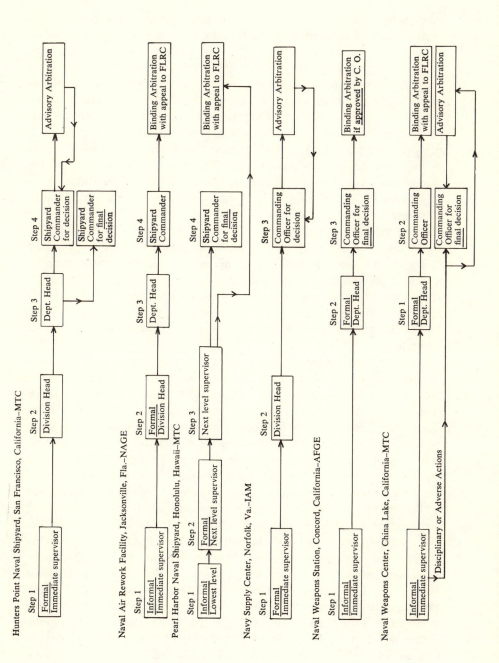

Hunters Point Naval Shipyard, San Francisco, California–MTC

Naval Air Rework Facility, Jacksonville, Fla.–NAGE

Pearl Harbor Naval Shipyard, Honolulu, Hawaii–MTC

Navy Supply Center, Norfolk, Va.–IAM

Naval Weapons Station, Concord, California–AFGE

Naval Weapons Center, China Lake, California–MTC

he does in the first. He has processed his disagreement through three steps of the chain of command by the time he must decide. At this point, it would seem that the employee would almost never choose shipyard commander as the final arbiter of his grievance. It would appear that the worker, having been ruled against three consecutive times by navy management, would choose an alternate route for the *final* decision. Nevertheless, the path to the shipyard commander is still in the agreement. One can only conjecture. Does management favor it as a method of circumventing third-party review? Do unions prefer it because it adds one more level of appeal in the grievance process, because the C.O. takes a broader view of the dispute and overrules subordinates, or because they can exert more pressure on the C.O.? Is there an idiosyncratic explanation at each installation? Only research can provide answers.

A final example is the Naval Weapons Center at Concord, California. Under this procedure, binding arbitration is provided but only if approved by the commanding officer. Thus, at this installation, the contract includes an *empty* binding arbitration clause. In practice, this grievance procedure affords the aggrieved employee about as much due process as a worker is afforded in the negotiated grievance procedure at the Navy Supply Center in San Diego. At San Diego, there is *no* provision for any type of arbitration.

Of the four unions in the sample, only one, the (AFGE) demonstrated either a desire or a noticeable ability to negotiate binding arbitration provisions in its agreements (see Table 5–5). Five of the seven AFGE contracts contained such provisions, while contracts of the other three unions were divided evenly between "advisory" and "binding" arbitration. At least part of the AFGE's penchant for binding arbitration provisions may be explained by the nature of the union itself. The AFGE is a public sector based union, and, as such, rarely if ever has the right to strike over disagreements with management. In the private sector, binding arbitration in the grievance resolution process frequently developed because both management and labor sought an alternative to frequent disruptive strikes over working conditions and the interpretation of the contract. In the public sector, federal management has usually opposed it, while unions have been more insistent on the inclusion of such provisions in labor agreements. The motivation, therefore, of federally based labor unions has been to strengthen the federal system of due process rather than to eliminate disruptions at the work site. The other federally based union in the sample was the National Association of Government (NAGE). Because only two contracts with this union were included, not even general conclusions could be drawn.

Table 5-5. Grievance procedures in selected navy contracts by type of arbitration and union representative

Union	Number of contracts with— advisory arbitration	binding arbitration	no arbitration
AFGE	1	5	1
NAGE	1	1	
IAM	1	1	
MTC	5	4	
Total	8	11	1

The geographic location of navy installations had even less influence on the type of grievance arbitration. These data are presented in Table 5–6. On the Atlantic coast, four contracts contained provision for advisory arbitration, while five agreements had binding arbitration clauses. On the Pacific coast, there was a split between advisory and binding arbitration with four contracts in each category. There was also one agreement with no provision for arbitration. Both contracts at installations situated inland had binding arbitration provisions.

In this sample of navy contracts, there were agreements with no arbitration, advisory arbitration and binding arbitration. Clearly, in civilian federal labor relations the trend has been toward third-party review with binding decisions. This situation is somewhat analogous to the uniformed segment of the navy. The major difference is that the development of third-party review for uniformed personnel, at present, is somewhat close to the advisory arbitration concept among civilian employees. The ombudsman is somewhat analogous to an arbitrator whose awards are only "advisory." Final decisions in the grievance process are still made by the top ranking line officer. However, if the experience with civilian naval workers can be applied to uniformed employees, "advisory" decision making by third parties will not suffice. By preferring the binding arbitration process over other methods of grievance resolution, civilian employees have signaled

Table 5-6. Grievance procedures in selected navy contracts by type of arbitration and geographic location

Location	Number of contracts with— advisory arbitration	binding arbitration	no arbitration
Atlantic coast	4	5	0
Pacific coast	4	4	1
Inland	0	2	0

their dissatisfaction with the bureaucratic system of due process in the federal service, if not with the bureaucrats themselves. If history repeats itself with uniformed personnel, the establishment of the office of the ombudsman must be viewed as an intermediate event in a trend toward a system of due process for uniformed personnel which includes binding arbitration by a third party.

Summary and Conclusions

This chapter describes a plethora of "due process" structures available to nonuniformed federal employees. The sources of these systems are found in laws, executive orders, administrative decisions and even court decisions. The expansion of collective bargaining for these employees added another structure with clout to insure protection. Although there may be some disagreement, it seems clear that the Civil Service Commission sits at the apex of all the systems.

In the "rights" area the Civil Service Commission occupies a unique and strategic position. Its power and authority extends much beyond the customary tasks of a personnel department, since it is a federal agency whose function is to monitor the personnel and employment practices of all *other* federal agencies and to guarantee the statutory and administrative rights of nonuniformed federal employees. During the past decade it has become heavily involved in all aspects of unionization from representation to collective bargaining. The challenge facing the United States, notes John W. Macy, former chairman of commission, "calls for an innovative pattern of relationships between [the civil service concept and collective bargaining] so that the benefits of both systems may be available to management, unions and the public."[12]

The full panoply of appeals rights is most impressive and suggests why federal managers feel rigidly circumscribed in managing the federal work force. At this point we should stress that the various executive orders, which unquestionably stimulated unionization, added significantly to the due-process rights of nonuniformed federal employees. Beyond this the executive orders and their implementation increased the number of subjects over which federal managers had to bargain with the unions. Combining the dues process protections with the enlarged scope of bargaining provides employees with just, equitable, and legally safeguarded treatment.

The expansion of collective bargaining adds another dimension to the protection of employees. By incorporating agency regulations into collective bargaining agreements, unions can challenge disparate and in-

---

12 "The Role of Bargaining in the Public Service," in *Public Workers and Public Unions,* ed. Sam Zagoria (Englewood Cliffs, N.J.: Prentice-Hall, 1972), pp. 5–19, 9.

consistent application of negotiated terms. Nurtured in a bureaucratic environment controlled by rules and regulations, employees and their unions are both ingenious and ingenuous in interpreting contract terms in their self-interest. This clearly demonstrates that public managers have not been effective in establishing trustful relationships between employee groups and themselves. What we find today, however, are various due process systems—unclear, overlapping, and made to order for litigation.

It is fair to characterize labor relations in the federal system as an evolving one. The large federal establishment comprised of many agencies with different missions, different internal structures and processes and diverse categories of employees is difficult to centralize and unify. There are so many plural pressures and interests that rationalizing labor-management relations is difficult. Moreover, the relationships are viewed one way by employees and quite another by managers; the latter, as their counterparts in the private sector, are continually faced with an erosion of management's capacity to manage. What will eventuate remains unclear although there are signs and hope that stable and fruitful relationships will emerge.

A specific indication that mature links are being forged between unions and management is the development of the grievance-arbitration procedures. Binding arbitration of grievances in the federal service is a growing trend even though advisory arbitration is found most frequently in agreements. Civil service workers prefer the former since impartial third-party review strengthens procedural and substantive due process when contrasted with unilateral determination by management. On the other hand, federal managers see in neutral and binding arbitration further encroachment on their managerial prerogatives.

To indicate the expansion of grievance and arbitration procedures, the basic structure of a due process system, we examined a sample of contracts between the United States navy and its civilian employees. More than half of the twenty agreements provided for binding arbitration with an appeal by either party to the FLRC. This is significant because the C.O. is not the final word when workers process grievances; this is also a harbinger for the type of system likely to be sought by uniformed personnel.

As noted earlier, federal employees are prohibited from striking. In the private sector, management and unions trade a no-strike clause for grievance/arbitration provisions. Such an exchange is unavailable in the federal sector. Nonetheless, the labor-management policies of the federal government encourage and facilitate inclusion of grievance-arbitration provisions in collective bargaining agreements. These practices and policies suggest the awareness and acceptance by the federal establishment of the crucial nature of such a due process system.

It is noteworthy that of the four unions in the sample, AFGE, is the only one that presses for and achieves binding arbitration. The explanation probably lies in the fact that AFGE, a militant and widely-based public sector union, recognizes that binding arbitration provides the best safeguard for insuring due process protection. Should AFGE succeed in representing uniformed personnel, it would undoubtedly seek a comparable system.

What does our review of rights systems, appeals processes and grievance/arbitration for nonuniformed federal employees suggest for the future of collective action for uniformed personnel? Some implications are clear and others are speculative. *First,* the experience of the navy, army and air force with its civilian employees provide a reservoir of knowledge, skills and institutional mechanisms useful for handling due process for uniformed personnel; *second,* there are the statutory, administrative and judicial precedents adaptable for achieving procedural and substantive regularities for uniformed personnel; *third,* many federal managers have accepted and implemented a full range of due process for nonuniformed personnel; *fourth,* notwithstanding the prohibition against strikes, the federal establishment, guided and monitored by Civil Service Commission, Congress, and employee organizations, believes that a rights system for nonuniformed employees is an essential feature of sound collective relationships; and *fifth,* the accommodation of due process with management's duties and responsibilities poses a complex and dynamic problem.

Somewhat speculative and conjectural are the following implications for uniformed personnel: *first,* the thrust of American norms, a voluntary armed forces complement and higher levels of education will require the development of an effective due process system for uniformed personnel; *second,* the Civil Service Commission will not play a centralizing, guiding and controlling role for the armed forces, and so a comparable structure will have to be developed; *third,* serious tensions will arise unquestionably between the disciplined and hierarchical structure of the armed forces and a due process system; *fourth,* there is the question whether the officers in the armed forces, comparable to the managers in the nonuniformed sector, will be able to adjust to and implement a similar rights system; and *finally,* is the overarching issue of developing a compatibility between the principal mission of the armed forces—vigilance and armed conflict—with a due process system.

No one can at this time hazard any assured predictions about the future of incorporating a well-articulated and effective rights system in the armed services. What we can be sure of, however, is that the problems identified above (and others not now perceived) will have to be faced. Armed forces personnel at all levels must understand and prepare for the ineluctable prospect of insuring rights, developing procedures for appeals and implementing a grievance/arbitration process.

6

Due Process and Bargaining
Rights in Public Education

CHARLES R. PERRY

Introduction

Public school teachers in the United States have long been organized and teacher organizations have long been active in representing the professional and economic interests of teachers. Until relatively recently, however, the representational activities of teacher organizations were focused primarily on lobbying at the national and state levels and generally confined to testifying before boards of education and/or consulting with superintendents of schools at the local level. It has only been within the past decade that teachers and teacher organizations have widely and actively sought a more powerful voice in the terms and conditions of their employment through collective bargaining at the local level as a complement to their political influence at state and national levels.

The emergence of demands for bargaining rights among public-school teachers came as both a surprise and a shock to the education establishment. Teachers, as professionals, were not regarded as a likely group to espouse the principles of "blue-collar" trade unionism and accept the adversary relationship and power orientation associated with collective bargaining. Furthermore, teachers enjoyed an elaborate set of rights embodied in state law and local practice which were felt to be sufficient to obviate any need for bargaining rights. Specifically, they enjoyed almost total job security under state tenure laws and procedures, extensive rights of redress of individual grievances under formal grievance procedures mandated by law in many states and adopted voluntarily in districts in other states and elaborate privileges of testimony and consultation for participation in decision making and redress of group grievances. Finally, the demand for bargaining rights constituted a frontal assault on the fundamental principles of employer sovereignty and lay control of education and an indirect challenge to the sanctity of the educational mission of the school system.

The dramatic success of the drive for bargaining rights among teachers has placed them at the forefront of the larger public employee bargaining movement and made public education the focus of considerable speculation and investigation as to the probable causes and potential effects of collective bargaining in the public sector. Thus, public education constitutes a fertile field for an examination of the forces and factors which shape the potential for collective action among groups of employees who, by nature, status, or tradition, have not been regarded as likely candidates for union organization and for exploration of the structural and substantive impact of collective bargaining in enterprises governed by the social, fiscal, and bureaucratic constraints which characterize governmental institutions. This chapter will undertake such an examination and exploration through an account of the history of teacher organizational activities and an analysis of the impact of those activities on the structure of decision-making processes in local school systems and on the scope of managerial authority and discretion in school systems.

Historical Perspectives

There are two major teacher organizations in this country—the National Education Association (NEA) and the American Federation of Teachers (AFT). The NEA was founded in the 1850s; the AFT was created in 1916 with the granting of a charter by the American Federation of Labor. Throughout their history both organizations have been more than occasionally concerned with teacher welfare, but prior to 1960 neither organizational activity actively encouraged the practice of collective bargaining or advocated recourse to the strike as a matter of policy.

There are isolated cases of "confrontations" between local teacher groups and local boards of education or other municipal governing bodies dating back to the turn of the century, but the earliest evidence of bargaining activity dates back only to the mid-1940s. The Eau Claire, Wisconsin, Board of Education is reported to have entered into formal negotiations with a union of its teachers as early as 1944 and to have signed a formal agreement with that union as early as 1946. In that same year, teachers in the Norwalk, Connecticut, school system engaged in a strike which resulted in formal recognition of an association as official bargaining agent for teachers, and the members of the Pawtucket, Rhode Island, Teachers Alliance (an affiliate of the AFT) were successful in forcing the board of education to negotiate on its proposal for salary increases through strike action.

Both the AFT and the NEA had long advocated teacher participation in the formulation of school district policies and practices but, prior to these post-war developments, neither had supported formal collective action of the type encountered in Norwalk or Pawtucket. In 1947, however, both organizations began to shift their stance. The NEA executive committee declared that, "Group action is essential today. The former practice where teachers individually bargained . . . for their salaries is largely past."[1] Later that year, the NEA convention passed a resolution recommending that, "Each member seek salary adjustment in a professional way through group action." The AFT advocated similar action in asserting: "Methods whereby various groups may participate in policy formation must be devised. Procedures which will permit successful democratic participation must be perfected."[2]

The true meaning and significance of these declarations of policy must be interpreted in light of the state of public policy regarding the rights of teachers to engage in collective action. In some states, the right of teachers to organize was prohibited or limited by statute. In most states, exclusive recognition of a teacher organization as bargaining agent was legally questionable on the grounds that it would interfere with the right of an individual employee, as a citizen, to petition his government and might constitute a discriminatory conferral of privilege to one organization, while bargaining was viewed as an illegal delegation of sovereign power. Finally, in all states, the strike was strictly illegal—a view not contested by either the AFT or the NEA at this point. The only major legal breakthrough in these legal constraints had come in the court case resulting from the Norwalk teachers' strike in which the judge firmly upheld the traditional ban on strikes by public employees but also indicated that he saw no legal barrier to the use of the discretionary power of the board of education to grant formal recognition to, or engage in bargaining with, an organization representing teachers.

The 1950s saw little change in this state of affairs. The AFT did resolve to "assist and support locals in establishing collective bargaining procedures," but did not commit itself to an active campaign to seek such procedures and did not even contemplate changing its long-standing no-strike policy.[3] The NEA undertook no comparable change in its policies,

---

[1] "The Professional Way to Meet the Education Crisis," *NEA Journal* 36 (Feb. 1947): 47.

[2] Lester A. Kirkendall, et al., *Goals for American Education,* (Chicago: American

[3] *Policies of the American Federation of Teachers,* (mimeographed report, Chicago: American Federation of Teachers, n.d.).

Federation of Teachers, 1948), p. 60.

and the courts continued to regard employer sovereignty and the public interest in uninterrupted service as paramount. In this context, it is not surprising that the only notable bargaining developments were the achievement of written agreements by AFT locals in a few districts, including Pawtucket, and the establishment of new bargaining relationships by union locals in some other districts including East St. Louis, Illinois, and Gary, Indiana. However, at the end of the decade, the State of Wisconsin took a monumental step, if little noticed at the time, in passing the first positive legislation with respect to the bargaining rights of municipal employees.

The turning point came in New York City in the early 1960s. Efforts to organize an AFT local in the New York City school system had been underway since the mid-1950s (possibly with at least moral support from the United Automobile Workers and the Industrial Union Department of the AFL-CIO), and these efforts culminated in a one-day strike in 1961 to force the board of education to hold a representative election. The mayor appointed a distinguished panel to investigate the feasibility and desirability of collective bargaining in the school system. The panel found no incompatibility between the system's mission and collective bargaining and recommended that the election be held. An election was held in December 1961 and was won by the United Federation of Teachers (Local 2, AFT) against a hastily organized NEA-supported coalition of teacher organizations. Contract negotiations began almost immediately after the election and led to another strike by the UFT which resulted in a virtual total victory for the union.

The New York City representation election was the first in which the NEA faced the AFT in a highly visible test of strength. The AFT victory in that election coupled with its success in the subsequent negotiations necessitated a positive NEA response. This response was not long in coming as the NEA at its 1962 convention adopted the following resolutions which signified its official entry into collective bargaining and announced its policy of "professional negotiations" as an alternative to "collective bargaining."

> The Association believes that procedures should be established which sional associations, through democratically selected representatives using professional channels to participate with boards of education in determination of policies of common concern including salary and other conditions for professional service.
>
> The Association believes that procedures should be established which provide an orderly method for professional education associations and boards of education to reach mutually satisfactory arrangements.[4]

---

[4] *Proceedings of the National Education Association* (1962), p. 394.

Almost immediately thereafter, two of the first "professional nego-tiation" agreements appeared in Denver and in Champaign, Illinois. In addition, to counter the AFT's success in New York City and in other major cities, the NEA created the Urban Project. At the same time, the AFT acquired membership in the Industrial Union Department of the AFL-CIO and began receiving financial aid from that organization for its organizing efforts. The result was intense competition between the two at all levels, but particularly at the state level where the state affiliates of the NEA sought to head off the AFT challenge through passage of "professional negotiation" statutes designed to create a favorable atmos-phere for the representational activities of their local affiliates.

The lobbying activities of state education associations and the com-petitive efforts of the AFT and its ally, the AFL-CIO, at the state level exerted strong pressures on the existing legal proscriptions regarding col-lective bargaining in the public sector. This pressure, coupled with the precedents inherent in the Wisconsin law, the report of the New York City panel, and President Kennedy's Executive Order 10988, resulted in fundamental changes in both the judicial and legislative view of the rights of teachers and other public employees to engage in collective bargaining. Thus, courts in virtually every state have come to accept the right of public school teachers to organize and the right of their organizations to be recognized and to engage in collective bargaining, although they have not been accorded the right to strike or engage in similar activities. More im-portantly, some thirty states have enacted positive legislation protecting the rights of teachers to organize, be recognized, and to engage in some form of bargaining, with two of these states according to teachers at least a limited right to strike.

The changing public policy framework altered and then mitigated the competition between the AFT and the NEA. Between 1962 and 1965 this competition was focused on individual representation elections. After 1965, it took the form of a contest over which party could take the greatest advantage of the rights granted under state laws and resulted in the virtually total organization of teachers in states such as Wisconsin, Con-necticut, Michigan, and Pennsylvania. In the course of this contest, it has become clear that the AFT enjoys a clear and probably permanent advan-tage in the major cities with the NEA prevailing elsewhere. Thus, the competition has become more fiction than reality and the two organiza-tions have begun negotiations for a merger which, if accomplished, could produce the nation's largest trade union.

The results of the developments of the 1960s are staggering when viewed in terms of the situation at the end of the 1950s. During the 1972–73 school year, well over a million public school teachers in over 4,000 school districts in the United States were working under some form of collective agreement, with about 2,800 of these districts under substantive, bilateral signed agreements which contained detailed provisions regarding salary schedules, teaching-duty requirements, and other working conditions. More importantly, perhaps, the number of work stoppages and man-days lost due to strikes has grown dramatically as indicated in table 6–1.[5]

Table 6–1. Teacher strikes: 1960–75

	1960–64	1965–68	1969–72	1973–75
Number of strikes	16	199	543	488
Teachers involved	42,320	276,420	356,147	341,370

In retrospect, it is clear that unilaterally granted participation rights and grievance procedures were sufficient only to forestall, but not preclude, the emergence of demands for bargaining rights among public school teachers. It is also clear that such demands did not wait upon the emergence of supportive organizational or public policy, but rather preceded and dictated changes in such policies. Thus, the causes of the so-called new militancy and aggressiveness of public school teachers must be sought in other forces. While any number of such forces may have been at work, the following merit particular attention:

Teachers desire more money and benefits, "a bigger share of the pie," which, they believed collective bargaining could deliver.

The percentage of males in the teaching force is increasing as is the extent of training and the degree of career commitment among teachers of both sexes.

The increasing size and bureaucratization of school systems has led many teachers to feel that they need a more effective way of protesting possibly discriminatory or arbitrary application of the rules and policies which control their daily activities.

Legislation granting bargaining rights to teachers has been both a cause and affect of teacher militancy, as have been the policies of the two major teacher organizations, the competition between them, and the interest of the larger labor movement.

The monumental problems of big city school systems and the disenchantment with and criticism of teachers and public education associated with Sputnik appear to be strongly correlated with the emergence of teacher militancy.

The 1960s were, in the words of one commentator, "An age of political activism, in which collective action, demonstrations, and thrusts

---

[5] Data compiled on the basis of information received from the two major teacher organizations.

for power are both fashionable and effective," and the drive for teacher power undoubtedly derived some strength from this cultural context.[6]

The Locus of Decision-Making Power

The substitution of collective bargaining for consultation or testimony as the basis for teacher participation in decision making at the local level has involved more than a mere change in form or procedure. The establishment of formal collective bargaining relationships in local school systems has dramatically altered the basic structure of the decision-making process and the distribution of decision-making authority within that structure.

In the absence of a collective-bargaining relationship, policy is formulated through a legislative process and implemented through a hierarchical command structure. A board of education enjoys the legal right to make final decisions on policy matters and a superintendent of schools bears the legal and organizational responsibility to execute such policy decisions. However, these rights and responsibilities are qualified by the political need to consider and accommodate, to some extent, the views of various constituent groups. Thus, in practice, decision making by school management can be viewed as a process in which managers mediate possibly conflicting interests among the following types of groups: taxpayers, parents, civil rights organizations, city officials, school administrations, classroom teachers.

Collective bargaining is essentially a bilateral decision-making process in which each party is expected to articulate and defend the interests of its own constituents vis-a-vis the goals of the other party, and public education has proven to be no exception. Local teacher organizations have been no less immune than unions in the private sector to the institutional imperative to seek out conflict between their members and management and pursue an adversary approach to the resolution of conflict in order to justify their existence. School management has resisted the adversary role, but, given limited resources and pressure from teacher organizations, has had little choice but to abandon its neutral role of mediator of multiple interests and to accept the active role of adversary to teachers.

The emergence of adversary approaches to decision-making has rendered untenable the traditional concept of the educational establishment as one characterized by common interests and congruent goals and shattered the image of a united profession. The result of this fragmentation of the educational enterprise has been public debate and private conflict

---

[6] Richard D. Wynn, *Policies of Educational Negotiation, Problems and Issues,* (Tri-state Area School Study Council Research Monograph, University of Pittsburgh, Oct. 1967), p. 4.

over the relative organizational roles and professional status of school boards, school administrators, and school teachers.

One of the manifestations of this phenomenon has been an ongoing conflict over the scope of bargaining. At a pragmatic level, this question has centered on the issue of whether collective bargaining will be limited to wages, hours, and conditions of employment or will extend to "anything that affects the working life of the teacher" or "all matters which affect the quality of the educational program." On a more basic level, the issue is one of the extent to which collective bargaining will alter the balance of lay and professional control in public education. This issue was raised early in the history of the collective bargaining relationship in New York City in the following statements of a union leader and a board member, respectively:

> The coming of age of the teaching profession, through collective bargaining, forces us to meet, head-on, the critical problem of the respective roles of teachers and civic and parent groups in the system of public education. . . . It is inconceivable that laymen will insist on keeping the educational process out of the control of educators, any more than they would think of depriving doctors, lawyers, and theologians of the ultimate control of their respective professions. Lay groups will have to recognize and accept the realities of the new world of collective bargaining by teachers in the educational system.

> It is the belief of our scheme of public education that the objectives of the school system, the basic emphasis in the teaching effort, the goals to be achieved, shall be determined by the community itself, and not by the professionals. . . . I do not believe that this philosophy is altered or modified by the fact that a board of education has entered into a collective bargaining agreement with an organization which represents the teachers in that system.[7]

A second manifestation has been the emergence of challenges to the colleague and leadership roles of administrative personnel—specifically, the superintendent and the building principal. The root of these challenges rests in the fact that administrators do exercise some control over the resources and rewards sought by teachers and are, therefore, a part of management—the adversary. As such, they cannot be accorded the status of a colleague to or spokesman for the classroom teacher, as is indicated by their exclusion from the vast majority of even the earliest teacher bargaining units. Three mechanisms have been used to articulate and institutionalize these challenges:

> Provisions in agreements for ongoing consultation between representatives of the teacher organization and administrative personnel at the central and the building levels;

---

[7] Unpublished remarks made available to the author.

Insistence that the teacher organization control or participate in the selection of teachers to serve on advisory committees; and,

The formal grievance procedure.

Each of these mechanisms, in theory, is designed to facilitate problem solving, but each has been used to question the professional judgment and administrative wisdom of superintendents and principals at least as often as they have been used for constructive purposes. The net result has been a tendency for administrative personnel to be confined to the role of manager or officer in the bureaucratic sense, as opposed to acting as leaders in the informal group sense.

The establishment of a collective bargaining relationship also alters the balance of power between teachers and the other parties of interest. In the absence of collective bargaining, the views of community leaders and community groups generally define the limits on the range of alternatives open to school management, and the views of the profession, as articulated by the superintendent, generally dictate the choice of specific courses of action within that range. The views of teachers constitute a second professional input, but one which may be accepted or rejected, in whole or part, at will. The emergence of a formal bargaining relationship dramatically alters this situation. At a minimum, bargaining assures teacher representatives effective access to the centers of decision-making power within the system. More importantly, collective bargaining in public education, as elsewhere, has carried a presumption in favor of compromise and accommodation which, in practice, has given teachers a significant measure of control over management in the decision-making process. Finally, collective bargaining has served to augment the political and economic power of teachers, legal proscriptions notwithstanding, and, thereby, to accord to teachers easier access to and stronger influence over the centers of power in the larger community which hold effective veto power over school management.

The most dramatic evidence of this shift in the distribution of power is to be found in the change in approach to salary determination associated with the advent of collective bargaining. Prior to collective bargaining, the amount of money available for teacher salary increases was determined primarily by "ability to pay," as defined by the resources expected to be forthcoming from state aid and local revenues less those expenditures required to maintain existing programs, salary commitments, class sizes, student services, and physical facilities. In short, teacher salaries were set on a residual basis which, in their words, "forced teachers to subsidize education" where the state and local community failed to do so adequately. With the advent of bargaining, teachers strongly resisted reliance on "ability to pay" as a valid basis for salary determination and advocated that salaries be set on the basis of individual and social equity and support levels determined by what the community "should" pay to maintain a truly "professional" salary scale and sound educational system. Beyond advocacy, local teacher organizations generally have been willing to pursue their salary demands to the point of impasse and support their position with collective action and generally with highly favorable results.

The success of teachers in forcing a change in approach to salary determination through the exercise of group power can be traced to the inability of school management to resist the political pressure for settlement generated by the exercise of power by teachers. The workings of these political pressures have been most easily discernible in those cases where city officials have been drawn into the fray by virtue of the fact that the board of education is directly dependent on the city for its resources but are a little different in other crises. In this context, the following examples may be enlightening:

> In the 1962 negotiations in New York City, a strike by teachers induced the governor to make available to the city an additional thirteen million dollars which the mayor agreed to appropriate to the board of education. The board of education asserted that these funds were granted for "educational purposes" and should be used, at least in part, to restore budget cuts made in nonsalary areas as part of the board's attempt to accommodate the demands of teachers short of a strike. The union rejected this argument, and the mayor pointedly refused to support it, and the entire thirteen million dollars was allocated to increases in teacher salaries and benefits which resulted in a final settlement which exceeded the union's prestrike demands.

> In the 1963 negotiations in the same city, the mayor was unable to provide additional funds for the schools, even in response to a strike threat but was willing to exert indirect pressure on the board to agree to sizeable salary increases in the out-years of a multiple-year contract in order to avoid a strike. The board sought assurances from the mayor that the funds would be forthcoming to cover the costs of those increases, but it received no such assurances. However, the board did sign the agreement as worked out by the mayor's mediators but openly charged that it was being forced to "mortgage the future" of the educational system. When subsequent increases in city support proved sufficient only to meet the costs of the deferred salary increases, the board publicly stated that it was being relegated to the status of a "caretaker."

> In the 1972–73 negotiations in Philadelphia, a prolonged strike by teachers and the threat of a sympathy strike by the larger labor movement in the city forced the mayor to make available additional funds for the school system. School management, however, was denied any opportunity to seek to use these funds as a trade-off to secure any of its goals in taking the strike and precluded from participation in even the decision as

to how the additional monies would be allocated among various teacher benefits.

The net effect of the exercise of power by teachers in the above cases was to escalate conflict and remove control over decisions from the hands of those responsible for the operation of the school system. This loss of control had implications well beyond the level of teacher salaries. Issues such as salaries and class size have significant fiscal implications, and concessions on such issues can easily absorb any budget margin in a school system and require cutbacks in other activities. Indeed, there is at least subjective evidence that in major cities concessions on these issues have resulted in abandonment of new initiatives, reduction in wage increases for nonteaching personnel, and cutbacks in staffing levels. Thus, it is not surprising that boards of education have come to regard collective bargaining as a challenge to their ability to set and effectuate educational policy nor that nonteaching personnel have also sought to organize and secure collective bargaining rights in many school systems.

The same phenomena of escalation and loss of control have affected administrative personnel in the area of "policy issues" and "working conditions." The distinction between these two types of issues is far from clear in the educational context, but among policy issues would be included staff and pupil integration, curriculum design, text book selection, pupil discipline, grading systems, and pupil-promotion policies, while such matters as class size, work loads, teaching assignments, and nonteaching duties are best characterized as working condition issues. The former issues traditionally have been the province of the superintendent; the latter, the province of building principals.

The most obvious challenge to the policy-making powers of a board of education lies in the demands of a teacher organization that so-called "policy issues" be the subject of joint determination through collective bargaining. While such issues have received attention in the bargaining context, there is little evidence that such attention has resulted in significant change in the policy formulation powers of boards of education, although there are isolated cases where such change appears to have taken place on a limited and perhaps temporary basis. This lack of impact stems from the inability of teacher groups to achieve a clear consensus on and strong commitment to specific substantive positions on such issues. However, they have been able to achieve such a consensus on and commitment to the position that they should have a definite voice in decisions on such issues and have been able to convince boards of education to grant them such a voice by according them equal status with the superintendent of schools as representatives of the professional view through explicit provisions for

formal consultation between the representatives of teachers and the superintendent and implicit promises to make no changes in existing practices
without the consent of teachers.

In the case of working conditions, the same type of shift in the locus
of influence and control has taken place, except that it has been the building principal who has been adversely affected. Bargaining over working
conditions has centered on the demands of teachers to formalize and
elaborate the set of rules defining the rights and responsibilities of teachers
and the procedures by which such rules are applied and enforced. In
general, neither boards of education nor school superintendents have resisted the formalization of rules or procedures, although they have fought
some changes in the substance of such rules and the scope of such procedures. The result has been the substitution of system-wide rules for
individualized decisions by building principals and the imposition of systems of due process (the grievance procedures) and participatory management (consultation at the school level) on those principals who have
sharply reduced their discretionary authority and administrative control.
Perhaps the best index of the true impact of these changes is the fact that
principals in many school systems have organized and sought bargaining
rights in an effort to secure a stronger voice in the bargaining process.

The Web of Rules

The initial thrust of collective bargaining over the terms and conditions of
employment is to formalize and institutionalize the status quo by bringing
existing employee policies and practices within the scope of bargaining and
incorporating them in the contract. In some cases, this has been done by
writing those policies directly into the agreement between the teacher organization and the board of education. In other cases, it has been done
through inclusion of a clause such as the following:

> With respect to matters not covered by this agreement which are
> proper subjects for collective bargaining, the board agrees that it will
> make no changes without appropriate prior consultation and negotiation
> with the union. . . . All existing determinations, authorizations, by-laws,
> regulations, rules, rulings, resolutions, certifications, orders, directives,
> and other actions made, issued, or entered into by the board of education,
> governing or affecting salary and working conditions of the employees in
> the bargaining unit, shall continue in force during the term of this agree-
> ment, except insofar as change is commanded by law.

The effect of such contractual arrangements is to deprive school
management of the authority to change existing policies and practices with-

out the consent of the teacher organization where such changes affect the rights or prerogatives of any teacher. Clearly this type of commitment constitutes a major concession in terms of what are traditionally thought of as "management rights." This concession has obvious implications for the ability of management to respond to changing conditions and circumstances, particularly since teachers constitute the major productive resource in the system. In addition, it has proved to have equally significant implications for the ability of school systems to innovate, largely because most systems lack the resources required to undertake innovative programs without altering the level or structure of the demands placed on existing teachers. For example, the Philadelphia school system asserts that it was effectively precluded by an arbitrator's decision from appointing house directors for three self-contained "houses" in a new experimental high school, designed to provide a more personal atmosphere and promote greater student identification with the school. The arbitrator declared that a clause similar to that cited above required that department heads also be appointed for the entire school system because this system could not afford both the house directors and the department chairmen.

The cornerstone of the system of rights spelled out in collective bargaining agreements is the grievance procedure, as it is that procedure which provides the mechanism for determination of the true rights of individuals in specific cases and contexts. In public education, the concept of a grievance procedure is not new or unique to collective bargaining. Many school systems had adopted such procedures either voluntarily or pursuant to legislative mandate prior to the advent of bargaining, and all systems took pride in their open communication channels within the system through which any individual could air his grievances and receive a fair hearing. Against this background, it is not surprising that school management did not resist, in principle, the incorporation of formal grievance procedures in their agreements with teacher organizations or strive to avoid or forestall the institution of binding arbitration as the final step in such procedures. Indeed, most school systems did not resist the transfer of the extremely broad definition of a grievance which had traditionally prevailed under unilateral procedures to bilateral procedures, and many made no real effort to restrict the range of grievances which would be subject to final adjudication by an outside party. In this respect, the following provisions of the agreement between the Philadelphia Board of Education and the Philadelphia Federation of Teachers are illustrative:

> A grievance is a complaint involving the work situation, that there is a lack of policy; that a policy or practice is improper or unfair; or that there has been a deviation from, or a misinterpretation or misapplication of a practice or policy; or that there has been a violation, misinterpretation,

misapplication, inequitable or otherwise improper application of any provision of this agreement.[8]
. . . may submit the matter to arbitration if the grievance, complaint or problem involves the compliance with or application or interpretation of this agreement, provided that a grievance concerning any board
action, not inconsistent with any provision of this agreement, taken under
any term of this agreement, requiring or providing for exercise of the
board's discretion or policy-making powers, may be decided by an
arbitrator only if it is based on a complaint that such action followed
throughout the school system in similar circumstances.[9]

In retrospect, it is clear that school management misestimated the significance of the grievance procedure and grievance arbitration in the bargaining context. Most were stunned by the number and range of grievances
which emerged, largely because they failed to perceive that the addition of
institutional support to the right of an individual to seek redress would
permit and encourage the expression of long-standing dissatisfactions which
individuals acting on their own in a hierarchical context were unable or
unwilling to articulate, however benevolent those in the hierarchy might
have claimed to be. Against this background, it is not surprising that school
administrators were shocked to find virtually all of their decisions and
actions being challenged, often successfully, and quickly began to feel that
they had lost control. While the loss of administrative control is debat-
able, it is clear that grievance procedures and the due process they provide
have served to grant teachers a measure of control over school operations
and a degree of protection against adverse actions far in excess of their
prebargaining rights as professionals. Indeed, in some systems, the grievance
procedure has been used to expand the tenure rights enjoyed by teachers
under state law and to extend comparable rights to those employees not
covered by tenure laws. Finally, management also failed to anticipate the
implications of institutional control over the grievance procedures for the
types of issues to be raised and pursued. In one grievance case, thirty-eight
fellow teachers signed a letter in which they indicated that they were
"chagrined and disturbed by the unilateral action" of the grievant and that
they felt that the principal against whom the grievance had been filed was
an "exemplary supervisor and sincere friend." The union responded in the
following terms:

> The collective bargaining agreement provides that every teacher,
> either alone or with others similarly situated, has the right to seek redress
> of grievance. Since [the grievant] is exercising her right as a teacher and

---

[8] Agreement between the Board of Education and the School District of Philadelphia and the Philadelphia Federation of Teachers, Local 3, American Federation
of Teachers, AFL-CIO, 1 Sept. 1970 to 31 Aug. 1972. Article IX, Section 1a.
[9] Ibid., Section 2, Step 3a.

[union] member in seeking redress of what both she and the union consider a proper grievance, it would be highly improper and contrary to [union] policy . . . not to support [the grievant] in this matter . . . the union . . . takes the view that [the principal] has, in fact, on numerous occasions violated the by-law . . . and that he should not, therefore, be upheld in violating the by-laws [in this instance] . . . the union takes the view that [the teachers' statement regarding the personal qualities of the principal] is irrelevant and immaterial since neither the proficiency of the principal as a supervisor nor his personal or professional relationships with staff members has any bearing on whether [he] has violated the by-law as alleged in [the grievant's] appeal.[10]

The major substantive areas of teacher interest and impact within the overall area of working conditions can be divided into four categories— the hours of work, work loads, the use of free time, and the method of assignment. In each of these areas teachers have been able, through collective bargaining, to achieve major gains in terms of limiting the demands administrators or the system can place on them. In some cases, these gains have involved only relatively minor costs; in others, they have required substantial additional resources. Overall, they have clearly reduced the amount of flexibility in the system and may have significantly impaired the ability of school systems to meet their basic educational goals.

In most school systems, teachers have pressed for a precise definition of the school day in terms of the clock hours a teacher may be required to be in school and on duty. In some systems, teachers have been able to secure a shortening of the school day through negotiations while in others they have been successful in resisting pressures to lengthen the school day. In Detroit, teachers were successful in achieving about a twenty-minute reduction in the length of the school day, and in Philadelphia teachers have been highly effective in resisting pressure from the board of education to extend their school day which is the shortest in the nation. At the same time, teachers in a number of systems have also succeeded in achieving limitations on the amount of time outside the basic working day that they can be expected to spend on school business. These limitations have taken a number of forms including limitations on the number and duration of after-school faculty meetings, provisions for parent-teacher conferences during the school day rather than during the evening as had traditionally been the case, and stipulation of either a weekly maximum for "expected" extracurricula service or a specific number of extracurricular functions per year at which attendance is expected.

The impact of these limitations on duties beyond the regular school day appear to have had significant impact. Individual teachers have been

---

[10] Unpublished letter made available to the author.

quite willing to utilize their rights in this area as is indicated by the case of one teacher who walked out of an after-school faculty meeting when the principal failed to conform to the specified forty-minute limit and then filed a formal grievance when the principal directed her to report to his office at the close of the next day of school to discuss those matters treated after she had left the first meeting. More importantly, teachers apparently also have been willing to exert informal group pressures to insure that individual teachers do not go significantly beyond minimum requirements in the area of extracurricular activities and school functions.

The second major area in which teachers appear to have recorded substantial gains through collective bargaining is in the area of work loads. These gains have taken the form of reductions in class sizes above and beyond those which would have taken place in the absence of bargaining, reductions in the number of hours of pupil contact during the school day through provision of duty-free lunch periods and preparation periods, and relief from nonteaching chores. The fiscal impact of these teacher gains can be significant, particularly in the larger cities. In Philadelphia, it costs about eight million dollars to reduce average class size by one pupil, and it is now necessary to staff the education program with teachers who are required to teach the equivalent of only three days. In New York City, as early as 1962, it required almost two million dollars to provide the personnel required to relieve most teachers of the majority of their nonteaching duties.

Duty-free lunch periods and relief from nonteaching chores, while expensive, have not been the subject of considerable grievance activity, largely because they are matters of vital interest to the teachers and have been somewhat difficult to implement quickly and totally. For example, a teacher in one system charged that she was deprived of her full fifty-minute, duty-free lunch period because she was required to escort the children from her classroom to the exits and lunch rooms—a process which required from seven to ten minutes—at the outset of her fifty-minute lunch period. In the same system, the decision of a building principal that two teachers instead of one were required to supervise the cafeteria during noon hour in order to adequately protect the health and safety of pupils was the subject of a grievance by the second teacher which was upheld by an arbitrator on the grounds that, in the absence of any proof of a particularly difficult discipline problem or any marked growth in the student population, the principal was required to at least try to use only one teacher in line with accepted practice in the system.

The provision of released time for teachers has resulted in some significant conflict over the extent to which the system can make demands on such time. In general, teachers have asserted, with a fair amount of success, that they should enjoy relative freedom in deciding how such time was to be used. In this respect, the following grievance cases are illustrative:

> A teacher charged that during a preparation period the principal called him to his office to discuss placement procedures for special progress pupils; that he spent the entire period at the office and that, since this was not an emergency situation, he was deprived of a preparation period in violation of the agreement. (Upheld)

> A teacher claimed that he was requested to visit the classroom of a teacher with greater experience and skill in order to improve his own teaching techniques during an unassigned period and that this request violated his rights under the contract. (Denied)

> A teacher claimed that the scheduling of department conferences during an unassigned period violated his right under the contract to use such period for professional work of his own choosing. (Denied)

The control of time gained by teachers as a result of relief from non-teaching duties has also come into question. In general, teachers have argued successfully that teachers so relieved should not be assigned additional teaching duties and had some success in limiting the discretion of administrators in making alternative assignments. For example, one agreement contains the following provision:

> Teachers relieved of administrative assignments by school aides should be programmed for the periods so relieved for professional duties and projects, and they should be permitted to select for this purpose activities among the duties and projects hereinafter listed, and others of a similar nature, with the understanding that the principal may make specific assignments from among the duties and projects listed, or others of a similar nature, as the needs of the school require.
>
> Appropriate activities in lieu of administrative assignments covered by school aides are:
>
> a. Duties and professional projects which are related to the instructional program of the teacher and his department, such as, but not limited to:
>
>> Curriculum development and adaptations
>> Review and selection of instructional materials
>> Long-range and unit planning
>> Preparation for departmental and other conferences
>> Construction of departmental and teacher tests
>> Correction of written work of pupils
>> Pupil conferences
>> Pupil interviews
>
> b. The planning of guidance and guidance materials for officials or subject class pupils and individual conferences with the teacher's

> pupil when in the judgment of such teacher such conferences are deemed desirable.[11]

The impact of collective bargaining on the staffing policies and procedures of school systems has closely paralleled experience in the private sector. In general, bargaining appears to have led to enhanced weight on seniority in decisions regarding the right of teachers to transfer between schools in the system, to qualify for administrative assignments and positions and to receive favorable subject matter, grade-level, or ability-group teaching assignments. At the same time, effective limitations have been imposed on the subjective evaluation of teachers with guarantees of the right of teachers to review and appeal their ratings by principals and any material placed in their personnel files. As a result, administrators assert that they have lost much of their authority to match teacher abilities with student needs, while teachers have gained a significant measure of protection against discriminatory or arbitrary treatment at the hands of school administrators.

Implications for the Military

The first and most basic lesson offered by the history of collective bargaining in public education is that it is not safe to discount the potential for collective action among groups of employees in a society which has given de facto and de jure recognition to such action as being legitimate in the search for job security, improved working conditions, and redress of grievances. The fact that less than twenty years ago collective bargaining in public education was inconceivable, while today it is an incontrovertible way of life, is impressive evidence in its own right of the breadth and depth of this potential. However, it is also important to note that there are compelling similarities between public education and the military which go well beyond the broad social context in which they exist. Specifically, the following points should be noted:

> Collective bargaining in education emerged in the face of a well-ingrained concept of employer sovereignty and strong commitment to the sanctity of agency mission.

> Collective bargaining in education emerged despite the existence of a strong concept of professional and organizational unity and an elaborate set of legal and procedural guarantees of tenure rights and due process.

---

[11] Agreement between the Board of Education and the City of New York and the United Federation of Teachers, Local 2, American Federation of Teachers, AFL-CIO covering classroom teachers and per-session teachers, 1 July 1965 to 30 June 1967. Article V, Section A, Part 4.

Collective bargaining in education emerged in the context of a complex set of economic and social changes which resulted in the recruitment of a better-educated, more professional group of teachers with higher economic and career expectations at the same time that school systems were coming under pressure to exercise greater bureaucratic control, and the entire educational system was coming under increasing social criticism for alleged failure to meet its obligations to society.

Collective bargaining in education emerged despite the existence of numerous organizations, some of which were performing trade-union-type functions. This circumstance has a relevant analogue in the number of types of organizations "representing" military personnel today.

The second of these points deserves some elaboration in light of the current situation in the military. Prior to the advent of collective bargaining, teachers had numerous avenues of appeal, including ones based on their informal, professional right to question the decision of their superiors, their organizational right to challenge such decisions through formal grievance procedures, their statutory right to appeal adverse actions to the state superintendent of public instruction, and the courts and their constitutional right to petition the board of education or other legislative authority. The existence of such avenues of appeal clearly did not obviate the perceived need for collective bargaining nor did the relative lack of use of such avenues indicate that there was insufficient conflict to support a bargaining relationship. The fact is that these rights and procedures were not adequate to encourage the articulation of grievances because they did not provide assured and protected mechanisms for the accommodation of conflict. Indeed, once such assurance and protection was forthcoming, these rights and procedures became a positive liability from the managerial standpoint, in marked contrast to the situation prior to the advent of bargaining.

Another lesson offered by the experience of public education is that bargaining brings with it fundamental changes in the locus of decision-making power. Collective bargaining effectively divides the organization and provides the employee group with the incentive to by-pass existing bureaucratic channels and the power to do so through their ability to escalate conflict and, thereby, compete successfully for attention, particularly in a political environment. At a minimum, the effect of such escalation is to induce the intervention of parties who have less knowledge of specific operational matters, less concern for long-run operational effectiveness and more interest in short-run accommodation than those who are responsible for management of the agency. The result may be decisions which severely impair the ability of management to set or effectuate basic priorities.

The implications of this change in the structure of decision-making may be significant in the military. The armed forces have long been subject to executive branch control and congressional oversight, but have been reasonably effective in keeping both bodies "at arm's length." The emergence of collective bargaining could dramatically alter this situation by forcing either the executive branch or the congress to mediate disputes between the command structure and the enlisted force over policies, procedures, and priorities. The result could be a very different set of decisions than would otherwise have prevailed, particularly in the face of something akin to a strike threat, with dramatic implications for the service especially during times when military budgets are receiving intensive and critical scrutiny. At lower levels a similar effect may occur, despite the fact that there is already considerable centralization within the military command structure. The ability of individual employees or groups of employees to challenge the decisions of their superiors and to pursue such challenges through or around the command structure with relative impunity will inevitably have impact on the role performance and role satisfaction of line officers. In the first instance, this impact may be felt in terms of their ability to lead and to respond effectively to the unique pressure situations which constitute the ultimate test of military effectiveness; in the final analysis it may be felt in the organization of line officers, as has been the case in public education.

The third area in which the bargaining experience of local school districts is of interest is that of substantive impact. In this respect, the ability of teachers to utilize collective bargaining to influence salary determination or policy formulation is not relevant, but their ability to impose restrictions on the allocation and utilization of human resources is crucial. The military is accustomed to relatively free use of its personnel on almost a twenty-four-hour basis and has not had, at least until recently, to be much concerned about the cost of those resources. However, given recent pay increases and increasing congressional pressure to cut total defense expenditures, the services can no longer be sanguine about personnel costs or labor productivity, and collective bargaining can profoundly affect both.

Teachers have been much interested in limiting the claims of their employers on their time in terms of the total working day, the amount of time during the working day that they are to face students, and the use of time not designated for student contact, and it may well be that members of a volunteer force will have a similar interest. The budgetary implications of such an interest can be staggering, as is suggested by the fact that teachers in the Philadelphia school system now face students for less than twenty hours per week. The implications for the United States military can be seen in the European experience with military unions presented in Chapter 8. Particularly in Sweden there has been increasing and successful pressure to limit the demands which can be placed on uniformed military personnel under nonemergency conditions. These pressures and the evoked resistance by the military command are resulting in a redefinition of command prerogatives. The parallel with the teachers' unions and school management is compelling.

7

Collective Bargaining in the Police and Firefighter Services

ROGER FRADIN

Introduction

Policemen and firemen represent distinctive groups in public employment. They differ from other municipal workers in the nature of their work, their place of work, their discipline, and their traditions. Police and fire fighters are two of the most highly organized groups of public servants, and their actions affect everyone as their services are the most visible and critical that a municipality provides.

They closely resemble military forces in the discipline and the dangers they must face. It is, therefore, instructive to study the progress of collective bargaining in both of these paramilitary forces to gain insight into the forms that an aggressive pursuit of due process may take in the uniformed military forces.

The International Association of Fire Fighters (IAFF), which was founded in 1918, is the oldest of all public employee unions. Collective bargaining between city and municipality management and fire fighters has continued for over fifty-five years. The joint decision-making process over terms of employment that characterizes collective bargaining is firmly ingrained in the firefighter tradition; just the opposite is true for the police. It was not until the sixties that the first signs of collective bargaining surfaced in the police service. The police labor movement lay dormant from 1920, after the Boston police strike, until 1960, when the turbulent environment of the decade caused collective bargaining to become a formidable force in police labor relations. Collective bargaining has been completely accepted in the firefighter service, and this acceptance took a relatively short period of time, while the police struggled for many years and are still struggling for the right to participate in decisions affecting their wages, hours, and working conditions.

In 1968 there were 496,000 paid policemen and 249,000 paid firemen in the United States. Police and fire-fighter employment is primarily a local phenomenon, with the federal and state governments employing only one sixth the total number of policemen and an even smaller portion of firemen. The size of a department can vary from a one-man municipal county police department to New York City's 27,671-man force. Fire departments also vary widely, from one paid fireman to the largest fire department in New York City with 13,781 men. Employment is growing in both departments. From 1955 to 1968 the average annual manpower increase for police was 4 percent, and for fire fighters the increase was 2 percent. Despite this growth, 60 percent of all American cities have vacancies in their protection forces. Both departments have recently been under pressure to increase their minority employment. Attempts to increase nonwhite membership have been met with limited success as a result of overt discrimination, hostility of nonwhites toward the public safety services, and the failure of minorities to meet entrance requirements. In departments with nonwhite membership, separate groups divided along racial lines, have tended to develop.

Police and fire-fighting work requires the use of physical effort, mental judgment, exposure to hazards, twenty-four-hour-a-day duty, and exposure to seasonal and climatic variations. A recent work-accident study revealed that the death rate for firefighters is 69 per 100,000, and the comparable police figure is 44 per 100,000. A policeman must be part lawyer, sociologist, sleuth, diplomat, and weapons technician. He must have a knowledge of drugs, evidence, identification, investigation, crowd and riot control, and first aid. Recent Supreme Court decisions require a policeman to match his skill in fighting crime with the obligation to maintain the integrity of a citizen's constitutional rights. A fireman must have a solid knowledge of fire control and prevention, as well as rescue techniques. He must be able to handle all types of equipment and understand the nature of various materials. The glamour attributed to police and fire-fighting work is greatly exceeded by the requirements of dull routine. For instance, 25 percent of a policeman's time is involved with traffic, while the rest of it is spent on patrol duty handling minor disturbances and domestic conflicts. Only 10 percent of the police force are detectives who are involved in formal investigations. Firemen respond to alarms and investigate causes of disasters. A fireman's typical day is comprised of three hours of housekeeping, two hours of drills, two hours of recreation, and one hour of calisthenics.[1]

---

[1] Michael H. Moskow, J. Joseph Lowenberg, and Edward C. Koziara, *Collective Bargaining in Public Employment* (New York: Random House, 1970), pp. 171–73.

The nature of police and fire-fighting work require different kinds of work organizations. Fire fighting is primarily a supervised group effort in units subject to paramilitary command, while police work involves very little group action except in mob control or similar situations.

Professionalization of the public protection services is advocated by both the International Association of Firefighters and the International Association of Chiefs of Police (IACP), both to improve job content and to upgrade fire-fighter and police images. There is some evidence that the professionalization movement is growing as fact finders have recently invoked professionalization to justify wage hikes. Institutions of higher learning are offering an increasing number of courses in police and fire-fighter science.

Both police and fire departments have pyramid-shaped authority structures. The structures are also paramilitary in nature, with the final power vested in a chief or commissioner. The number of ranks depends on the size of the department, the number of men per shift, and the available physical facilities. The individual precincts or firehouses are respectively commanded by a lieutenant or captain. The chief exercises more authority and delegates less than his counterpart in private industry or most other areas of public employment.

History of Fire fighter Organization

Fire fighters have long emphasized the need for collective bargaining in deciding terms of employment; in recent years, the IAFF has conducted seminars to educate both labor and management on the proper role of bargaining. The first fire department with paid personnel was established in Cincinnati, Ohio, in 1853. During the latter part of the nineteenth century, other major cities recognized the need for full-time, trained firemen, and they began to replace the volunteer forces with career firemen. Early societies were formed by these firemen for fraternal and benevolent purposes because at that time firemen could not get insurance because of the risk entailed in their work.

The first firemen's union was organized in Pittsburgh, Pennsylvania, in 1903.[2] By 1916 there were seven cities with unionized fire fighters, and by 1918 eighty-two fire departments were organized; these locals represented 10,000 out of the 40,000 paid firemen in 1918. On 28 February 1918, the various locals sent representatives to Washington, D. C., to form a national union of fire fighters, the International Association of Firefighters. The IAFF was chartered by the AFL during the same year. The original purposes behind the formation of the IAFF were the "pure and simple" trade

[2] David Ziskind, *One Thousand Strikes of Government Employees* (New York: Columbia University Press, 1940), p. 33.

unionism motivations that spurred the formation of the classic private sector "business" unions; the IAFF was concerned with raising fire fighter wages, securing the twelve-hour work day, improving working conditions, and eliminating political assessments that were made upon firemen.

Like most unions of the period, the IAFF did not have an easy time gaining management acceptance of their locals. Organizing the workers into a national union, though, was relatively easy for the IAFF because fire fighters throughout the country had organized themselves in a "grass-roots" movement, and the only effort expended by the IAFF was to negotiate the affiliation of these groups. City officials opposed organizing attempts by the IAFF, and the militancy of the firemen grew; there were thirty strikes, lockouts, and mass resignations in the 1918–19 period. This militancy subsided as a result of the 1919 Boston police strike, and in 1930 a no-strike clause was put into the fire fighters constitution. The switch to more conservative tactics by firemen, e.g., lobbying and de facto negotiations, during the fifties, netted considerable gains. With the onset of the turbulent sixties, though, firefighter militancy in negotiations was becoming more and more prominent. In fact, the IAFF rescinded its no-strike clause in 1968.

Over time, a change in fire fighter collective bargaining strategy may be noted. For forty years after the mid-1920s, organized fire fighters pursued a strategy of accommodation and conciliation in dealing with municipal administrators. This strategy emphasized the development of community and political support for the IAFF demands. A conciliatory bargaining strategy was used in this period because, after 1919, there was a strong public antipathy towards public sector unions in general, and militant job actions by public protection employees in particular. By the mid 1960s municipal labor relations environment changed, so that fire-fighters found it possible to reconsider their alternatives in dealing with their employers. Two more strategies have come into use by the IAFF today, a cooperative and a conflict-oriented strategy. The conflict-oriented technique centers around the use of coercion and pressure to enforce bargaining demands while the cooperative approach emphasizes the use of educational and persuasive tactics in negotiations. The reasons for the change in negotiation strategy include the rapid growth and acceptance of collective bargaining for all municipal employees; a number of public employee interest groups, (e.g., teachers and sanitation workers), have successfully employed militant tactics to achieve their goals, and there has been little public repression of them or their unions; the fire fighters have found themselves in a declining relative economic position with the rise of the widespread disparity between police and fire fighter salaries.

Contrary to the policy of most unions, the IAFF includes super-

visory personnel. In a normal local, all ranks up to, but not including, chief are in the bargaining unit. The one exception to this rule is in Michigan where fire chiefs are permitted in the same unit with the rest of the fire department. By 1970 the IAFF had 150,000 members in 1,550 local craft units; this represents 90 percent of the nation's uniformed firemen.

History of Police Organization (1830–1919)

In the late eighteenth and early nineteenth centuries urbanization proceeded at a rapid pace, and more and more village constables and town marshals were replaced by police departments. The wages and working conditions of the police in this era depended solely on the ability of the police administrator to secure legislation to improve the policeman's lot. This method often failed, and benevolent organizations soon formed to speak for the police. The superiors in the department did not object to these organizations for many of them were controlled by the superiors themselves. Currying favor through the political machine was the method whereby the police got "more." Exploiting their strategic position, the police, working closely with local politicians acquired a substantial degree of political power.

From 1890 to 1915, police in most big cities were organized into fraternal organizations that provided fringe benefits, including life insurance, and lobbied with the city for higher wages and the fulfillment of their social needs. Some of these early associations still exist today: the Patrolmen's Benevolent Association formed in New York City in 1892, the Erie Club in Buffalo founded in 1894, and the Milwaukee Policeman Protective Association formed in 1908. The first recorded attempt at police trade unionism was in Cleveland in 1897. A group of special police petitioned the AFL for charter and the AFL's response in denying the charter was, "It is not within the province of the trade union movement to especially organize policemen, any more than it is to organize militiamen, as both policemen and militiamen are often controlled by forces inimical to the labor movement."[3] From 1897 to 1919, all requests for AFL charters for police locals were denied on the basis of the 1897 ruling. The World War I era with its general labor unrest, rampant inflation, rising private sector wages, and fixed police wages caused the police to become more aggressive in pursuing their self-interest activities. The conditions of the times coupled with the many and persistent requests from police organizations to affiliate with "bread-and-butter" unionism caused the AFL to

---

[3] Allen Z. Gammage and Stanley L. Sachs, *Police Unions* (Springfield, Ill.: Charles C. Thomas, 1972), p. 33 and pp. 30–57.

rescind its prior ban on police unions. The AFL said that they now "favored" the unionization of policemen and that they saw no difference between police and other civil service workers.

During this period, the police organized in thirty-seven cities including Boston, Los Angeles, Jersey City, and Portland. There was great public hostility towards these organizations for the police were viewed as symbols of authority, guardians of law and order, and the representatives of the state. Therefore, any alliance with the purveyors of collective bargaining was considered a direct attack on the roots of the state.

The New York Police Department serves as a good example of why police did turn to unionization. The New York policeman was hurt badly by the wartime price rises; his living expenses, uniform costs, and arms and equipment were skyrocketing in price. The police saw other groups in society turn to unionism to keep their economic status from declining, and the policeman wanted his fair share of the pie too. "If the patrolmen and firemen were employees of a private corporation instead of the City of New York, their demands for salary increases would be enforced by a strike just as organized labor on the railroads and elsewhere compelled recognition."

The Boston Police Strike

The first police strike occurred in 1880 in Ithaca, New York. The mayor unilaterally decided to lower police wages from twelve dollars a week to nine dollars a week. The five-man department struck for seven days until the city council restored their wages to twelve dollars a week. The next major police labor disturbance was in Cleveland, in 1918, when 450 police struck for a salary increase from $1260 a year to $1500 a year. There was no disorder, amnesty was granted to the strikers *and,* within a few months, their salaries were increased!

The Boston police strike of 1919 attracted the most attention until the present time. Before the strike, the Boston policemen's morale was low, they worked in vermin-infested station houses, their low wages were exacerbated by inflation, they worked from seventy-three to ninety hours per week, they paid for their own uniforms, and political favoritism was used in work assignments. The Boston Social Club, the fraternal organization of the patrolmen, had its petition for an AFL charter accepted in August 1919. Police Commissioner Curtis responded by banning police affiliation three days after the AFL had issued its charter.

The commissioner proceeded to suspend nineteen patrolmen for violating his directive, and, on 9 September a police strike was called to support the nineteen men. The immediate cause of the dispute was the right of the Boston police to affiliate with organized labor, but the long-run causes were low wages, long hours, poor working conditions, and poor communication within the department.

The policemen stayed out for four days, during which time their function was taken over by the Massachusetts State Guard. Governor Calvin Coolidge made at the time, the now famous statement, "There is no right to strike against the public safety by anybody, anywhere, anytime."

A number of significant results of this strike followed: First, the 1,200 striking policemen were summarily dismissed, never to be rehired despite lengthy litigation. Second, the Boston police union was smashed. Third, the city dropped the police entrance requirements and incurred a large training expense to restore their police force. Finally, not only was the Boston police union destroyed, but the strike dealt a severe blow to police unions everywhere. "The Boston Police Strike dealt a blow to police unionization. . . . police unions everywhere were obliged either by municipal officers or the force of public opinion to relinquish their charters."

The negative effects listed above may be noted on the liability side of the strike's balance sheet. There were, however, some side benefits derived from the strike. The striking policemen, in effect, won the strike for their successors. Salaries were increased by $300 per year, entering recruits were given free uniforms, and a pension system was instituted. The strike also caused underpaid policemen in cities like New York and Washington to be hastily granted pay increases.[4]

The strike served as the vehicle to make Calvin Coolidge vice president. His statement, "the obligation of a policeman is as sacred and direct as the obligation of a soldier . . . and he has no right to prefer any private advantage to the public safety," has been carried down through the decades as the classic argument against police unions. Nevertheless, police strikes have taken place since this time in such cities as Atlanta, Kansas City, Madison, Montreal, and, in the summer of 1974, in Baltimore and San Francisco.

The Next Forty Years

There was no police union associated with organized labor until 1937. Fraternal and benevolent associations filled the void left by the fledgling unions; they acted mainly as lobbyists with local and state legislatures in an effort to gain better pensions and welfare benefits for police. In 1937 organized labor began to turn towards municipal workers as a source of

---

[4] John H. Burpo, *The Police Labor Movement: Problems and Perspectives* (Springfield, Ill.: Charles Thomas, 1971), pp. 3–15.

union membership, and this resulted in the first police local being chartered by the American Federation of State, County, and Municipal Employees (AFSCME-AFL) in Portsmouth, Virginia. By 1944, thirty-nine locals received AFSCME support, and, by 1953, AFSCME claimed fifty-eight locals.[5]

The important point about these early AFSCME locals is that they were *transitory* in nature:

> In July 1957 questionnaires were directed to the cities which had reported police unions in 1944. Within 13 years, 28 unions or 68% of the total replying are no longer in existence; 16 cities still have a union, 4 of these are small in membership and considered inactive, and one is associated with a police benefit and protective association. Thus, leaving 11 police departments of the 44 having unions at this time.[6]

In cities where AFSCME locals did not die from apathy, their demise was brought about by various legal and management pressures. For example, the AFSCME local in Chicago folded in the face of an adverse court ruling. The police in St. Louis (1945) were ordered to quit the union, and they did. The Wichita, Kansas, local (1946) was pressured out of existence. Thirty-six policemen were dismissed from the Jackson, Mississippi, department (1946) for union activity. The action was over-ruled by a jury trial, but the State Supreme Court reversed the lower court, and stated that police had no right to unionize.[7]

Today, AFSCME has approximately 11,000 members, with its locals concentrated in Colorado, Connecticut, Illinois, Maryland, Massachusetts, Michigan, Minnesota, New York, and Wisconsin. AFSCME has been fairly successful in negotiating contracts without resorting to a strike. For instance, the Omaha police garnered a 15 percent wage hike after the AFSCME local published a wage survey (1966). The Bridgeport police local obtained a $920 per year increase by the use of a vigorous public relations campaign. AFSCME's early, but limited, victories may be attributed to the fact that the AFSCME did not threaten the police administrators' ability to manage. That is, they did not "rock the government boat."

During this forty-year period that marked the low point in police collective bargaining, two professional organizations arose to represent the police. The Fraternal Order of Police (FOP) experienced slow but steady growth; in 1943 they had 169 locals, and by 1954 they had 194 locals.

---

[5] Hervey A. Juris and Peter Feuille, *Police Unionism* (Lexington, Mass.: Lexington Books, 1973), pp. 15–40.

[6] Carl E. Huestis, "Police Unions," *Journal of Criminal Law, Criminology and Police Science* 48 (November 1948): 643.

[7] *City of Jackson* v. *McLeod,* 199 Miss., 676 Sc. (2nd) 319 (1947).

The International Conference of Police Associations (ICPA) also was established to represent police. Neither the ICPA nor the FOP was affiliated with the trade union movement, and, for the most part, they were considered nonthreatening by police management because of their professional themes. Nevertheless, it is difficult to distinguish their current activities from those of any labor union.

The classic antiunion argument was expounded by the International Association of Chiefs of Police (IACP) in 1959.

> We have found unionization of police to be contrary to the basic nature of police work. Because police work is semi-military in nature, policemen must forego certain personal privileges enjoyed by employees in private industry. It is the responsibility of the police to enforce the law without fear or favor or prejudice . . . unionization will create such prejudices unacceptable to the public's desire for fair and impartial police work.[8]

The arguments against police unions do not stop here; public and legal opinion from the turn of the century until the sixties have been consistently against police unions. "Despite a longer history of paid public service, policemen have experienced more difficulty than firemen in organizing themselves. Legal restrictions and public antipathy to police unionization have been major deterrents to police unionization."[9] A public opinion poll that asked the question, "Should the police unionize?" received the following responses in 1959. Fifty-five percent of the respondents answered no, and only 27 percent answered in the affirmative.[10]

A series of court cases demonstrate the legal animus to police organization. In *FOP* v. *Harris,* 306 Mich. 68 (1943), the court upheld the decision of the Lansing Board of Police and Fire Commissioners prohibiting FOP membership. In State Lodge of Michigan *FOP* vs. *City of Detroit,* 318 Mich. 182 (1945), an order by the Detroit police commissioner banning membership in a fraternal order was held to be proper. The Lansing police tried to organize again, this time with the Teamsters (1948)—but they were prohibited. An attempt to organize New York policemen in 1951 was struck down. The New York police commissioner said in 1958, after an unsuccessful attempt at organization by the Teamsters, "You might as well try to organize the Army, Navy, Air Force, and

---

[8] Audrey M. Davies, "History and Legality of Police Unions," *GRA Reporter* 5 (July–August 1953): 41.

[9] Arthur Sackley, "Trends in Salaries of Firemen and Policemen," *Monthly Labor Review* 88 (Washington, D.C.: Government Printing Office, February 1965): 159.

[10] Edmund P. Murray, "Should the Police Unionize?" *The Nation* 188 (13 June 1959): 530–33.

FBI as to organize the police!"[11] Indeed, well they might! For it was a supposed Teamster interest in unionizing enlisted men of the United States armed forces that may have precipitated the introduction of S. 3079 discussed in Chapter 1.[12] Even though police unions were generally banned, other factors encouraged the formation of benevolent, or social organizations. Most of these organizations were readily accepted by the paternal police administrators because they helped to build morale, satisfied the policemen's social needs, and could be manipulated by political leaders.

What is most interesting about these fraternal organizations is that, though they were organized as fraternal organizations and, as such, were seen as no threat by the same commissioners who would not tolerate unions, within a short time these organizations (like the Policemen's Benevolent Association of New York) had evolved into classic collective bargaining organizations that make all of the same demands as a labor union. In other words, many of the functions performed by trade unions were now taking place under organizations with a different name. Grassroots needs for decent working conditions and for a recognition of human rights implicit in adequate due process procedures assert themselves under the most varied types of auspices. The very organization which may be created in response to an adversary's dislike for another kind of organization will turn into the very unwanted organization under a different name.

In summary, we may say that by the 1960s firemen had been fully immersed in the trade union movement and its philosophy, while the police were asking for the same thing under an assorted variety of labels. With the onset of the sixties, "Police employee organizations emerged from a forty-year period of relative dormancy to become a driving force in the quest for better salaries and working conditions," and militancy became the method for achieving these goals.[13]

Organizations Today: The Fire Fighters

The largest and most influential of all fire fighter organizations is the International Association of Fire Fighters. The IAFF was formed and received AFL affiliation in 1918; its membership includes all paid firemen except those in shipyard fire departments and nonuniformed department employees. The IAFF is a member of the National Fire Protection Association, so they are constantly advocating the implementation of new and

---

[11] *New York Times,* 12 December 1958.
[12] Mike Causey, "Senate Heading off Unions for Military," *Washington Post,* 24 April 1976.
[13] John H. Burpo, *The Police Labor Movement,* p. 6.

better fire-fighting equipment and techniques. Rival unionism is a problem that the IAFF does not face. Fire-fighter unionism is widely accepted, and, unlike police management, the professional association of fire chiefs (International Association of Fire Chiefs), officially endorses collective bargaining. The IAFF, throughout its history, has always supported and lobbied for expanding the scope of collective bargaining.

The IAFF attitude toward the use of the strike has changed with time. In 1918 the IAFF policy was that strikes were "inadvisable," but no local was sanctioned for striking. After the Boston police strike, fifty IAFF locals, including those in Boston and Washington, D.C., were dissolved. This led the IAFF strike policy to change; if a local struck without the consent of the international, they lost their charter. The 1930 IAFF convention incorporated a prohibition on strikes into the constitution which remained there until 1968. Several factors caused the IAFF to rescind its "no-strike" clause. These include the success that the firemen of Atlanta, Youngstown, St. Louis, Kansas City, and Lansing all achieved by striking in the 1964–1968 period. The large gains made by teachers, nurses, sanitation workers, and even police, by the use of the strike, encouraged a "why not us, too?" feeling among firemen. Finally, the rank-and-file fireman was unhappy with the union leadership.[14]

Organizations Today: The Police

National associations, local unaffiliated associations, local unions belonging to exclusively public-sector unions, locals affiliated with mixed unions, and an independent police union all compete to represent the police at the bargaining table. Police employee organizations are fast becoming a big voice in city government-police relations; The traditional feeling that police service is a calling like the military; and that police officers, by the nature of the institution, are expected to forego certain privileges enjoyed by employees in occupational careers, is no longer valid.

Police organizations are more likely to be fragmented on a rank basis than are fire fighters. Rank-and-file patrolmen jealously guard their associations from management interference. It is not uncommon for each rank above patrolman (sergeant, detective, lieutenant, and captain) to form their own separate employee groups. An example of this is seen in New York where the patrolmen have the Patrolmen's Benevolent Association, the sergeants have the Sergeant's Benevolent Association, the detectives have a Detectives Endowment Association, the lieutenants have a benevolent association, and the captains have a separate endowment association.

---

[14] Jack Stieber, *Public Employee Unionism: Structure, Growth, Policy,* (Washington, D.C.: The Brookings Institution, 1973), pp. 177–79.

Police locals, similar to the IAFF locals, are the locus of police labor power. The dominance of the local is caused by the inability or unwillingness of the national to become involved in local affairs and the monopolistic nature of the police service. The labor market for police, as with firemen, is local in nature. The combined FOP, AFSCME, and ICPA membership in 1968 was 250,000 out of a total of 315,000 municipal police.

The police have organizations vying to represent them on the national, state, and local levels. Nationwide, the FOP, ICPA, AFSCME, and national AFL-CIO police union, and various private sector trade unions compete for police membership. At the state level, state employee clubs and state research associations have police membership. The major local police organizations are the nonaffiliated associations. There are also a number of fraternal, benevolent, and social clubs that perform a number of nonbargaining functions on the local level.

The Fraternal Order of Police is the largest and most geographically widespread police organization with nationwide status and membership. Its membership spans forty-two states but is mostly located in Florida, Illinois, Pennsylvania, and Ohio. It has 125,000 active and 80,000 associate members in 465 lodges. The FOP was founded in 1919 to attain civil service protection for police along with better pension benefits. It had no significant membership until the thirties. Membership is open to all police, with associate membership being granted to members of the general public. FOP lodges are completely autonomous from the national, thus constituting a loose confederation.

The FOP engages in vigorous federal lobbying; its most important cause to date is the passage of a bill that would compensate families of men killed while apprehending a federal criminal. Local and state FOP lobbying ranges from an aggressive Pennsylvania lobby to an ineffective and apathetic North Carolina group. The FOP is on firm financial footing, and it is in good standing with most politicians.

The FOP, as conceived by its leadership, notably John Harrington, is not associated with the trade union movement. He stated that professionalization of the law enforcement service was incompatible with unionization. An interesting commentary on this position is his defeat in the last election by a much more militant leadership.

The International Conference of Police Associations was formed in 1953 by a number of independent police associations that rejected invitations to join the FOP. ICPA is an "association of associations" that, in contrast to the FOP, does not offer individual membership. It is not a union, and it has joined with the FOP in condemning police unions. Its raison d'etre is "to collect, study, standardize, summarize, and disseminate factual data for the purpose of promoting professionalization of the police service and to stimulate mutual cooperation between law enforcement agencies." It has been accepted by both police administrators and their professional organization, the International Association of Chiefs of Police, because it is considered nonthreatening.

ICPA is strongest in the south, and, nationwide, it is the coordinating agency for 275,000 police in autonomous organizations. There is a great deal of FOP-ICPA membership overlap, as it is possible for an individual to belong to the FOP and also hold ICPA membership via a local association. Without a doubt, the FOP and ICPA are more loosely structured than is the IAFF.

There is little doubt that the same forces that are changing the nature of the Patrolmen's Benevolent Association are at work within the ICPA, and, again, what must be looked at is the nature of their activities rather than the nature of their rhetoric which is designed to gain acceptance from the very people against whom they will find themselves in an adversary position.

AFSCME's 11,000 police members represent organized labor's most significant foothold in the police service. AFSCME is an all-public-employee union, but admitted police locals are kept separate from other AFSCME bargaining units. Its police membership is centered in Connecticut and Illinois. Membership has been static since 1954, when AFSCME had sixty-five police locals, until 1971, when they had sixty-eight locals.

There are two nonpublic employee national unions that claim some police membership, the Service Employees Union and the Teamsters. The Service Employees had a very small number of policemen until its merger with the National Union of Police Officers. After a total failure in 1958 to organize police, the Teamsters have chartered a number of small city locals, and in 1970 they claimed a police membership of 2,300. The Teamster police charters are revokable if the local strikes.

The local unaffiliated associations, not the national organizations and their locals, have been the real "hotbeds" of police-labor militancy in the sixties. These associations shun AFL-CIO affiliations because they do not want to be bound to the "no-strike" clauses that the AFL-CIO unions demand as a prerequisite for membership. They have no interest in joining national associations like the FOP and ICPA; they feel that these organizations would only serve to weaken local political clout.

The Detroit and New York associations, in particular, have shown little hesitancy in taking job actions in support of contract demands. In 1962, 1966, and 1968, the New York Patrolmen's Benevolent Association called slowdowns and "sick-ins" at negotiation time. In 1967 the Detroit police caught the "blue flu" and ended up being the highest paid police in the nation for that year.

A final phenomenon in police organizations is the rise of Afro-American associations that are more concerned with the black and his problems as a policeman than with job conditions. Internal police and fire-fighter racial dissension has led to the formation of groups known as guardians. In Hartford, Connecticut, the local guardians called a three-day sick-out to protest departmental discrimination; they also demanded desegregation, more vigorous recruitment of nonwhites, and a grievance procedure for special nonwhite problems. Other cities, too, that have black men on their forces, have witnessed the segregation of the blacks into organizations like the St. Louis Black Police Officers Association and the New York Guardians.

Causes of Union Formation and "The New Militancy"

Police and firemen in the sixties have increasingly turned to collective bargaining and militant labor tactics. The standard reasons for police dissatisfaction are usually couched in terms of a "hostile external environment" and "low economic benefits." The hostile environment for police includes the civil rights movement, black militancy, Supreme Court decisions restraining police action in favor of individual due process, the cry for civilian review boards to act as "watchdogs," increasing violence directed at police, and a great public command to "do something."

Four factors contribute to police job dissatisfaction. *First,* the "hostile external environment" described in a context of increasing public hostility towards police and a feeling of lack of support for police actions by city officials. *Second,* the pressure applied to the police, to achieve "law and order" in a situation in which they can neither prevent nor control crime, puts them in a "no-win" situation. *Third,* low pay further contributes to job dissatisfaction. For the period from 1938 until the early 1960s Bureau of Labor Statistics' data indicate that the police experienced a decline in economic status compared with earnings of federal and municipal employees. Using Consumers Price Index figures discloses that the earnings of police lagged. Indeed, the average metropolitan patrolman's salary in 1938 was 23 percent less than the Bureau of Labor Statistics' standard for a family of four in a large city. With the advent of collective bargaining, "much of the improvement in the relative positions of firemen and policemen has taken place in the past decade when their salaries rose proportionately more than earnings of factory production workers and urban teachers and more than three times as fast as the CPI."[15] The *fourth* contributing factor to job dissatisfaction is the poor personnel practices of police departments. There is a lack of internal civil and constitutional rights for a policeman accused of misfeasance or malfeasance. A grievance procedure

---

[15] Arthur Sackley, "Trends in Salaries," p. 159.

is also lacking. Police are often called to duty and held on standby without pay. Shift transfers come without advance warning, overtime premiums are not paid, and the patrolman is often the object of demeaning treatment by superior officers. Most of these practices have been eliminated in departments where police labor organizations have been established.

Job dissatisfaction is *one* cause of worker organization, but what are the causes of the "new militancy" and confrontation tactics that the police have adopted in the last decade? What may be termed a "demonstration effect" explains one part of police militancy. The police witnessed first-hand the confrontation tactics of students in the 1960s who, by these tactics, succeeded in gaining a voice in university governance. The police saw black militants riot to their advantage; after the 1967 Detroit riots, companies sought out and employed thousands of nonwhites. Other organized groups of public and private employees became more militant in the sixties and gained large wage hikes.

A *second* cause of police militancy is the influx of young police recruits in the sixties. Around 1965, large numbers of men who were hired in the World War II era began to retire; younger police, who were used to the "confrontation politics" of the sixties took their places. One-half the manpower of many departments is under thirty with less than five years experience. They are less socialized into the militaristic atmosphere of the police service, and they are more critical and less receptive to orders. An example of this propensity on the part of the younger policemen is the New York wildcat police strike of 1971, where the younger patrolmen put pressure on the older police officers to join the strike.

Ethnic and religious cohesion provides the key to a *third* cause of police (and fire fighter) militancy. This cohesion is reinforced by a common outlook arising from frequent social and professional contacts, shared interest, and shared dangers. Such cohesive, established groups actively promote their self-interest when they perceive a violation of their concept of equity or a change in their environment from supportive to threatening. Thus, considering the milieu of the sixties, it is quite natural for police and fire fighters to be militant in the pursuit of better employment terms. The similarity in circumstances to the social context of the United States armed forces is apparent.

A number of additional factors came together in the sixties and seventies to create environment more supportive of police and fire-fighter collective bargaining. A liberalization of public opinion towards public-sector unions in general, and police unions in particular, made rapid police organization possible. A 1967 Gallup poll found that six in ten Americans supported police unions.[16] This represents a shift in opinion from a 1959

---

[16] *New York Times,* 12 Jan. 1962.

poll that concluded that six in ten Americans *opposed* police unions. A change in legal opinion towards police union membership can also be noted. In 1966 a Wisconsin court ruled that police had the right to join the American Federation of State, County and Municipal Employees, AFL-CIO. In *AFSCME* v. *Woodward, Commissioner of North Platte, Nebraska,* the United States Court of Appeals for the Eighth Circuit concluded that union membership for policemen is protected by the right of association under the First and Fourteenth Amendments.[17] By 1967 seventeen states had "little Wagner Acts" for public employees and police.

The decade of the sixties brought with it, for police, a realization that the prestige and status that went with the badge and blue uniform were no longer there. A survey of the police departments in Boston, Chicago, and Washington, D.C., reveals that 59 percent of their respondents believe that police prestige is lower than it was twenty years ago.[18]

Declining working conditions, a failure of police agencies themselves to professionalize, often unfair liberal criticism of the police, an increased desire of the rank and file to have a voice in management, and the policemen's fear that American morality and patriotism was deteriorating all added to police dissatisfaction and caused them to organize. The head of the Boston Police Patrolmen's Association declared, "We are sick of being thrown to the dogs. Our militancy started when everyone else's became accepted. . . . Militancy [of the police] just had to come. There's nothing wrong with the word. What it means is that you're not sitting on your dead ass."[19]

President Kennedy's Executive Order 10988, granting collective bargaining rights to federal employees, set the tone for the decade. Unions devoted more time to organizing police. A police administration leadership problem also contributed to the growing number and militancy of police labor organizations. Not only has the traditional quasi-military command structure, which permitted many police chiefs to operate in a dictatorial fashion, become inappropriate for today's younger officers, but its inherent rigidity has been self-defeating when confronting departmental dissension. The New York City police disorders of September and October 1976 point to chaos in the department's management. The chiefs and supervisors were unable to deal with defiance by patrolmen. The department projected an image of indifference to job performance and an emphasis on routine paperwork. Commanding officers lamented the disappearance of the "loyal blue line" tradition and the emergence of a "shop-steward mentality."

---

[17] 406 F. 2nd 137 (CA-8, 1969).
[18] Gamage and Sachs, *Police Unions,* p. 109.
[19] *Boston Sunday Globe,* 15 June 1969.

Managerial and leadership inadequacies, coupled with economic pressures, had made police service "just a job."[20]

The Nature of Police and Fire-fighter Collective Bargaining

Collective bargaining in the public sector operates in a different context from private sector bargaining. The private sector labor-management relation is shaped by economic constraints; for each bargaining unit, a bilateral relation exists between the representative of the employee's and the representative of the employer's interest; private sector bargaining power depends primarily on the union's ability to impose economic costs on management. In the public sector, the context of labor relations is one of many conflicting interests; multilateral relations exist between the employees and the government; a public union's bargaining power depends on its ability to inflict both political and economic costs on management.

In examining the nature of police and fire-fighter bargaining, we will first look at the legal framework in which the process operates. Next, the problem of recognition and unit determination will be considered. Then the scope and conduct of bargaining, grievance procedures and discipline, strikes and other pressure tactics, impasse resolution, and the use of lobbying by both police and firefighters will be considered.

Because police and fire fighters are not covered by federal collective bargaining statutes, they must rely on state laws. Although the latter legislation varies among the states, all states prohibit police and fire fighters from striking. Most of this legislation has been passed since 1958. Despite the ban against strikes, police and fire fighters have used such surrogates as collective sick leave, literal enforcement of rules, picketing during off-duty hours, etc. Under Act 111, the Commonwealth of Pennsylvania requires compulsory arbitration of unresolved issues as a substitute for the strike prohibition for police, fire fighters and guards.

The three issues that frequently arise in police and fire fighter unit determination include the distinction between public-protection employees and other employees. Problems are usually not encountered with this first issue since either a state law or the "community of interest" of police and firemen prevents nonprotection and protection-service employees from being in the same unit. The second issue is whether nonuniformed and uniformed employees in police and fire-fighting work may be included in the same bargaining unit. The answer is not clear, as sometimes uniformed and nonuniformed employees within a department are allowed to be in the

---

[20] Selwyn Raab, "Top Officers Say Police Protests Have Lead to Chaos in Department" *New York Times,* 17 October 1976.

same unit, and sometimes they are not. The third, and most frequent, issue in bargaining-unit determination, is whether to include supervisory and nonsupervisory personnel in one unit. The IAFF places all ranks up to, and often including, assistant chief in the same unit. The police, on the other hand, are more likely to have separate units for separate ranks. State labor-relations boards are reluctant to make the "appropriate unit" policemen of all ranks, but have chosen to follow the National Labor Relations Board's self-determination principle; different ranks within the department must vote separately to be in the same appropriate unit encompassing an entire police department.

Negotiating is conducted by an employee bargaining team and the municipality's bargaining team. The employee organization bargaining committee draws up bargaining demands and submits them to the rank and file for approval and amendment. In lieu of maintaining a professional bargaining staff, the police and fire fighter organizations generally hire a lawyer to represent the organization at the bargaining table. The municipality team most frequently is made up of city administrators in charge of labor relations, personnel, and finance. Less often an elected official is on the bargaining team, and rarely are the police or fire chiefs on the team. The reason that chiefs are not included is that they identify closely with their men, and they may even be in the same bargaining unit, so that city officials neutralize the chief's bargaining role by excluding him.

The scope of bargaining or subjects covered by collective bargaining parallel those found in private sector bargaining except for such special items as uniform allowances and use of department facilities. In some situations municipal management has granted substantial wage increases to police and fire fighters to sustain morale and assist in recruiting. However, in the more recent period financial stringency has limited the amount of increases for police and fire fighters.

With respect to managerial rights, municipal administrators refuse to negotiate over such items as the size of the force, number of men per squad, assignment selection, manning of work stations and moonlighting. Their position is that such matters bear upon efficiency, a managerial prerogative. Despite this view, there has been a slow expansion of the scope of bargaining to encompass items deemed within the sole purview of management.

Because members of fire fighter services have had a longer time in which to refine their grievance procedures, these are more developed than are those of the police. Typical IAFF bargaining procedure is multistepped, beginning with a complaint filed with the company captain, with appeal rights through the battalion and deputy chiefs, and ending with the fire chief. There is no standard procedure for policemen. Pressure from an employee organization affects the grievance procedure in three ways. First, the organization usually demands a role in representing the grievant through all steps of the procedure. Second, changes in the procedures that would benefit the employees are sought. Third, the organization will usually demand binding arbitration by a third-party neutral as the terminal step in the procedure. Grievance arbitration is becoming more common in the protection services. For instance, Detroit and New Haven policemen and Rhode Island firemen now arbitrate unsettled grievances. It is also common, especially with policemen, to settle grievances in a more informal manner ("the chief's door is always open"). Discipline and the chief's ability to make rules affecting working conditions are excluded from the grievance procedure because of the demands of a paramilitary organization. Typical grievances include complaints about procedures, pay for work outside of the craft boundary, and other questions regarding application and interpretation of the collective agreement.

When negotiations break down, police and fire fighter organizations employ various pressure tactics to raise the costs of disagreement to management. The forms of protest when bargaining fails include lobbying, picketing, civil lawsuits, and publicity campaigns. Picketing is used to alert the public to the dispute in an effort to gain their sympathy. In recent years, the New York, Detroit, and Omaha police departments used picketing to enforce demands for higher wages. Boston patrolmen also used picketing to effectively protest an order requiring the wearing of name tags. The New York City Patrolmen's Benevolent Association went to the courts in a civil action to successfully recover overtime pay for riot duty in 1964. They also succeeded in securing an injunction against the implementation of an overlap shift or "fourth platoon" in Bronx high-crime areas.

Stronger actions when bargaining fails are work slow-downs and speed-ups, concerted refusals to perform voluntary overtime, requests for emergency leaves to take care of family business and slow-down in non-essential work. Police work slow-downs involve a refusal to write traffic tickets; this action is designed to hit the city in the pocketbook. "Super" enforcement of the law characterizes speed-ups; the action is directed at the public to put pressure on police management to accede to the employee's demands. Firemen use slow-downs in nonessential work, e.g., refusal to perform hydrant maintenance, in order to put pressure on management.

The Role of the Strike

The ultimate union pressure tactic is the strike. Recent police and fire-fighter militancy is reminiscent of the first quarter of the century when there were at least three police and thirty-five fire-fighter strikes; from the end of the Depression to the mid-sixties, work stoppages were virtually non-existent. Since 1967 there have been strikes lasting from five hours to five days in the police departments of Joliet, Illinois; Indiana, Pennsylvania; Pontiac, Michigan; Detroit, Michigan; Youngstown, Ohio; and the fire departments of Atlanta, Georgia; Kansas City, Missouri; Danville, Illinois; Lansing, Michigan; Madison, Wisconsin; and others. Police and fire fighters are hesitant to walk off the job and call the action a "strike" because many states, cities, and all department rules prohibit it; they do not want to place themselves in a blatantly illegal position because they would alienate public opinion. In an effort to subvert the antistrike statutes, work stoppages appeared in the form of mass resignation, sick-ins, and continuous professional meetings.

With few exceptions, everyone agrees that police and fire fighters should be prohibited from striking. A minority view was expressed by attorneys Theodore W. Kheel and Donald H. Wollett who argue that without the right to strike, police and fire fighters are placed at a bargaining disadvantage.[21] But the predominant position is that such strikes in essential services endanger the public health and safety, and leave the city defenseless, and they are illegal. Significantly, AFSCME excluded police and other law enforcement officers from the right to strike. And even those who like Professors John F. Burton, Jr., and Charles Krider support the right of public employees to strike agree that police and fire fighters must be prohibited from striking.[22]

As indicated earlier, police and fire fighters have developed various substitutes for the strike. An unusual approach in striking but not calling it a strike was a threatened "pray-in" by the Knoxville, Tennessee FOP. The police threatened to attend evangelist Billy Graham's meetings continuously to dramatize their demands.

Have the militant job actions been effective? The answer seems to be yes. The New York City Patrolmen's Benevolent Association, which is characteristic of the new militant police labor organizations, was instrumental in achieving significant gains for its membership between 1958 and 1969. The salary of a patrolman increased from $5,800 to $11,000 per year. Death benefits increased from $400 to $16,500; longevity pay was implemented, eleven paid holidays were secured, health and welfare pro-

---

[21] Wollett, "The Taylor Law and the Strike Ban," in *Public Employee Organization and Bargaining,* ed. H. Anderson (Washington, D.C.: Bureau of National Affairs, 1968); and Kheel, "Strikes and Public Employment," 67 *Michigan Law Review* 931 (March 1969).

[22] John F. Burton, Jr. and Charles Krider, *The Role and Consequences of Strikes by Public Employees* (Washington, D.C.: The Brookings Institution, 1970), pp. 437–38.

grams were created, increased retirement benefits were secured, and shift differential pay was obtained.

Reactions of the public employer to these actions have sometimes been strong, but, in the vast majority of the cases, few reprisals occurred. A strike of an independent employee organization led by the two captains against the Atlanta Fire Department (1966) resulted in suspensions and dismissals for over one half of the force. Two thirds of the Kalamazoo Fire Department were fired for participating in a 1969 strike.

AFSCME has been the only protection employee organization to take repressive actions against striking locals; they revoked local charter of the Joliet police for striking. Neither the FOP nor the IACP has taken action against striking members, and the IAFF (1968) also cut the "no-strike" clause from its constitution.

Impasses are particularly critical in police and fire-fighter negotiations and they characterize many bargaining situations.[23] For example, two thirds of the mediations in Connecticut during the first eight months of 1967 involved policemen or firemen. Mediation, fact finding, and arbitration are all used in attempts to break deadlocks in police and fire-fighter bargaining.

In addition to collective bargaining, police and fire fighters use lobbying and other political strategies to get what they want. The amount of lobbying is a function of legislative history, response of elected officials to past lobbying efforts, the organization's resources, and the effectiveness of other means for objective attainment. Police and fire fighters are effective lobbyists because they are highly visible, tightly organized, and often have the public's and the legislators' sympathy. Lobbying at the local level exemplifies the multilateral nature of public labor relations for police and firemen; when unsuccessful at the bargaining table, they will often attempt a legislative "end-run" to achieve victory elsewhere.

Police and fire-fighter political actions have also been adapted to the special requirements imposed by law in certain jurisdictions. In Denver, Colorado (1967), the charter said that police and fire-fighter salary increases might be made only with voter approval; police and firemen campaigned vigorously and succeeded in gaining a 10-percent salary hike. In 1970, local 109 of the National Union of Police Officers, Service Employees International Union joined with local 858 of the IAFF to amend the Denver city charter to allow collective bargaining on wages and other terms of employment. The St. Louis firemen (1966) spent over

---

[23] J. Joseph Loewenberg, "Compulsory Arbitration for Police and Fire Fighters in Pennsylvania," in *Collective Bargaining in Government,* eds. J. Joseph Loewenberg and Michael H. Moskow (Englewood Cliffs, N.J.: Prentice-Hall, 1972), pp. 347–62.

fifty thousand dollars in the winning of a referendum to achieve parity with the police.

The primary method for fire fighters and fire departments to agree on employment terms is collective bargaining, but there are really four types of police negotiating. First, there are informal talks through normal police channels. Second, there is lobbying. Third, the police employee organization can attempt to convince the chief to make recommendations to the city council. The fourth method is direct labor-management bargaining, including compulsory arbitration.

The Impact of Collective Bargaining on Police and Fire Departments

When employer-employee bargaining begins, the most controversial issue is the impact of this new form of decision-making on resource allocation and management's ability to manage. "In both public and private sectors, organized employees use power to affect the distribution of resources and the management of men and materials. In the private sector, they do this primarily as *employees*. In the public sector, they exert influence as *employees,* as *pressure groups,* and as *voting citizens.*[24] In this review of impact, we will first look at the impact of employee organization on the various stages of the employment process, i.e., hiring, selection, promotions, and training. Next, the impact on training, grievances, discipline, position classification, methods of pay setting, and fringe benefits will be discussed. Finally, police and fire-fighter unions' impact on work management, working conditions, work assignment, and the impact on the chief's "traditional" authority will be examined.

Police and fire-fighter organizations have had some effect on departmental hiring policies. They may attempt to change entrance qualifications to benefit their members or resist changes that threaten their constituency, but resistance to changes in qualification requirements is more common. The New York IAFF successfully opposed a city proposal to lower the minimum height standard to five feet, six inches; this change would have led to an increase in the number of Puerto Rican firemen. The police organization resisted attempts by the City of Tacoma to lower minimum entrance height from five feet, ten inches to five feet, nine inches!

The union impact upon selection methods has been to limit management's freedom to choose among candidates for a job. Under civil service the top three qualifying candidates are ranked by exam score, and the department head may choose among the three; the theory behind this is that

---

[24] David T. Stanley, *Managing Local Government Under Union Pressure* (Washington, D.C.: The Brookings Institution, 1972), p. 20.

the exam is not always 100 percent accurate in choosing the best man. Employee organizations, by way of collective bargaining, have attempted to eliminate possible subjective errors on management's part by making the department head select the man with the highest score. In some municipalities police and fire-fighter unions have resisted the employment of blacks and women.

Fire-fighter and police worker groups have had only modest impact on the promotion process, but that impact has been greater than that in the hiring area. Employee goals in bargaining with respect to promotions have been to reduce subjective management judgment, limit competition for the job to the organizational unit where the job is located, and use specialized job content material in exams, thereby favoring people already in the organization. On the whole, policemen and firemen tend to support established merit procedures, but they try to "load" the promotion process in favor of longer service employees. For instance, admission to the promotion qualifying exam under civil service is contingent upon serving a certain period of time in lower jobs. Union impact upon this system has been to raise the time-in-grade requirements. In addition, the method of determining who can be considered for promotion and who will actually be promoted are matters of management prerogative in most cities and are usually governed by civil service provisions. Police and fire-fighter organization effect here has been to narrow the areas of competition for promotion, to increase the weight of seniority in promotion exams, and to place more emphasis on written tests as opposed to oral exams and performance appraisals.

A significant case came up regarding a fire department's right to unilaterally institute a change in promotion procedures. On 17 April 1968, the State of Michigan's labor mediation board (Case no. 067-F-58), City of Detroit and Detroit fire fighters (local 344, IAFF) ruled that the city's change in the promotion process was an unfair labor practice because the changes were not duly bargained with the certified representative of the firemen. The case arose when the most senior battalion chief was denied advancement because he had no high school diploma, failed written exams and did not complete certain civil service courses. The mediation board found that Detroit's Board of Fire Commissioners tried unilaterally to change the basis for promotions. Thus, the union won a victory in its battle against advancement based on quantified measures of merit.

Grievance matters have been a fertile field for influence of employee organization. With the advent of fire-fighter and police collective bargaining, the general consensus is that the number of complaints have increased, and these complaints are handled in a more formal manner. There is a trend away from civil service grievance procedures, while the use of third-party neutrals to adjudicate unsettled complaints is becoming more common.

Like the grievance procedures for private sector employees, grievances for police and fire fighters may arise over a contract violation, breach of an established practice, violation of a rule or regulation, differences over the meaning and application of contract terms, or a violation of an employee's rights. The customary steps proceed upward, subject to time limits and terminating with a neutral arbitrator. Although these procedures are widespread for fire fighters, they are less frequent in police departments because many complaints are handled informally. Moreover, grievance procedures in police departments are not fully used because lower level supervisors have little motivation to settle since they know that the chief will eventually make the final decision.

The impact of public protection service employee organizations on discipline has been to regularize procedures, minimize ad hoc decisions on punishment, and eliminate certain types of punishments, like penalty tours and long suspensions, without appeal rights. Arbitrary or unjust discipline is more likely to be questioned, and so management exercises greater caution in taking action. Recently, the police of Pittsburgh, Buffalo, Boston, San Francisco, and New York have made bold moves to secure such rights.

Employee organizations do not fight position classifications. However, they do attempt to get jobs reevaluated to higher grades as a means of gaining wage increases, and they do insist on pay for out-of-title work.

Only the fire fighters have shown concern about the hours of work. Holding salaries constant, the firemen hope to get more for each hour worked by reducing hours. They also have more time to take on a second job. Demands for fewer hours means that departments must replan shift assignments and increase manpower (which means spending more money). Via direct pressure, the IAFF has reduced the workweek in Boston from forty-eight to forty-six hours in 1970. In Hartford (1968), the workweek dropped from fifty-six to forty-four hours, and it was scheduled to fall to forty-two hours in 1971. In Wilmington (1967), the hours' reduction was from fifty-six to fifty-two to forty-eight in 1971.

The impact that police and fire-fighter employee organizations have had on management prerogatives has, perhaps, the most far-reaching implications for the military of any of the single effects of unionization. Two New York City cases, one involving firemen and the other involving police, will serve as examples as to the potential impact of labor organizations on workload and manning decisions. The New York IAFF in 1969 claimed that the workload per man was improperly high, and they demanded that the city hire 2,500 more firemen. The City refused, claiming that manning was a management prerogative and nonbargainable; the city also wanted the flexibility to assign additional fire-fighting units to high-risk areas. The firemen threatened to stop performing all nonfire-fighting duties. The city hired 500 additional men and agreed to submit the issue of the negotiability of workload and manning to a tripartite collective bargaining board. The board ruled, "Any management determination having a practical impact on the working conditions of employees may ultimately become the subject of collective bargaining if the City does not act expeditiously to relieve the impact."[25] The city was also ordered to hire 840 men in addition to the original 500.

The two-man patrol car controversy points up another potential effect of employee organizations on manning. The New York Police Department told its men that one-man patrol cars would be used in "safe" neighborhoods. The Patrolmen's Benevolent Association resisted, but the arbitrator found that this was a management right not subject to negotiation. Winning the arbitration award may have some nice theoretical implications, but the Patrolman's Benevolent Association soon threatened the department with a "job action" if one-man cars were instituted. Today, the City of New York has 300 never-used one-man patrol cars sitting idle.

Both through collective bargaining and arbitrator's awards, public protection employee organizations have had a significant impact on work assignments (the "when" and "where" question). In some situations, such as those involving stabilizing days off, these unions have forced management to minimize the transfer of personnel between shifts and duty assignments which would result in changing the number of working hours in any fixed working period.

The issue of work assignment arose in the form of a "fourth platoon" dispute in the New York City Police Department in 1966. The mayor and police commissioner sought the repeal of a fifty-eight-year-old State law limiting the number of shifts to three, each lasting eight hours; the city wanted to use the fourth shift in high-crime areas. The act was repealed despite strong opposition by the Patrolmen's Benevolent Association. The association proposed a compromise; they would work a fourth shift but on a volunteer basis. The city objected, stating that the volunteers could too easily be used in a "job action." The end result was that the fourth platoon was instituted on a volunteer basis even though the city had the clear legal right to compel a mandatory shift.

Protection service labor groups have had some effect on work jurisdiction. The organizations want to get more pay for performing higher-rated work; they do not want to work below their skill level; and they jealously guard against "outsiders" doing their work in addition to refusing

---

[25] *New York Times,* 18 Sept. 1969.

to do another union's work. Boston and San Francisco policemen have stopped the practice of allowing nonpolice department personnel to direct traffic. Dade County firemen refuse to do any major hydrant maintenance, and Cincinnati firemen will not do any maintenance work.

What has been the employee organization's impact on the chief's traditional authority? The "traditional" department chief was an autocrat who exercised sole authority with respect to directing the work force, discipline and discharge, and rewards. In an industry patterned after the military model, and with no lateral entry, the chief had ultimate power in personnel and policy matters. A great deal of this power has been lost because of employee organization, a high personnel turnover and decreasing average age, and the various factors that gave rise to militancy in the sixties. The two roles of the union have been, first, to negotiate a new set of operating rules which move toward management by policy, protection of employees against arbitrary or inconsistent treatment, and the institutionalization of the mechanism of collective bargaining for continuing power-based interactions. And, second, in the police service, to provide a voice for the rank-and-file police officer within the boundaries of these new policies. The chief is left to manage, subject to these procedural constraints, and with an additional demand upon his time.

The impact of a protection service worker group varies by region; it is stronger in New York than in New Orleans. The impact varies by function; union effect is greater on grievance procedures than on civil service tests. The impact of police and fire-fighter organizations is growing; the number of issues determined jointly is increasing. In law enforcement,

> the demands of police unions seem to be consistent with the traditional demands of trade unions representing other production and maintenance workers with respect to wages, hours, and conditions of work. For all their talk of professionalization, the police are conceptually indistinguishable from steel workers or auto workers in their on-the-job concerns. . . . We would agree from this that the real impact of the union has been to force shared decision making in the allocation of resources, whether the resources discussed are monetary or human resources.[26]

No longer do police or firemen work overtime without receiving time-and-a-half; police are no longer called to stand by without being paid their normal wage. Of course, department management has a large role to play here too, for collective bargaining is *shared* decision making. Management must demand quid pro quo at the bargaining table; they must seek innovative solutions to mutual problems; they must oppose demands that would

---

[26] Juris and Feuille, *Police Unionism*, p. 146.

create intolerable burdens; and they must "rationalize" the bargaining process so that all union gains are limited strictly to the bargaining table.

Instances of "Red" and "Blue" Power

This section will present examples of police and fire-fighter strikes. The reactions of the city administration, the causes of the strike, and the various impacts of the strike will be discussed.

Before 1969 the only police work stoppage that allegedly resulted in serious damage to life and property was the Boston police strike. On 7 October 1969, 3,700 Montreal policemen walked off their jobs, throwing the city into total anarchy. The issue causing the strike was the failure of an arbitration board to settle a year-long wage dispute in favor of the police. Montreal was left with a skeleton law enforcement force; only forty-seven officers stayed on duty, and two hundred Quebec provincial police were called in. The five hundred cars had either been disabled or taken by the strikers. The Quebec provincial police had no working knowledge of the 1.25 million population metropolitan area; this problem was compounded by striker tactics, which included the jamming of police radio frequencies, assaults on the Quebec police, and false alarms. The above-named arbitration decision also affected firemen, and they too chose to strike, thus worsening an already terrible situation. The firemen, though, did maintain "emergency" teams on duty.

All the ingredients for a criminal rampage were present, and, before the police returned at 12:30 A.M. on 8 October, at least 34 armed robberies and 456 burglaries occurred. These figures were far above normal daily Montreal crime. The absence of authority set the scene for the surfacing of long-standing hostilities. Taxi drivers attacked the office of a limousine service that held the exclusive franchise to Montreal International Airport. French-Canadian separatists destroyed downtown buildings associated with the "English establishment." Social radicals took the opportunity to vent their hostilities by vandalizing the city. The mob action swept up honest citizens who also participated in the looting and vandalism. Two people were killed, and forty-nine others were injured in strike-related incidents; property losses were greater than one million dollars.

The state legislature of Quebec was in session that day, and they passed a bill requiring the strikers to return to work or suffer severe penalties. The police returned, and order was restored. Sixteen days after the strike, a new contract was negotiated to supersede the arbitration decision; the settlement provided for salary increases that were $720 above the amount awarded by arbitration.[27]

---

[27] Los Angeles Herald Examiner, "The Day the Police Went Away," 30 Nov. 1969.

Two thirds of Atlanta's five hundred-man fire department struck in defiance of a Georgia state law and stayed out in the face of a court order. On the day of the strike, 2 September 1966, the mayor not only refused to negotiate with the firemen, but he began hiring permanent replacements. The city's reaction to the strike was to regroup the remaining fire fighters and assign these men extra shifts. The Atlanta Fire Department also formed "mutual assistance" pacts with neighboring cities.

The trouble first began in the spring of 1966 when firemen demanded that hours be reduced from sixty to fifty-six. To enforce their demands they broke away from the IAFF, which still had a "no-strike" clause and formed an independent association. The association struck in June but immediately decided to submit the issues to mediation; the mediator, through shorter hours and wage hikes, recommended a 16 percent pay increase for firemen. The city agreed, but charter provisions prevented implementation of the recommendation until 1 January. The firemen were adamant in demanding immediate implementation, so they struck. The results of the strike were: it took one year to rebuild the department; no striker was rehired; and two major fires occurred along with numerous false alarms.

Five weeks of less-than-normal law enforcement in Detroit in 1967 was climaxed by the first major United States police strike since Boston. Detroit's mayor triggered a ticket slow-down when he claimed that no funds were available for police salary increases. 50 percent fewer tickets were written by the patrolmen which hurt the City revenue-wise. The independent Detroit Police Officers Association was demanding minimum base salary increases from $8,335 to $10,000 for police with more than five years service. On 13 June 1967, sixty-one police were suspended for the slow-down. The suspensions caused a "blue-flu" epidemic during which hundreds of police officers called in sick. An injunction against the mass sick call was secured (at least one third of the 2,668-man force participated), and the situation began to improve. The city reacted to the strike by instituting overtime, juggling men and assignments, and alerting the National Guard and state police. The nonstrikers did an amazing job during the dispute, and the number of major crimes committed actually dropped! Four months after the strike, a fact-finding panel's recommendation for the $10,000 minimum base salary was implemented.

Vallejo, California (population 70,000), endured a five-day joint police–fire fighter strike in the summer of 1969. The ninety-man police force and eighty-eight–man fire department struck for increased wages and fringe benefits, pay for home standby and a better pension plan. The strikers picketed, violated a restraining order, and broke the California "no-strike" law. No real disruption occurred because surrounding cities' police and firemen helped to protect Vallejo. The strikers were granted amnesty upon returning, and the city agreed to their demands.

In January 1971, 85 percent of New York's 27,400-man police department participated in a six-day wildcat strike inspired by the Patrolmen's Benevolent Association. The strike was caused by "frustration," "humiliation," and "anger" that had been building up for years. The "final injustice" was a court's refusal to act on a lawsuit by the association on the proper relationship of a patrolman's and a sergeant's pay. There was no breakdown in law and order as was the case with Montreal's crime and riots. A combination of cold weather and nonstrikers, along with officers placed in strategic spots, averted a "crime wave." The strike ended when the judge agreed to expedite the investigation into pay ratios.

Other strikes include one by Rockford, Illinois, firemen in 1968 in pursuit of higher wages. Gary, Indiana, firemen struck in 1969 while a major fire blazed. Police in Indiana, Pennsylvania, walked out when the city council refused their wage demands. A strike in January 1971 by Milwaukee policemen failed because of public apathy and the city's ability to maintain a "police presence" on the streets. Pittsburgh policemen caught the "blue flu" in April 1970 to protest racial transfers; management's right to transfer was subsequently upheld. Rochester policemen successfully broke a bargaining impasse in May 1970 with an eight-hour work stoppage.

> A brief strike by San Francisco's police and firemen ended on August 21, when Mayor Joseph Alioto invoked emergency powers to override the Board of Supervisors' rejection of a settlement he had negotiated. The settlement provided 1,935 policemen and 1,780 firemen with a 13-percent wage increase and total amnesty for the strikers. The increase was to be effective October 15, rather than the traditional July 15. The police strike began on August 18, after the Board offered a 6.5-percent increase to both groups, and the firemen walked out 2 days later.
>
> According to the city's charter, uniformed employees cannot be paid more than comparable workers in other large California cities. In practice, the San Francisco employees had always received the maximum permitted by the charter provision. In the current bargaining, policemen and firemen, whose starting pay was $16,044, asked for a 13-percent increase to equal the pay of one of Los Angeles' three patrolmen ranks. The Board of supervisors offered a 6.5 percent to match the pay of a lower rank. San Francisco has a single rank for patrolmen.[28]

Of the fifty-one police strikes that occurred between 1965 and 1969, three were AFSCME affiliated, nine were by FOP groups, six were by organizations like the Patrolmen's Benevolent Association, and the rest were by independent associations. Eighteen of the thirty-nine fire-fighter strikes in the same period were IAFF-instigated, and the remainder in-

---

[28] *Monthly Labor Review* 98 (Oct. 1975): 62–63.

volved independent associations. The duration of these 1965–69 strikes is tabulated below:

Length in days	1	2	3	4–7	8–14	More than 15	
Police strikes	14	9	7	12	6	3	(total 51)
Fire-fighters strikes	8	7	7	9	2	6	(total 39)

During the above period the average duration of police strikes was 4.5 days and strikes by firemen, 5.3 days. In 1974 the police averaged 3.0 days lost due to strikes and the firemen averaged 5.4 days.[29]

The main issues involved in fire-fighter strikes early in the century were the right to join a labor organization, wages, hours, and working conditions. Early police strikes, with the exception of Boston, were also incident-free and were caused by disputes over wages, hours, or other terms of employment. The same generalization has held true in the sixties and will probably continue to hold true for the ensuing decades. City administrators are becoming more adept at mitigating harmful effects of public protection service strikes. For example, the number of major crimes dropped in the Detroit issue, no major incidents occurred in the Youngstown police-fire strike, and the police in Pontiac were able to deploy enough officers and nonstrikers to maintain a "police presence."

There is a question of whether protection service employee strikes have brought hardship to the general public. Their actions are frequently short in duration. The strike most often involves less than the full work force. Furthermore, job actions short of total work stoppages are many times employed. Finally, the employee associations themselves tend to terminate the action if strong negative public reaction is encountered.

Implications

The experiences of the police and fire fighters with collective bargaining have direct implications for the military. *First,* it is not realistic to discount the possibility of the emergence of a shared decision-making system in any group in society. The rank-and-file firemen and the fire departments "grew up" with collective bargaining as the means to find solutions to mutual problems. In contrast, joint labor-management decision making only surfaced in the police service in the sixties; collective bargaining is not yet fully accepted by all police departments, as only one half of the police departments in the United States use it. Still, the police model has a number of lessons for the military:

[29] *Analysis of Work Stoppages, 1974* (Bulletin 1902, U.S. Department of Labor, 1976), Table 18.

Collective bargaining emerged in the police service despite a hierarchical structure and strong management-rights views. As previously discussed, the police chief traditionally exercised more power and delegated less than his counterparts in the public service or private industry. The comparison between the chief in a paramilitary, pyramid-shaped, authoritarian organization such as the police and a commander in the military is inescapable.

Shared decision making surfaced in the police even in the face of a growing movement towards professionalization of the service.

Elaborate civil service protection for police and firemen forestalled, but did not prevent, the appearance of collective bargaining. In the pre-bargaining era, both services were quite adept at securing better terms of employment through political tactics, but now political action is used mainly to augment bargaining power.

Collective bargaining emerged despite an alleged acceptance by police recruits of a military command structure which demanded unquestioning obedience and imposed rigid discipline. The conclusion may be that today's young man is just not willing to blindly follow orders that deviate from his conception of what is "right."

Groups exposed to stressful and dangerous situations tend to become cohesive; the police reputation for group cohesiveness has aided the growth of shared decision making.

Poor police leadership was a major cause of police unionization since police commanders were insensitive to the patrolman's dissatisfactions and his need for an outlet to handle job grievances.

An important lesson that police bargaining has for the military is that workers will organize when they perceive a decline in their economic or job status compared to other employees.

The troublesome strike issue can be resolved constructively by providing compulsory arbitration for unsettled issues.[30]

A *second* implication that the police and fire-fighter experience has for the military has to do with the nature of unions. The presence of a worker group attempting to attain certain due process rights for its members puts pressure on management. Management directives and orders, especially arbitrary ones, are more likely to be challenged; and the right of management to decide unilaterally certain matters may come under attack. For instance, military managers have always been able to reach unilaterally decisions on "critical" issues like work management, work assignments, manning and workloads, and hours of work. If the experience of police and fire fighters with collective bargaining is any guide, we may expect an enlisted personnel work group to encroach on the "sacred" management

---

[30] James L. Stern, *et al., Final-Offer Arbitration: The Effects on Public Safety Employee Bargaining* (Lexington, Mass.: D.C. Heath and Co., 1975).

areas. Joint employer-employee decisions on force assignment and manning were inconceivable in the police service only ten years ago, but, today, policemen through arbitration awards and sheer bargaining power have forced some shared decision making on these and other "management rights" areas.

The impact that police and fire-fighter unions have had on resource allocation provides a final inference for the potential impact of codetermination on the military. Police and fire department manpower resources are increasing in costs; unionization has succeeded in putting a higher and higher price on manpower. The imposition of collective bargaining brings with it the realization that manpower has costs and must be carefully allocated among competing ends, an attitude that is certainly consistent with our current military posture. A compensating factor is that collective bargaining impels management to reexamine its structure, organization, rules and operations; to become sensitive to the needs and desires of employees; and finally, to manage more effectively and efficiently its nonhuman and human resources.

8

European Military Unions

EZRA S. KRENDEL

Introduction

The following presents the background and present status of military unions in the Federal Republic of Germany (FRG), Sweden and Norway.[1] Although military unions also exist in Denmark and Austria, examining them will provide no additional implications for American policy. A distinction is made between these military unions (which are akin to trade unions in their philosophy, goals, and strategies) and soldiers' organizations (which may formally represent military personnel but are not part of a trade-union tradition). These European military unions are unions of commissioned and noncommissioned officers; the soldiers' organizations, such as the Union of Conscripted Soldiers in Holland, which have been referred to in the press in this country, are for conscripts only.[2] Because of the transient nature of their membership, associations of conscripts lack a commitment to military service as a career, unlike the military unions which are an expression of a career commitment on the part of their members. This difference makes for a fundamental distinction in the nature and attitudes of these two types of organizations. The consistent theme which

---

[1] Earlier examinations of this topic are presented in: Ronald V. Grabler, Maj., USAF, "Military Unions: An Analysis of Unionization in Norway and Germany as it Relates to the United States" (Masters thesis SLSR-17-71B, Air Force Institute of Technology, Wright-Patterson Air Force Base, Ohio, August 1971; Joseph P. Mockaitis, Capt., USAF and Donald E. Johnson, Capt., USAF, "An Analysis of Military Unionization in Austria, Denmark and Sweden" (Masters thesis, SLSR-10-72B, Air Force Institute of Technology, Wright-Patterson Air Force Base, Ohio, September 1972).

[2] Bowen Northrup, "This is An Army? Well, It Has Arms, Marches—Sort Of, But Thanks To Their Union, Dutch Soldiers Can Forget About Salutes and Reveille," *The Wall Street Journal*, 1 October 1974; Phil Stanford, "Would Soldier's Unions Cripple U.S. Defense?" *Parade*, 11 April 1976.

emerged from interviews in the fact-finding trip from which much of this chapter derives, is that, in addition to union negotiations for economic issues, there is a growing pressure for codetermination in decision making by junior officers. While respecting the need for and principle of command prerogative, these officers want to be more fully involved in those decision-making processes that concern them directly. This attitude of professional responsibility toward sharing management prerogatives has also been expressed by unionized teachers, and to a lesser extent by policemen and firemen, as discussed in the preceding chapters. The northern European experience will be traced briefly from a cultural and historic perspective to detect trends with parallels in the United States.

The Swedes and Norwegians exhibit a homogeneity which is exceptional even for old, established European states. Although cultural residues of regionalism exist in the FRG (i.e., there is a Schwabian dialect, Hessians differ from Bavarians, and both differ from Hamburgers), these differences are insignificant compared with the ethnic diversity of the United States. Save for the FRG, these countries are small. Norway's population of 3.9 million is comparable to that of our smallest states. In these countries, the Social Democratic presence in the parliamentary form of government has been strong since World War II, even though the Social Democrats did not enter the ruling coalition of the FRG until 1966. The labor unions have had strong, proprietary stakes in the various national Social Democratic Parties.

All of these countries have a system of conscription and ready reserves rather than large, standing military forces. Sweden has not been at war in 150 years. The other nations have post–World War II armies which differ from their World War II predecessors. None of these new armies has seen combat. The military personnel, officers and noncommissioned officers, who constitute the cadre about which the military forces are expanded in times of emergency, are the candidates for union membership. A unifying principle in the evolution of northern European military unions, as in the development of unions in general, is the progression from technical interest group to a group-welfare–oriented position, usually manifest by lobbying, and, finally, to an organization having the negotiating powers, adversary capabilities, and membership benefits and responsibilities which are characteristic of a trade union. This progression has been seen in the public sector in this country among our teachers; and it is slowly evolving for engineers in response to recent economic downturns in that profession. The economic and social forces which have prompted this evolution in the past may provide a predictive capability for the future.

There are factors which are more directly visible in the European military experience. These are the recognition of the need to democratize the military—with different techniques used for regulars than for con-scripts—and the pressures from the officers and men for an institutionalized voice in many of the matters which concern them directly.

The FRG is the largest, militarily most significant, and, (in respect to size, industrial power, and relative heterogeneity) the most similar to the United States of all the countries which have military unions. The FRG will be discussed first, followed by the Scandinavian countries.

The Federal Republic of Germany

Historical Perspective

Unlike Norway and Sweden, the FRG does not have a stable, continuous political and military history extending back for the last hundred years or so. The German experience has been one of industrial development, tur-moil, war, and disaster. In order to understand the present position of col-lective bargaining and trade unionism within the German military, it is well to review some of the salient aspects of the German experience. The unified German nation, which terrorized much of Europe in World Wars I and II, was created in 1871 when Bismark engineered the formation of the German Empire, the First Reich. Prior to this, Germany had been a collection of principalities, kingdoms, and other independent states whose main con-necting link was a common language, albeit colored by local dialects and usages. The German Empire did not have the religious homogeneity which characterizes the Scandinavian countries. Germany was split between Protestants and Catholics, and this spirit was reflected in political divisions. In the year of the formation of the First Reich, all the individual German armies were converted into units of the imperial army. The Imperial German Army, which basically evolved from Prussian army traditions of command and organization, developed and flourished until 1918 when it was destroyed by the Allies at the end of World War I. In 1919, the Second Reich, the so-called Weimar Republic, was founded. The military forces, modest as the terms of the Versailles Treaty demanded, were con-stituted as the Reichswehr. The Imperial German Army, deriving as it did from the Prussian army (which has been referred to as the army that owned a state), had been responsible to the Kaiser and not to the political machinery. The Reichswehr, in a similar fashion, was an entity within the state, independent of political control and reporting to a Reich's minister. It was the power of the rising German labor unions, demonstrated by a series of general strikes in 1921 and 1922, that prevented the reactionary forces which were in control of the Reichswehr from staging a coup d'état against the struggling young republic. From its commander, General Hans von Seeckt, came the concept of an "army of leaders" and "the iron framework for the Reich." From the very start the army was an expandable device for once again exerting German military power. The Versailles Treaty limitations were subverted in many ways. The Reichswehr's officers were trained in the Soviet Union in the use of forbidden military equipment. The air force, which was forbidden by treaty, trained under the shelter of civil aviation and Soviet aid. When the Nazis overthrew the Weimar Republic and created the Third Reich in 1933, the Wehrmacht, the Nazi replacement for the Reichswehr, was easily built upon the Reichswehr's "iron framework." The Reichswehr regiments were expanded into divisions. The complement of officers had been planned with this in mind by the German general staff well in advance of the actual event. In 1945, at the conclusion of World War II, the formidable Wehrmacht had been destroyed. Germany was divided into two nations: the German Democratic Republic under Soviet control and the Federal Republic of Germany which was oriented toward Western Europe. The FRG, whose present population is 62 million, was founded in 1949 and remained under Allied control until 1955 when it became a sovereign state and entered NATO as a member of this military alliance. In April 1957 the first Bundeswehr recruits reported for service and the history of the army of the FRG begins at this time.

The Bundeswehr and FRG Political Parties

The Bundeswehr employs both uniformed soldiers and civilians attached to the armed forces or to NATO. There are 186,000 civilians working for the German defense establishment of whom 132,000 work for NATO. The uniformed members of the defense establishment total approximately 490,000. Of this number, over 40,000 are in the navy, and 120,000 are in the air force of the FRG. This number includes 15-month conscripts as well as regular professional soldiers and so-called soldiers *auf zeit*. The soldiers *auf zeit* are soldiers who are basically specialists with a technical skill who enlist for two-year intervals. When these two-year periods have aggregated up to 15 years, the *auf zeit* soldier is in much the same position as the professional soldier who sees the army as employment for his complete working life until his retirement at from 52 to 60 years of age. In the army there are a total of 210,000 regular soldiers or nonconscripts. These 210,000 include 52,000 soldiers who have enlisted for life, and the rest are soldiers *auf zeit* who reenlist if they so wish on the two-year period basis. In addition, there are 32,000 civilians employed to perform what would normally be jobs of uniformed soldiers, such as aircraft repair and maintenance. These persons are in the civilian structure, so that their wage scale can be compatible with that outside of the military without breaking the wage structure for their particular rank and seniority in the military. These civilians become uniformed soldiers in the event of war or an emergency. The similarity to the United States National Guard civilian technicians is clear.[3]

The FRG has been ruled by the Christian Democrats, Christlich-Demokratische Union (CDU), a right-to-center party, from 1949 to 1966. From 1966 to 1969, a coalition of the Social Democrats, Sozialdemokrat-ische Partei Deutschlands (SPD) and the CDU ruled Germany; from 1969 until the present, the ruling coalition has been the dominant SPD and the Free Democratic Party, Freie Demokratische Partei (FDP). In 1955, the SPD objected to the formation of the Bundeswehr, but it was not until 1966, when they had a responsible role in the government that this objection could become effective. When this occasion arose, however, the objection remained more a verbal principle than a basis for action. The SPD has close ties with the German Trade Union Federation, Deutscher Gewerkschaftsbund (DGB), which has seven million members. The DGB has been depoliticized in that formal ties with the SPD have been severed and the substantial DGB contributions to the SPD treasury are a thing of the past. Nevertheless, there is a large overlap of basic interests and personnel between the DGB and SPD.[4] The FRG's constitution gives all citizens the right to form unions, and this was reaffirmed for soldiers in a defense minister's decree on 1 August 1966.

Trade Unions and Military Unions

Labor unions in Germany grew rapidly after World War I; by 1939 they had reached a total membership of well over eight million. These unions ended their role as free labor organizations in May 1933, when they were suppressed and merged with the German labor front of Robert Ley under Nazi auspices. Even under the Nazis, however, a considerable emphasis was put on making available to the German working man many of the advantages of "the good life." For example, the Kraft durch Freude organization was a Nazi effort to make vacations, cruises, and other recreational activities available to the German workers after the "glorious victory" of World War II. These background facts indicate, if not the power of German labor, at least the concern with which German governments, however totalitarian, viewed the labor component of the German nation. The trade union move-

---

[3] *Zur Sicherheit der Bundesrepublik Deutschland und zur Entwicklung der Bundeswehr* (Bonn: Press—und Informationsamt der Bundesregierung, Weiss Buch 1973/1974).

[4] Barbash, *Trade Unions,* chap. 5.

ment between World Wars I and II, except for a large block (roughly half of the total) of membership in the DGB, was a fragmented group of industrial unions, craft unions, religion-oriented unions, and so forth. After World War II, when the FRG was created, democracy in the labor movement was encouraged by the Allies with the formation of many unions at a decentralized, grass-roots level. It was not until some time later that the major labor confederations which presently exist in Germany appeared. These unions, because of the political attitudes of their members and because of the traditions of distrust of the military and the class structure it represented, were oriented toward the SDP which was a minority party in the early days of the FRG. The SPD's early objections to the formation of a German military machine derived not because of a sympathy with the "socialist block" in the East, but because of a profound distrust of what the military had done to Germany in the past and what it might do again if given the authority. Bernhard Fleckenstein of the FRG Ministry of Defense has written an excellent analysis of the antecedents and history of these attitudes.[5]

Military unions in the FRG are overwhelmingly officers' unions, because the officers, commissioned and noncommissioned, constitute the skeletal cadre about which the army is expanded in times of emergency. They are the permanent force who have a long-term interest in the stability of their jobs and the conditions surrounding them. The conscripts are not allowed to join these unions. They may, of course, maintain their membership in whatever union to which they may have belonged prior to entering the service. The Bundeswehr officer corps preserves many of the old traditions, one of which is the notion of responsibility for the men, as modified by the concept of "Innere Führung," which basically means generating leadership qualities from within a person. Its purpose is to encourage enlisted men and officers to develop more questioning minds and to humanize the military by moving it farther from the feared Prussian model of older times. A device for achieving the same end is the institution of the elected representative of the soldiers, the Vertrauensmann. In effect this is a formalized grievance procedure. In a sense the soldiers' representatives are a military parallel of codetermination in industry which the DGB strongly supports for three major reasons: "to restrict existing positions of power and to subject them to effective control"; to humanize "the whole of our social and economic life," that is, the workshop as not only a "place of production" but also "a place of human association"; and

---

[5] Bernhard Fleckenstein, "The Military and Labor Union Organization in Germany," *Armed Forces and Society* 2 (Summer 1976): 495–515.

to put "formal democracy" into practice "in a decisively important sphere of life."[6]

German officers appear to be dedicated to developing a new, democratic armed force. The "citizen in uniform" image for the German soldier came up repeatedly in the author's conversations with German officers. This means that the soldier is part of the nation and does not exist as a privileged, separate class within the nation. He has the same basic rights and responsibilities of any other citizen, whether or not in uniform. This, in itself, is a break with past German tradition and a point of similarity of the Bundeswehr with the current United States armed forces. No longer do United States regular officers maintain the exaggerated apolitical stance which was traditional before World War II.

Two major organizations compete for the loyalties of German military personnel and the right to represent them. By far the largest is the association of the German army, Deutsches Bundeswehr Verband (DBwV).[7] The DBwV is not a union but a vocational organization of career members of the armed forces who have banded together so as to lobby more effectively for improvements in their compensation and working conditions. In a variety of ways, because of shared politics and philosophy, the DBwV is associated warmly with the German Civil Servants Association, Deutscher Beamtenbund (DBB), which organized *tenured* civil servants, or *Beamten*. Compensation for *Beamten* and military personnel is established by law in the FRG, not by collective bargaining. Neither *Beamten* nor military personnel have the right to strike. They do not regret this since they derive from a tradition of service to a government of which they are the bureaucratic and military mainstay. The FRG follows the concept of linkage in a unitary pay scale for all employees of the state. A pay raise for one class of employees is reflected in the pay scales for all other employees of the FRG. Thus, military personnel, officials of the FRG bureaucracy, and professors *all* may get salary increases as the result of a successful strike by trash collectors or train men, both of whom are nontenured civil servants.

This introduces the organization that is competitive with the DBwV, the Public Service Transport and Communication Workers Union Gewerkschaft Öffentliche Dienste, Transport und Verkehr (ÖTV). About 50 percent of the nontenured civil servants are organized by the ÖTV. The ÖTV has a union membership of approximately one million and is the largest

---

[6] Wilhelm Haferkampf, *Codetermination in the Basic Programme of the German Trade Unions* (Dusseldorf: DGB, 1964) as quoted in Barbash, *Trade Unions*, p. 91.

[7] Herman Giesen, *Der Deutsche Bundeswehr-Verband,* Amter und Organizationen der Bundesrepublik Deutschland (Bonn: Boldt Verlag, 1970).

component of the DGB federation. The DGB membership, on the order of seven million, represents a powerful force in bargaining with the government. It is this force in bargaining which precludes the need for the strike as a weapon by either the DBB of the DBwV; they are cost-free beneficiaries of the DGB's aggressive union posture in negotiating with the State. These two protagonists, the DBwV and the ÖTV, with different political and social philosophies, constitute the main lobby for soldiers' rights, welfare and pay. Both steadfastly affirm their allegiance to the FRG constitution and the concept of a civilianization of the FRG military. The rivalries between these two groups, though papered over in public, run deep and lie in the historic and cultural events which led up to the founding of the Bundeswehr.[8]

The DBwV claims that roughly 70 percent of the military personnel who are eligible are listed in their "union." The number who would be eligible is 210,000 soldiers. The ÖTV began organizing the military later than the DBwV, has significantly higher dues, and by 1975 could claim only 8,000 members. Members range widely in rank, from privates to the Inspector General of the Bundeswehr in the DBwV, and from privates to a lieutenant general in the ÖTV. The great majority of members in the ÖTV military union are junior officers, lieutenants and captains. They come from a weak but growing tradition of officers who depart from the old officer corps' philosophy and attitudes. Their number is small because of the former reluctance of the DGB to become involved with anything relating to German military. A new attitude is rising, however, and many in the ÖTV have assumed an almost missionary attitude toward involvement in the Bundeswehr. This ÖTV attitude, as extracted from several interviews with ranking ÖTV officials may be summarized as follows:

There is a need to institutionalize democratizing influences within the Bundeswehr in much the same sense that there was a need to institutionalize democratic influences in German industry. An effective way of doing this is to encourage young men from trade-union backgrounds to become officers. Once this has been accomplished, it is necessary that they maintain a formal operating contact with trade-union ideals and not be seduced into rejecting their heritage by assimilation into the traditional officers' corps. The DBwV represents, to the ÖTV, the source of a beguiling siren song of German militarism and privilege. Thus are the philosophical battle lines drawn.

Apart from political philosophy, the ÖTV accepts current trends in trade-union thinking, modifies them when appropriate, and attempts to apply them to the military. Codetermination, or *Mitbestimmung,* is a strong

---

[8] Informationen für Alle Soldaten, (Stuttgart: ÖTV, April 1973).

and lively issue in German labor–management relations. The ÖTV leaders find the concept not only admissible in a military context but appropriate as well. This position follows directly from their commitment to a democratization of the military. There exists a variety of living rather than work-associated aspects of the military where the appropriateness of co-determination is deemed clear. The DBwV, on the other hand, is rigidly opposed to any dilution of command prerogative. The central issue, however, is not whether a commander consults with his men on certain issues. Only an incompetent would fail to sense or would ignore the attitudes of the men in his command. The question is, "Should such a procedure be institutionalized in the military and, if so, under what conditions and how?"

Norway

Historical Perspective

Although Norway and Sweden have much in common—a remark which might be contested vigorously by nationals of either country—they will be treated separately in what follows. More detail will be presented on the development of the military trade unions in these countries than on that in the FRG, because the history of trade union power in Scandinavia is larger, more continuous, and provides a better basis for extrapolation than the current, perhaps ephemeral, German experience.

Norway is a small country affiliated with NATO which shares a border with the Soviet Union. In 1905 Norway separated from Sweden administratively, in a bloodless assertion of independence. The military establishment had been separate from Sweden since 1814; although both the Swedish and Norwegian military were under the joint command of the King of Sweden.

The Social Democratic Party has been in power in Norway since 1935, except for the period of German occupation during World War II. The labor unions, which exert enormous influence in this country, are part of this ruling party, and, in this sense, trade unionism in Norway *is* the establishment. This perspective will make it somewhat easier to understand the role of trade unions in their military forces.

As in the FRG, the Norwegian military system is based on conscription and expansion by mobilization about a cadre of regulars. For convenience, we can separate the military personnel on active duty into two groups. The first group, or regulars, consists of officers and noncommissioned officers and a small group of enlisted corporals who volunteer for one or two three-year periods as technical specialists, usually in the air force. The second group consists of the draftees who are called up for twelve to fifteen months initial service, depending on the branch of the service to which they are assigned.

The issues and problems which arise, and the mechanisms which have been developed to handle them, differ for these two groups of military personnel. The first group is represented by the military unions, and the second by soldiers' representatives. The development of military unions proceeded as follows:

The oldest Norwegian union, although not a trade union in the modern sense, was started in 1835 and was a union whose membership was restricted to commissioned naval officers. Their first negotiations were held with the Defense Department in 1837 over uniforms and appearance. They began as a social/professional association which, as time passed, found itself assuming the attitudes and activities of a trade union.

In 1880, the noncommissioned officers in the Norwegian navy formed a union devoted to improving on board working conditions, living quarters, and food. In 1900, the army commissioned officers established a union affiliated with the Embetsmennenes Landsfordbund (EL) to which the senior servants of the government belonged. The noncommissioned officers became affiliated with the Norwegian Trade Union Confederation, Landsorgenisasjonen i Norge (LO). From 1911 to 1935, there was considerable conflict between the army commissioned and noncommissioned officers. It should be noted that the term noncommissioned officer in Norwegian usage generally is equivalent to the United States term "company grade officer." In their usage commissioned officer is sometimes called "regimental officer" and refers to majors and higher ranks. The legal distinctions between so-called commissioned and noncommissioned officers were abolished in 1933 by the Norwegian parliament (the Storting). Although there is no legal distinction, class differences are still present. One can assume that these differences evolve from social class distinctions; the commissioned officers coming from the vestiges of the nobility and the gentry, and the noncommissioned officers coming, in the main, from the middle classes and, perhaps, below.

Norwegian Military Unions

There are two main federations to which the various Norwegian military unions belong: the Joint Organization of Officers and Sergeants, the Befalets Fellesorganisasjon (BFO) and the LO. These federations carry out negotiations over wages and working conditions on a two-year cycle with the National Price Board on behalf of their member unions. The BFO is an apolitical grouping of unions whose leadership maintains that the LO is actually a participant in the government; thus unions affiliated with it are constrained in their negotiations with management (the government) by dual loyalties, and they become, in effect, company unions. The position of the leadership of the LO affiliates is that since the LO represents the overwhelming majority of other Norwegian labor unions in their national negotiations, non–LO-affiliated unions are getting a free ride on LO negotiating efforts.

The BFO, which represents by far the majority of officers and noncommissioned officers, developed after World War II when officers and noncommissioned officers sensed a need for an organization to represent groups of officers from all arms and services. The Norwegian high command concurred, and, in a statement of October 1946 to the various officers' groups, the Minister of Defense said:

> Working in my Department and traveling through the country, my impression has been that officers in the Norwegian Forces lack an organization which could represent their common interest versus the Department of Defense or the State, and to which the Department of Defense or the State could refer in cases concerning officers' pay, working conditions, etc.[9]

In 1947 the "Officers-Association Common Board" was established to encompass all groups of organizations within the armed forces with the exception of "Norges Befalslag," an old organization of noncommissioned officers which represents less than five percent of the Norwegian noncommissioned officers.

This was one of many halting steps toward the formation of the BFO. A variety of personal interests and institutional and jurisdictional rivalries had to be overcome before the meeting in Oslo in September 1957, at which the BFO was established. Much of the bickering and maneuvering for political power by the member unions resulted because of a law in Norway that no umbrella federation can participate in negotiations with the National Price Board unless it represents at least 13,000 members. This law was an effort on the part of the LO-dominated Storting to weaken the non–LO-affiliated unions by eliminating their negotiating capability.

There has been LO pressure on member unions in BFO to secede. In fact, resulting defections seriously threatened BFO's negotiating legitimacy, and BFO elected to affiliate with a compatible organization—The Central Board of Professional Trade and Civil Servants Organization of State Employees, Yrkesorganisasjonenes Hovedsammenslutning (YH)— whose interests were basically similar to officers and noncommissioned officers groups. The affiliation became formal in May 1964. Thus, union members in the military are represented in negotiations with the state by EL, BFO/YH, or LO. In addition to wages and certain working condi-

---

[9] *Kalendar* (Oslo: Befalets Fellesorgaisasjon, 1973), p. 9.

tions, the issues they address are a variety of personal problems arising from reorganization and moving orders, such as living quarters for families, schooling, and a number of problems not unlike those which would be faced by career civil servants in the Norwegian government.

Conscript Representation

The conscripts' problems are different. Starting in 1931, continuing until the late forties, and culminating in 1968, a series of bills were passed by the Storting which legitimatized an institutional form of representation for the soldiers. Draftees elect a representative, or *tillitsman,* as spokesman for their unit which is normally of company size. Thus, a battalion of a thousand men would have five *tillitsmen*. They, together with five officers of the battalion; the commander, the deputy commander, the chaplain, the doctor, and one additional officer, combine to form a so-called battalion board of trustees, with the commander of the battalion serving as its chairman. In a sense, this is an elaborated and institutionalized version of procedures having similar goals in the United States armed services, such as the United States navy's human relations councils. Complaints and problems arising through the network of *tillitsmen* which were not resolved at a local level could be presented to the ombudsman for the armed forces. The ombudsman's origin goes back to World War I, but the formal tie-in with the *tillitsman* organization did not occur until the late forties. In 1968, the *tillitsman* organization was empowered to hold a national convention of *tillitsmen* representing all battalions. The national stage, which the organization thus acquired, served to invest what had been a welfare-oriented organization with the potential for political power.

Shortly afterwards, both the Red Youth Group of the Workers' Communist Party (Marxist-Leninist) as well as the Kommunistisk Ungdom (KU), the Communist youth group of the regular Norwegian Communist Party, became aware of the political opportunities inherent in the *tillitsman* system. Previously, the radical left had adamantly opposed NATO and the Norwegian military and had attempted to avoid serving in it. In a turnabout of policy, these groups determined to seek national service so as to infiltrate the *tillitsman* organization and to either radicalize the military or, at a minimum, to achieve a credible-sounding platform for agitprop purposes.[10]

Infiltrating and dominating the *tillitsman* organization is relatively easy since a company *tillitsman* is elected at the end of the first week the

---

[10] *Study Outline for Politics in the Military,* translation of internal document circulated by Red Youth Group of the Workers' Communist Party (Marxist-Leninist) of Norway, 1973.

draftees spend in camp. A trained, dedicated radical leftist can easily become elected because it is rare for the average draftee to be actively concerned in these matters. By more or less standard radical-left tactics, the Marxist-Leninist group gained control of the *tillitsman* organization at local and regional levels. At the national meeting, at which eight representatives were elected to form a type of overall council, six came from the Marxist-Leninist group, one came from a fringe leftist group, and the final one was a centrist. This council provided a respectable sounding cover for a variety of agitprop actions. This phenomenon has disturbed many in the Norwegian trade-union movement, and in 1974, as a consequence, two bills were put before the Storting to address this problem in different ways; one by forbidding political activity by conscripts, and another by encouraging an open competition of political ideas.[11]

Future Trends

In the near future the Norwegian military unions can be expected to address the following issues:

There is a sharp difference between the attitudes of the conscripts, be they politically indifferent or politically radicalized, and the establishment-oriented attitudes of the unionized cadre of officers. Union leaders are seeking ways to bridge the cultural and generation gap from which the difference arises.

Industrial democracy, codetermination, workers' councils, and other devices for greater participation by employees are becoming increasingly important in labor-management relations in Norway. There is an apparent and increasing pressure toward some form of codetermination in the military service. An example is in matters relating to living conditions and barracks life. The limits of command prerogative will be defined as a result of the biannual adversary negotiations including codetermination issues on the agenda along with the conventional issues of working conditions and compensation.

Sweden

Background

Sweden, which is larger and richer than Norway, is a nation of approximately 8.2 million people who enjoy one of the highest standards of living in the world. The Swedes have not been at war for over 150 years and

---

[11] Jan Böhler and Arne Teige, "New System of Elected Representatives in the Defense," in a privately circulated Norwegian journal, *Dagbladet* (May 1974).

maintain a traditional policy of nonalignment in time of peace with the objective of preserving neutrality in time of war. Unlike Norway, they are not members of NATO. The Social Democrats, with Communist support, passed a bill over unified nonsocialist opposition in the spring of 1972 that envisages an eventual substantial reduction of their country's armed forces and overall military defense. There are fiscal reasons for this change as well as the belief that détente in Europe is a credible posture. Except for a few months in 1934, the Social Democrats, either alone or in coalition, have controlled the Swedish Government from 1932 until September 1976.

The Swedish Trade Union Confederation, Landsorganisationem i Sverige (LO), provides the major financial support and membership of the Social Democratic Party. Membership in LO automatically confers membership and dues-paying responsibility in the Social Democratic Party. Consequently, as in Norway, the trade unions are not mere contenders for political power. They are a significant component of the ruling establishment. This position, however, was achieved only after much strife and turmoil. Trade-union attitudes toward management responsibilities, job security and employee rights permeate the current Swedish culture. In what follows, we will discuss the Swedish military briefly, the union movements in some detail because of the publicity attendant on the 1971 strike of Swedish State employees, and, finally, the developing trends we have perceived in Swedish military unions.

As in Norway, the Swedish defense forces consist of a skeletal training and maintenance cadre with a modest operational capability. The army consists of approximately 12,000 regular officers, noncommissioned officers, and civilian military employees. These personnel staff the various headquarters and provide the cadre for forty-nine training centers where the annual conscript class of about 39,000 men is processed. The navy is quite small; personnel strength totals some 4,600 officers and enlisted personnel. Approximately 4,300 conscripts are trained annually. The air force has an inventory of over 900 aircrafts, including trainer support aircraft and those stored in underground hangers. The maximum strength averages 12,000 including career military, civilian employees, and conscripts.

As in Norway and the FRG, conscripts cannot be members of the military unions that are discussed here. These unions represent 99 percent of the personnel in the regular Swedish armed forces. Conscripts are represented by means of a variety of committees. Each regiment has a committee which the commander consults when appropriate. In addition to this, on a national level, conscripts have a congress—one or two representatives from each regiment who meet once a year. This organization, the Conscript's Working Group, Värnpliktigas Arbetsgrupp (VAG), has been radicalized as has its Norwegian counterpart.

Labor Unions and the Military

As in Norway and the FRG, labor unions negotiate with the state under the auspices of umbrella federations. Their structure and relation to the military unions follows.[12] Of the three major federations to which Swedish unions may be affiliated, the largest, LO, which was founded in 1898, consist of 25 trade unions and represents 1.9 million blue collar workers. The Union of Swedish Government Employees, Statsanställdas Förbund (SF), is the chief organization for government-employed LO members and negotiates with the State Bargaining Office, Statens Avtalsverk (SAV). The second major federation of unions is the Central Organization of Salaried Employees, Tjänstemännens Centralorganisation (TCO). Within the TCO, there is a section of approximately 200,000 civil servants, Statstjänstemannasektion (TCO-S). There are ten unions within this particular federation. The Swedish Confederation of Professional Associations, Sveriges Akademikers Centralorganisation (SACO), includes government and private industry employees, owners of business enterprises, such as lawyers, doctors with private practice and so forth. Certain groups with lower academic degrees (status credentials are important in Sweden) are also connected with SACO—physiotherapists, reserve officers and so forth. The National Federation of Government Officers, Statstjänstemännens Riksförbund (SR), represents about thirty unions of state officials in the higher and medium salary grade who have taken up the "matriculatory careers," that is, those careers open to those who have an upper school education—in the post office, customs office, state railways, etc. The largest individual union is the Swedish Union of Officers, Svenska Officersförbundet (SOF). SACO and SR merged in 1975 to form the third federation and have a current membership of just over 165,000.

Swedish military unions had their origin in 1907 when a company grade officers' union was founded, followed by the formation of a union for noncommissioned officers in 1918, and, finally, a union for regimental or field grade officers and higher ranks. The emerging unions had three goals: first, to improve the salary position of the officers for whom they were responsible, second, to improve working conditions, and third to extend the retirement age. These goals have been achieved, the last of them, the exten-

---

[12] Lennart Forsebäck, *Industrial Relations and Employment in Sweden* (Stockholm: The Swedish Institute, 1976). Annika Brickman, "Military Trade Unionism in Sweden," *Armed Forces and Society*, 2 (Summer 1976): 529–35.

sion of the retirement age, in 1952. It was not, however, until 1936 that
the right of association and collective bargaining was made explicit by
Swedish law. The SOF is for regimental officers; that is, officers of the rank of
major or lieutenant commander and above. About 5,000 military-academy–
educated active officers of different salary grades, as well as about 300
cadets, are members of the SOF. Nonactive members are retired officers
numbering perhaps a thousand. There are about 100 locals of the SOF.
Trade union responsibilities of the SOF, such as negotiations, are carried
out by about five full-time employed members of the SOF who operate in
accordance with instructions from the board of the SOF which consists of
sixteen officers from the different defense forces, from different parts of
Sweden, and holding varying ranks.

The Union of Company Officers, Kompaniofficersförbundet (KOF),
consists of officers from the rank of ensign to lieutenant, and is affiliated
with the TCO-S. The KOF has about 6,000 active members, 2,500 of
whom are civilian employees of the military, mainly technicians, who have
the assimilated rank or equivalent standing of so-called company officers.

The Union of Noncommissioned Officers, Plutonsofficersförbundet,
(POF), is also affiliated with the TCO-S. This union consists of 9,300
active noncommissioned officers of whom about 3,000 are, in fact, aviation
technicians working for the military.

The SACO and the SR are politically neutral. The SF, which is
affiliated with the LO, is firmly tied to the dominant Social Democratic
Party. SF represents various blue-collar state employees including about
19,000 employed by the military, and consists, in total, of approximately
80,000 members in such services as the post office, state railway, state
power board and so forth.

Strikes Against the State

Strikes and the definition of negotiable issues is central to a discussion of
military unions. The sources for what follows is material published by the
National Swedish Collective Bargaining Office's Information Service in
1971 and conversations at TCO-S Headquarters in 1974.[13]

In connection with the general round of negotiations in 1971, SACO
and SR, two of what were then four main labor federations, arranged
selective strikes. Three thousand SACO members were involved: high
officials in the administration of justice and the county administration, the
Board of Civil Aviation and other central administrative boards. The SR
action involved a thousand members of the state railways, custom admin-

---

[13] National Swedish Collective Bargaining Office of Information Service, *Negotiating Machinery Applicable to State Officials* (Stockholm, August 1971).

istration, etc. The SACO-SR induced strike basically protested rising inflation and the inadequacy of an aggregate 17 percent increase in salary which the government proposed to meet the increase in the retail index of the cost of living. This was the overt complaint. The covert issue, which was actually dominant, was that the salary differential between the blue-collar and the white-collar workers was diminishing. That is, the LO-dominated government insisted that the low-paid state employees get a larger share of the budgeted 17 percent increase than the non-LO-affiliates of SACO and SR. A government-approved mediator was appointed, and his new proposal still favored the lower salaried grades. This forced the strike. Two weeks after the beginning of the first strike, the collective bargaining office responded with lockouts against the SACO and SR. A total of 28,000 SACO members and 2,500 SR members were locked out. The biggest group locked out comprised 24,000 teachers in SACO. Further strikes and lockouts ensued. Simultaneously, SACO arranged strikes in local government sectors, embracing among others a number of social welfare officers. The state responded by threatening further lockouts, including military officers on training and nonvital missions. The strikes and lockouts in the federal government and local government sectors involved more than 40,000 public officials. Five weeks after the first strike started, the government intervened in the dispute by issuing an order declaring a six-week cooling-off period. A temporary special enabling law allowed the government to delay offensive actions threatening vital interests of the citizens for a period of six weeks. The purpose of this legislation was to provide a climate more conducive to successful negotiations. The issue of whether the military can exercise the right to strike has not been resolved. The government initiated an offensive action against the military affiliates of SR by threatening a lockout which was never implemented. The military unions threatened a retaliatory action, which never took place.

Future Trends

In Sweden, movement from negotiations over work rules to institutionalized codetermination is further advanced than it is in Norway. The erosion of what had been considered management prerogatives gained momentum in a law passed in 1971 in which the forty-hour work week was established for the military, with overtime limited to 150 hours per year. In the event of a war or an emergency, this limit on overtime work in the military is suspended. Civilians working for the military won the right to negotiate overtime conditions in a 1972 decision of the labor courts. They negotiated a forty-hour regular week plus two hundred maximum hours of overtime for nonwartime emergencies. As yet, there has not been controversy as to what constitutes an emergency. A common example would be searching for a lost aircraft. The notion of a limited military day and of a limitation on military overtime appears bizarre at first blush. It should be remembered, however, that the Swedish army is a garrison army devoted to training. The need for overtime often arises because of poor planning on the part of the commanding officer or of the training command. Many senior officers protested this limitation at first, but the situation appears to have worked out well. The additional planning imposed on management was relatively minor. Prior to this regulation, the union influence was such that the union representative on a post, who acts as a form of shop steward, was routinely consulted by the commander on matters affecting the men.

The foregoing limitations on command prerogatives are perceived by both management and the unions as a step toward codetermination in some areas of military decision-making. The issue of a military equivalent of "industrial democracy" is presently very much in the forefront.

In March 1974, TCO-S and SF issued a document entitled "Union Requirements and Democracy in the Defense Organization." It is of interest to quote the principles upon which the requirements are based.

> A series of measures must now be taken for improving democracy within the defense organization. The main objective here shall be to ensure that the individual's influence within the defense organization shall be much the same as on the civil labor market.
>
> In addition to information and mutual consultation rights, employees within the defense organization must be guaranteed the right of codetermination as soon as possible.
>
> This right of codetermination must be built up according to an established pattern and be relevant throughout the hierarchy of the defense sector.
>
> The right of codetermination shall have a trade union foundation and shall be developed through collaboration among the union organizations.[14]

The Netherlands

There is no trade union movement in the Netherlands armed forces. There has been wide publicity about the Union of Conscripted Soldiers, Vereniging voor Dienstplichtige Militairen (VVDM), founded in 1966, and the Conscript Association, Bond voor Dienstplichtigen (BVD). Neither of these groups is, in fact, a trade union because of the inability to negotiate

---

[14] TCO-S and SF, *Fackliga Krav Pa Demokratin Inom Forsvaret* (Union Requirements and Democracy in the Defense Organization) (Stockholm, March 1974), p. 1.

pay and working conditions as well as the lack of a career commitment to the military by the members. The VVDM consists of 30,000 members, and the smaller BVD has approximately 600. They address the interests and needs of the conscripts from a variety of political and economic points of view, the BVD being much more leftist and activist than the VVDM. The VVDM has various issues which concern it; the first is whether they should limit themselves to the promotion of the direct material interests of the conscripts or occupy themselves explicitly with a clearly defined political position. "Long-term interests" are subjects such as the democratization of the armed forces, emancipation, freedom of expression for conscripts and improvement of their legal status.[15] Since both the VVDM and the BVD are associations of conscripts, it is extremely difficult for them to maintain institutional continuity. In fact, under the argument of the need to democratize the armed services, the VVDM staunchly supports conscription and opposes an all-volunteer force.[16] There exist other organizations in the Dutch army for noncommissioned officers, officers, and so forth. These are not unlike the organizations in the United States, mentioned in Chapter 1, which perform a variety of social services for their members and attempt to present their interests before the general public as positively as possible. In many ways, the VVDM emerged from the political ferment of the sixties because there was no *tillitsman* organization in the Dutch military. There does exist in Dutch military and civilian affairs, however, the concept of joint consultation between management and labor. The Dutch Department of Defense has a syllabus on joint consultation and in it mentions a variety of approved organizations which can be used to generate representation for joint consultation.[17] Joint consultation is defined by the Dutch as an institution through which elected representatives of officers, enlisted men and conscripts consult with representatives of the Defense Ministry on matters of general importance to the legal status of personnel before competent authorities make a decision. The advice of these committees is not binding. It has not worked as successfully as was intended; otherwise the VVDM would not have arisen. Consultation with the VVDM has existed since 1966 but has been difficult because of the rapid turnover of officials within this organization.

---

[15] Walter Kok, *Dienstplichtigen en hun Vakbondsproblematiek,* undated descriptive memo on organization of and issues concerning the VVDM and BVD, contained in material supplied in April 1974 by T. L. J. Brouwer, Col. RNLA, Military Attaché Royal Netherlands Embassy, Washington, D.C.

[16] Ger Teitler, "The Successful Case of Military Unionization in The Netherlands," *Armed Forces and Society* 2 (Summer 1976): 524.

[17] The Netherlands, Defense Department of Military Personnel, *Syllabus on Joint Consultation* (Course on Personnel Affairs, 1972–73).

Implications of the European Experience for the United States Armed Forces

The European experiences with military unions can be better understood after considering the historical and traditional relations between the labor movement in a particular country and that country's government. In the Scandinavian countries this relationship, however stormy its beginning, is now close and of long standing. In a real sense the labor movement, and the political parties which they have dominated so long, *are* the establishment. In Norway and Sweden, therefore, it is not surprising that military unions are a readily accepted extension of public sector unions for state employees.[18] France, on the other hand, has a tradition of union politicization, confrontation with established government, and a polarization of economic interest. It is thus consistent with French history and traditions that Prime Minister Jacques Chirac in a speech in the National Assembly in November 1975 bluntly accused the Socialists of undermining national security by encouraging the formation of labor unions in military units. Although the Socialists and Communists both officially oppose military unions, the Socialist leadership accused the government of Valéry Giscard d'Estaing of failing to fulfill its promises of military reform. M. Chirac declared that military officials considered the unions as a "mortal danger" for both "military institutions and democracy itself." He added: "The Government will not tolerate the creation of such committees in French military units."[19] Between the polarized positions of France and the Scandinavian countries, we find the Federal Republic of Germany. Military unions had their effective beginning in the FRG after a two-year legal dispute which ended on 1 August 1966 with a defense ministry decree permitting the unions to recruit on base. The impetus behind the interest of the Deutscher Gewerkschaftsbund in achieving a trade union presence in the armed forces of the FRG resulted more from the DGB's commitment to strengthening democracy in the institutions of the FRG, and particularly in the military, than from the more traditional trade-union issues which predominate in the Scandinavian negotiations and appear to underly the sporadic beginnings of a drive toward military unions in France.[5, 20]

American trade unions exhibit many strong differences from their European counterparts which have been discussed in the foregoing pages. The trade-union movement in the United States is neither as highly politicized nor as potent politically as in the European countries to which we

---

[18] James L. Quinn, Lt. Col. USAF and Ronald V. Grabler, Maj. USAF, *Military Unions: The Advantages and Disadvantages of Unionization Within the Armed Forces* AD-734 746, (Air Force Institute of Technology, Wright-Patterson Air Force Base, Ohio, September 1971).

[19] "France Fighting Military Unions," *New York Times,* 30 November 1975.

[20] Lucien Mandeville, "Syndicalism and the French Military System," *Armed Forces and Society* 2 (Summer 1976): 534–51.

have referred. The procedures by which wages, benefits and working conditions are determined in the European countries differ drastically from those in the United States. The umbrella labor federation, negotiating on the behalf of its member unions with either the state or an industrial federation, is unknown in this country. Yet it is just this method of negotiation, which obtains in those countries where military unions exist, that has the structural capability of avoiding the use of the military union as the leading edge in a confrontation with the state following a deadlock in negotiations. Thus, these military unions can achieve their goals without ever having to strike, or threaten to strike.

In the FRG a need was perceived by elements in the DGB to institutionalize the influence of civilian democratic traditions upon the armed forces by means of military unions. In this country there are no such pressures from the trade unions. Such pressures, however, were in the rhetoric of the left-wing, politically activist American Servicemen's Union which may have achieved six to eight thousand members before it disappeared in the early 1970's. The issue has been raised recently in the liberal press, but there is no indication that the intellectual arguments have the support of significant numbers of servicemen or the trade-union movement.[21]

It is difficult to see why a unionized, all-volunteer military would provide a more reliable safeguard for civilian democratic values and processes than would a nonunionized all-volunteer armed force. A plausible and somewhat frightening argument can be summoned against the unionization of the armed forces in American society, namely, that it creates the potential for creating a "Praetorian Guard" attitude on the part of its members. Such an attitude could result in grave economic as well as political problems for this country.

The most significant and inescapable distinction between the European military experience with trade unionism, and analogies with the armed forces of the United States, lies in the differences in the strategic roles of the respective forces. A hesitation in the command and control capabilities—or a lapse in the effectiveness of the combat arms of a European democracy—might bring comfort and delight to Soviet planners, but it would likely have little influence on the dynamics of the United States-Soviet military confrontation. Evidence of similar hesitations or lapses on the part of the United States might provide an invitation to Soviet military adventures and perhaps to Armageddon.

Despite the many differences which serve to weaken analogies between the European military unions and possible similar activities in the United States, three useful implications may be drawn from this chapter.

---

[21] David Cortright, "The Union Wants to Join You," *The Nation* 222 (21 February 1976): 206–9; Tod Ensign and Michael Uhl, "Soldiers as Workers," *The Progressive* 40 (April 1976): 37–39.

First, these unions have all evolved from the orderly maturation of public-sector collective bargaining. The behavior they represent is not a freak episode in the recent history or culture of their countries. This lends support to a theme of this book, which is that by observing national social trends and developmental forces, an alert and knowledgeable observer can become able to extrapolate these trends.

Second, despite the national differences discussed above, it is unlikely that the goals and aspirations of the individual unionized European military personnel differ widely from those of their American counterparts. In this event, the subject matter of European union negotiations may either help American observers to anticipate issues in this country or else substantiate the presence of issues which are just beginning to emerge in this country. An example may be found in the growing pressure throughout Scandinavian countries and the FRG for participative management in military officers in matters where command prerogatives were not threatened. In a similar vein efforts were also evident on the part of the unions to distinguish the working conditions of military personnel, both normal and emergency, from the living conditions of military service.

Third, and finally, what effects, positive or negative, do unions have on military performance? Their immediate impact is in the eye of the beholder. Long hair, a nonmilitary presence, and the deemphasis of drills and other traditional observances are the images frequently found and cited with alarm in descriptions of unionized armed forces. Nothing in the open literature, however, indicates that performance in; for example, NATO exercises, has been affected by the appearance of the troops or the presence of unions.

Close-order drill had tactical military application in the eighteenth century. The ability of parade ground drill to develop an almost instinctive group action which enabled small units to prevail while fighting in limited space under great confusion even with little or no direct leadership, has been presented in vigorous defense of such seemingly inappropriate drill in World War I.[22] Different methods of training and leadership may be required to produce disciplined and effective responses in combat by today's soldiers implementing today's tactics. Time spent in traditional military observances might better be applied to perfecting combat skills. Military traditions and national rituals could be maintained cost effectively by the use of special ceremonial troops. The European unionized armed forces might well induce a productive examination of the priorities for discipline, training, and personal appearance in the United States armed forces.

---

[22] Robert Graves, *Good-bye to All That* (Garden City: Doubleday, 1957), pp. 187–88.

9

The United States Armed Forces

National Values and the Modern Military

In previous chapters we have described the developmental trends, the precedents and the legal structure which have resulted in the present status of public-sector collective bargaining in the United States. An implicit assumption has been that the social values and the economic pressures in the nation determined when and how such collective bargaining developed. A corollary assumption was that the armed forces respond to these same pressures, perhaps in a distorted fashion, perhaps with a time-lag generated by institutional inertia, but they *do* respond, and these pressures shape the organization of the armed forces, their deployment and the personnel whom they attract. It is instructive to illustrate this, first by a historic example, and then by reference to the United States Armed Forces.

The first modern professional army was created in the United Provinces of the Netherlands, the Dutch Republic, in the sixteenth century when the values and economic outlook of middle-class Dutch Calvinists molded an army into a form designed for their needs.[1] The mediaeval armies prior to this event, notwithstanding the technical and tactical skills represented by soldiery such as English bowmen and Spanish swordsmen in formation, were, in spirit and organization, essentially raiding parties. Professional support was available from mercenaries who ranged from the highly trained, combat-proven Swiss free companies to the *condottieri,* or contract soldiers, of Italy, who specialized in protracted expensive engagements with as little physical risk to the participants as was feasible. Mer-

---

[1] M. D. Feld, "Middle-Class Society and the Rise of Military Professionalism: The Dutch Army 1589–1609," *Armed Forces and Society* 1 (August 1975): 419–42.

cenaries, when needed, were hired for the duration of the campaign. Warfare, though regarded operationally as a form of self-liquidating venture capitalism, was dominated by aristocratic tradition which held that a soldier fought for glory and out of fealty to his chief. His rewards were the gratitude of his liege lord, and plunder, which, rather than deferred pay, were his traditional due. Mutinies were frequent and victories were aborted by soldiers striking for their expected rewards. The Dutch Republic changed this state of affairs for their army by providing annual employment and regularly paid wages. Since this army was accountable year round to its commander, periods between campaigns could be devoted to intensive training. A precise repertory of behavior and commands was developed. The competence of soldiers, NCOs and officers could be evaluated by the extent to which they could execute required maneuvers rapidly and effectively. The preferred weapons of this army were firearms rather than pikes. The individual inaccuracy of the musket, and the relative ease with which recruits could be drilled in its use in mass formations, put a minor value on individual prowess, but a high premium on the ability to control a system of men and machines. In many ways the Dutch innovations in warfare were precursors of the change in industrial production from a craft to an assembly line mode. In Feld's words:

> Investment in an armed force was regarded as one of the fixed expenditures of that trading company in extended form, the Dutch city. Commerce, not war, was the major occupation of the state and of its rulers. In marked contrast with the Spanish, the strategy of the Dutch was guided by their economic base.
>
> The reduction of Dutch forces to a size consonant with the state's financial resources laid the groundwork for a series of radical military reforms. By placing their army on a salaried basis, the Dutch changed its social outlook. The organization was to be held together not by its sense of honor and its loyalty to his sovereign but by the terms of its contracts. The root of its discipline was no longer an inner code but the objectively verifiable standard of regular work for regular pay. Its members were literally brought into line by a materialistic standard that determined the value of their services. Regular pay destroyed the aristocratic ethos. A salaried worker was not a gentleman.
>
> These changes transformed the mercenary composition of the Dutch forces from a source of weakness to a pillar of strength. Wages regularly paid were a stronger inducement to faithful service than honor intermittently satisfied. The regularity of pay also systemized the concept of military duties.[2]

In the United States political policy, economic forces, and national values have established a climate in which the collective bargaining rights

---

[2] Ibid., p. 423.

enjoyed by industrial workers, public-sector employees, and some professionals may be extended to the armed forces. The stage was set for this event, whose occurrence was no more anticipated than was the unionization of the National Guard civilian technicians as a result of Public Law 90–486, on 27 March 1969. On this date President Nixon appointed an advisory commission on an all-volunteer armed force under Thomas S. Gates, Jr., a former secretary of defense. One year later this commission brought forth a report.

The charge to this Commission read in part:

> . . . to develop a comprehensive plan for eliminating conscription and moving toward an all-volunteer force. The Commission will study a broad range of possibilities for increasing the supply of volunteers for service, including increased pay, benefits, recruitment incentives and other practicable measures to make military careers more attractive to young men.[3]

As a result of both the disenchantment of a large proportion of the electorate with the Vietnam War and this report, conscription ended in June 1973 and the All Volunteer Force (AVF) came into being. The personnel comprising this force, their values, organization and management reflect our society and its government in much the same way as did the army of the sixteenth-century Dutch Republic.

Although a variety of backgrounds and disciplines were represented among the fourteen active members of the Gates Commission, six of them had careers which emphasized either finance or economics. This numerical dominance is consistent with the commission's charge and reflected in the report's content. Conscription is described as a discriminatory tax-in-kind that is of questionable morality, regressive, and exploits young able-bodied males. Specific recommendations are presented to increase total military compensation so that free economic choice will enable the services to meet their need with volunteers. The emphasis is on presenting military service as a financially attractive occupation to young men so as to maintain a viable AVF.

As a concrete example, the manpower projections developed for the commission predicted that a 10 percent increase in first-term regular military compensation (RMC) would produce a 12.5 percent increase in the voluntary enlistment rate of seventeen to twenty-one-year-olds. A 40 percent increase in RMC would yield a 50 percent increase in enlistments from the same cohort.[4] The report does note that there are other motivations:

---

[3] *The Report of the President's Commission on an All-Volunteer Armed Force* (Washington, D.C.: Government Printing Office, 1970), p. vii.

[4] Ibid., p. 56.

Pay is not the only, and perhaps not even the primary, motivating force for joining or remaining in the military services. A sense of duty, a desire for adventure or travel, society's esteem for military service, a desire for training, the quality of military life and the general conditions of military service—all affect individuals' decisions.[5]

Adequate pay based on a military/civilian comparability measure is still the sine qua non of a sustained AVF.

The commission may have been both recognizing reality and promulgating a self-fulfilling prophecy: the emergence of military service as an occupational role. The increasing ascendancy of this role, and the parallel increase in the similarity between industrial and military managers, will generate a variety of constraints on military managers which were not anticipated.

By way of sharp and fascinating contrast with the Gates Commission's concept of the values of American youth is a voice from another country and another generation. In 1934 Charles de Gaulle described a mechanized army which was to be the defense of France against an increasingly populous and powerful German enemy. This force was to be manned by 100,000 elite volunteers. Drawing upon Pascal's summary of the human condition and his own experience and observations, he felt that the desire of young men to compete, to excel, to find excitement, and "to seek a new object in life beyond the horizon," would suffice to generate the needed volunteers. His treatise mentions pay only once, and then in the context of rewards for unit proficiency in war games: "By the award to the winners of the banners, special places in reviews, parades, billeting and even in the grading of pay to winners. . . . "[6] The troops themselves were described as follows: "These master troops, well fed and clothed, carefree celibates, a source of envy on account of all the flywheels, cylinders and rangefinders they will have at their disposal, ranging the country from April to November and touring France while on maneuvers, will be easily recruited."[7]

General de Gaulle's AVF of 100,000 represented about 1 percent of the pool of French males between the ages of fifteen and forty-four, adjusted for the disastrous losses of World War 1, in the year 1934. In 1975, the American AVF totalled 2,130,000, which represents 5.1 percent of the males in the fifteen- to forty-four-year pool. The economic, rather than romantic appeal selected by the Gates Committee, may have been a realistic recognition of the need to appeal to a larger population pool in order to recruit the relatively large numbers of troops needed to sustain the United

---

[5] Ibid., p. 49.
[6] General Charles de Gaulle, *The Army of the Future* (Philadelphia: J. B. Lippincott Company, 1941), p. 119.
[7] Ibid., pp. 111–12.

States AVF. Yet there is evidence that the romanticized estimate that Pascal and de Gaulle held of the goals and values of young men was as realistic as that held by the committee.

The attitudes and values of 860 men in the sixteen to twenty-two age group were recently studied in order to establish their criteria for enlistment or reenlistment in the United States Navy. Their preferences for a variety of incentive packages and career options were examined. In a dramatically counter-intuitive finding the group preferred a $1000 enlistment bonus to a $3000 enlistment bonus! The preferences were elicited from ratings of selected groups of incentives so that a patently absurd comparison was not made directly. In a variety of related studies the research team confirmed a general finding that neither more financial incentives nor bigger financial incentives were dominant factors in the decision to enlist or to reenlist. A cluster of career and working condition-related attributes, characterized as "fate control," appeared to dominate the enlistment or reenlistment decision. In the main, a desire for "fate control" indicated a dislike for authoritarian leadership, petty regulations, and the illicit use of power.[8]

Occupations, Professions and Callings

The foregoing discussion of the motivations of volunteers cannot be complete without introducing the potential recruit's expectations and model, or image, of military service. His model of service life will influence his enlistment decision. His actual experiences in the service will shape his attitudes and his actions. Three terms which are useful in understanding the image that military service has for both its members and society at large are *occupation, profession,* and *calling.*

An *occupation* is legitimated in terms of the *marketplace,* i.e., "What are prevailing monetary rewards for equivalent skills?" In a modern industrial society employees usually enjoy some voice in the determination of appropriate salary and work conditions. Such rights are counterbalanced by responsibilities to meet contractual obligations. The occupational model implies first priority inheres in self-interest—rather than in the task itself, or in the employing organization. A common form of group interest is the trade union.

A *profession* is legitimated in terms of *specialized expertise,* i.e., a skill level achieved after long, intensive, and formal training. The prerogatives of a profession center around conditions supportive of maintenance of professional skills, career achievement, and intrinsic satisfaction with one's work. The obligations of the professional are responsibility to

[8] Albert S. Glickman *et al., Navy Career Motivation Programs in an All-Volunteer Condition,* (Washington, D.C.: American Institutes for Research, June 1974), p. 4.

one's clientele or constituency. The modal form of advancement of group interest is the professional association.

A *calling* is legitimated in terms of *institutional values,* i.e., a purpose transcending individual self-interest in favor of a presumed higher good. A calling usually enjoys high esteem in the larger community because it is associated with notions of self-sacrifice and complete dedication to one's role. A calling does not command monetary reward comparable to what one might expect in the general economy. But this is often compensated for by an array of social benefits which simultaneously signals the institution's intent to take care of its own, and which sets the institution apart from the general society. Members of an institution do not organize into self-interest groups. If redress is sought, it takes the form of "one-on-one" recourse to superiors or a trust in the paternalism of the organization.[9]

The terms *occupation, profession,* and *calling* are clearly idealized, and we can expect to find a mixture of each characteristic in the members of a social organization as large and varied as the United States armed forces. Nevertheless, it is inescapable that the concept of the AVF, and its subsequent execution, have served to emphasize and enlarge the extent to which the occupational model characterizes the armed forces. The institutional, or calling model, had some validity when the selective service system was operating because, however imperfectly and unfairly the system might work in practice, the system itself was predicated on the existence of a citizen's obligation to serve his country and to subordinate his well-being to a higher cause. The professional model has meaning mainly for officers, and to some extent for NCOs and technical specialists, but even in these instances the occupational mode is strongly in evidence. In fact, as Professor Moskos cogently argues, the emergent military organization in this country may develop along a civilianized line of occupational and technical specialties which act as infrastructure for the fighting military.[10] The civilianized military would conform to the occupational model (the National Guard union experience is particularly pertinent), whereas the combat arms units would conform more closely to the institutional values of a calling. Even within combat arms, there is a tendency for the institutional values to be ascendant over occupational values in proportion to the "eliteness" of the unit, as was demonstrated by soldiers from battalions which ranged in increasing eliteness—infantry, tank or armored, airborne infantry, and ranger battalions. An attitude survey of a sample of approximately four hundred of these troops revealed that the more elite the unit, the more committed were its members to the institutional values of the military, and the more willing to serve in combat. On the other hand, for the less elite combat units, the occupational model was stronger and there

---

[9] Moskos, *Military Social Organization,* p. 2.
[10] Moskos, "The Emergent Military, pp. 270–71.

was less of a disposition to serve in combat. It is clear that within the armed forces, in both technical support and combat arms, there exists significant differentiation, in social composition as well as in military commitment.[11]

Despite the foregoing indication that within the armed forces there are many camps, it is valuable to examine the similarities overall both in work attitudes and in values held by military personnel and by civilians. Such comparisons bear directly upon developmental arguments relating forces at work in society as a whole to the military, and upon the pragmatic effectiveness of the marketplace economic values of the Gates Commission.

Such a comparison was made in late 1972 and early 1973. David G. Bowers presents the survey results obtained from a carefully selected sample of 2,522 officers and enlisted navy personnel drawn from both ships and shore stations, and 1,855 employed civilians, all over the age of sixteen.[12]

In a rank ordering of fourteen characteristics of a job, both the navy personnel and the civilians gave the highest preference to "opportunity to control personal life" and "good pay" in this order. Among the least important characteristics was "opportunity to serve my country," which ranked tenth for both groups. The navy and civilian rankings correlated highly (.90). When the civilians were grouped by age, their rankings still correlated highly with an average correlation of .90. The findings, did, however, reveal a striking set of differences within the navy which point to an "age gap" in career values. Navy men of forty-three years and older, both enlisted and commissioned, have rank-ordered profiles on preferred job characteristics which are unlike those of young enlisted men, young officers (who closely resemble young enlisted men), and civilians of their own age. These dissimilarities can be attributed to the importance ascribed to "opportunity to control personal life" (which the older navy men do not value as highly as do others) and "opportunity to serve my country" and "challenging work" (which older navy men value more highly than do others). Neither the region of the country from which the respondent came, nor race, had much influence on the rank ordering. Greater education, however, was found to correlate with lesser concern for both economic issues and with serving one's country, but with greater concern about having challenging work. The consistent and compelling finding of this survey was that, except for the generation gap characteristic of navy men,

[11] Charles W. Brown and Charles C. Moskos, Jr., "The American Volunteer Soldier—Will He Fight?" *Military Review* 56 (June 1976): 8–17.

[12] David G. Bowers, *Navy Manpower: Values, Practices, and Human Requirements* (Ann Arbor: Institute of Social Research, University of Michigan, June 1975), chapt. 2.

the civilian and military respondents had *very similar values and attitudes* toward their careers. For young men in the navy and for those who might enlist, military service has become an occupation which they evaluate as any other occupation. Although there may be special units within the armed forces for whom a calling or a professional career model predominates, as in the aforementioned elite battalions, the attitudes of young members of the AVF appear to be no different from those of their counterparts in the civilian work force. The prophecy of the Gates Commission, that an AVF could be sustained by economic competition, has fulfilled itself. The AVF is both a reality and an occupation. As such, it is plausible to assume that, if conditions are unchanged, collective bargaining in the public sector and the professions will become attractive to the career personnel of the United States armed forces.

Facing the Possibility of Military Unions

Congressional concern over defense manpower costs, over the effectiveness of the AVF, and the possible need for new approaches and reforms in defense manpower management and utilization resulted in an Act of Congress which created the Defense Manpower Commission in November 1973. The commission, with Curtis W. Tarr as chairman (a business executive and a former assistant secretary of the United States Air Force for manpower and reserve affairs), was sworn in on 19 April 1974, with two years in which to submit its final report to the president and the Congress. It was mandated to conduct a broad and comprehensive study of the overall management requirements of the Department of Defense.[13]

At a public hearing on 18 August 1975 in New York City, the commission heard a portentious prediction: military unionization by 1980! The source was Richard A. Beaumont, former assistant secretary of the navy (manpower and reserve affairs) who was further quoted by *Navy Times* on 3 September 1975:

> "The military is fantastically naïve about what individuals will suffer. . . . The fact that the military has not organized is one of the great perplexing phenomena as far as I am concerned. One of the major tasks that the United States faces is to prepare military leadership for the fact that they may organize. The concept of absolute command," he continued, "to do this or that under any set of circumstances, simply doesn't work. This is so in regard to lower and junior grade officers even more than with the enlisted men."

The commission had heard rumblings on incipient military union sentiments before, in the main from servicemen who felt that real or per-

---

[13] Defense Manpower Commission, *Defense Manpower*.

ceived benefits were in jeopardy. The complaints were real, but the rumblings were sound with little substance. The statement, quoted in Chapter 1 by the late Clyde M. Webber, president of AFGE, to the commission and the large percentage of union members among the civilian technicians in the National Guard, both served to make military unions in the United States a credible issue. The commission faced the issue forthrightly in its report. After emphasizing the requirements for military personnel to be responsive to a single chain of command, the strong distinction between civilian employment and military service, and the nation's dependence on the unswerving obedience of each member of the armed forces, the commission then presented its beliefs and recommendations:

> The Congress not only has the duty to raise and support armies and navies, but also to take appropriate and necessary legislative action on matters related to the armed forces. It therefore has the power to discourage a member of the armed forces from joining a union or similar organization, if membership entails disobeying lawful orders.

The commission further suggested:

> In view of the unique obligations of the members of the armed forces, their civilian leadership should not give them any reasonable grounds for believing that there should be divided authority over them, or that they perhaps need representation in order to be fairly and equitably treated, or that there has been any erosion of expressed and implied commitment previously made to them. The attitudes of the members of the armed forces in this regard are shaped primarily by their perceptions of the attitude toward them of the President, the Congress, and the Secretary of Defense.

The commission went on to applaud the role of noncommissioned officers, in the discipline and performance of the armed services and to state that the NCO corps is an integral part of the command and management of each service. The commission felt the NCO's authority depended on their remaining part of the supervisory echelon and that joining a union would dilute, if not destroy, their authority. The commission concluded that:

> The Services must enhance the status of the noncommissioned officers, encouraging further education to gain professional knowledge, raising prestige, and affording opportunities for upward mobility and the achievement by some noncommissioned officers of commissioned status.

The commission then recommended:

> Whereas all officers, either commissioned, warrant, or noncommissioned, are an essential and integral part of command and management, the Secretary of Defense should prepare and publish a regulation throughout the Services that membership in any union by any such officer is

expressly prohibited, and that in the event any such officer in violation of such regulation joins a union, charges shall be preferred against him under the Uniform Code of Military Justice to the effect that such officer has committed an offense against good order and discipline. The term "union" should be defined as any organization of any kind, or any agency or employee representation committee or plan, in which employees participate and which exists for the purpose, in whole or in part, of dealing with employers concerning grievances, disputes, wages, rates of pay, hours of employment, or conditions of work.[14]

The commission followed its statements of principles with recommendations, ranging from the specific to the highly general, which could serve to thwart possible union activity. A direct approach, mentioned in Chapter 1, was to reorganize the National Guard so as to eliminate the need for the presently unionized civilian technicians. A more long-range approach was to strengthen the professional and calling values in military service so that the occupational model would no longer dominate. Thus, a variety of programs for professional training for officers and NCOs was recommended, as was a "bill of rights" for service personnel, so that benefits could only be changed prospectively without application to those already in the service. In further direct response to the possibility of unions recruiting in the armed forces, and subsequently raising the issue of who represents the interests of the serviceman at the seat of government, the commission strongly advocated that the individual service chief personally be the ombudsman for his service. On a more general level, the commission stressed the need for greater public appreciation of the armed forces, and, in the epilog to their report, the commission stressed the primacy of human considerations in planning for the nation's defense.[15] The epilog combines apprehension, wisdom, innocence, and hope. Despite the lack of significant pressures from servicemen, the issue of United States military unions is with us more strongly than ever before.

Summary Comments and Recommendations

Due Process and Grievance Procedures

In Chapter 2 and in subsequent chapters we have discussed the two pillars upon which the structure of collective bargaining has been based: the desire for equity in compensation, and the desire for due process at the workplace. In Chapters 4 and 5 we have described how these two goals of organized labor have been addressed by collective bargaining in the federal civil service. In this section we will examine the recommendations of the

[14] Ibid., pp. 62–64.
[15] Ibid., pp. 433–38.

Defense Manpower Commission, which were intended to forestall any movement toward unionism by the armed forces, to determine if they are realistic.

Whether the issue in dispute is compensation or conditions of service, the manner and extent to which due process is involved in its resolution is important. The commission's recommended "bill of rights" for service personnel addresses both equity in compensation and the conditions of service. This "bill of rights" was intended to protect members of the armed forces against capricious changes in what they perceived as contractually established rights. It cannot, of course, influence the political process in the Congress which determines military compensation. This "bill of rights" does not as yet exist. If and when it comes into being, its substantive content and basic objectives will constitute a *necessary* condition, but not a *sufficient* condition for providing the intended protection. The *sufficient* condition, whose joint presence will enable the desired protection to be achieved, is some form of institutionalized structure for interpretation and enforcement. The national Bill of Rights, the first ten amendments to the United States Constitution, have had a powerful and pervasive effect on American life, not only because of the principles which they express, but because this nation was conceived as a government of laws. The adversary process of litigation, the court system, and a responsible executive authority operating together, were able to strive for the objectives of the Bill of Rights. The Constitution *and* this support system together were the *necessary* and *sufficient* conditions for accomplishing the expressed intentions of the framers. Similarly, procedures or devices must exist or be established if the servicemen's "bill of rights" is to be effective.

The Uniform Code of Military Justice is a well-developed device for guaranteeing fair treatment to servicemen but it addresses an entirely different set of questions from those which might arise in grievances about conditions of military service. In addition, as is characteristic of procedures under criminal or civil law, since no need exists for a rapprochement after legal action, the procedures are inappropriate. In a criminal case, the accused, if convicted, will be punished. In a civil case, a plaintiff, if sustained, may receive damages. After judgement has been delivered, the principals separate. The adjudication of grievances about conditions of service or employment is more similar to the operation of a domestic relations court. In such a court, in general, the goal is to keep the principals together in a more viable relationship than before. Should a separation be indicated, the goal is to accomplish it with equity and humane treatment.

The armed services have evolved a large number of different devices for addressing grievances. These range from the formal exercise of the chain of command, intervention by the Inspector General, notifying the navy ombudsman on up to the citizen's right to request his congressman or the president to intervene. How these various devices for redressing grievances work in practice is an issue which has not been examined fully. Clearly, this plethora of devices implies that many are ineffective. A requirement exists for institutionalizing a limited number of grievance-resolution devices that are *perceived by their users* as insulated against retribution and that are timely, effective, and fair.

In a sense, this requirement is incompatible with the calling model of military service, although it is compatible with an occupation or profession. Inherent in a calling is a trust in and reliance on the paternal benevolence of the institution and an emphasis on one-on-one interactions; e.g., the formal exercise of the chain of command. This flows naturally from the demands of combat, and the military ethos which is more akin to that of a government of men than one of laws. It is the kind of thinking which results in the following statement:

> The Commissioners are of the opinion that there is no satisfactory alternative to the individual Service Chief personally being the ombudsman for his Service. The Executive Branch, the Congress, the Services, and the public should recognize that this is a principal duty of the Service Chief. He should feel free publicly to express his dissent from policies he believes would adversely affect his Service.
>
> It is important in the national interest that the men and women of his Service perceive the Service Chief as their ombudsman. This role cannot be delegated. The Service Chief should declare himself on these issues which will greatly affect the morale of the men and women of his Service.[16]

Notwithstanding a strange misinterpretation of the role of an ombudsman—an impartial official, rather than a protagonist—the foregoing excerpt from the epilog of the Defense Manpower Commission's report is the epitome of paternalism. This approach is also found in the firm support and praise awarded NCOs. There is no doubt that *good* NCOs and capable dedicated officers can make a paternal and autocratic system work. Institutionalized safeguards and quality assurance devices are not needed because of them, but because of the average and *below* average NCOs and officers, in order to correct and improve their performance.

A compelling analogy exists with the stereotype of an autocratic plant manager—"My foremen know their business, and they can handle any trouble makers on the floor"; "My door is always open to my employees." A junior executive with ambition for advancement would be foolhardy to avail himself of this "open door" policy. Indeed, the blue-collar worker, with the protection of a union and a collective agreement, has more

---

[16] Ibid., p. 435.

guaranteed due process protection in his job than does the exposed and vulnerable career executive. In the military, despite the formal availability of due process for redress of grievances, the career officer is in much the same situation as the career executive. Availing himself of the process will probably serve to select him out of further consideration for advancement.

A grievance procedure is attractive on the face of it for reasons of equity and fairness to the grievant, but it has a larger and more important role to management. If used properly it can be a negative feedback system for insuring that the organization performs as planned. The evidence is quite persuasive that, where collective bargaining exists, foremen are impelled to rationalize their relationships with employees, thereby improving their performance significantly.[17] Unskilled and incapable foremen neither can cover their mistakes nor meet the needs of their superiors or subordinates. On a higher management level much the same happens:

> The challenge that unions presented to management has, if viewed broadly, created superior and better balanced management, even though some exceptions must be recognized. . . . The need to compromise conflicting interests within the firm shows that collective bargaining tends to make exacting demands on management and to increase the need for wise and well-balanced executives and for effective collaboration in policy making between operating officers and staff executives.[18]

Collective agreements and trade unions are not *necessary* to attain the foregoing goal of improved performance, although they help make it possible by providing a form of quality control. It *is* necessary that the performance standards be stated by management and monitored by management so as to be achieved by the entire organization. There are a variety of possible alternatives for providing the sufficiency condition which do not involve the intervention of trade unions. In 1972, for example, the Danish armed forces began the use of a survey feedback program. Once a year all personnel in operational, technical and school units answer a questionnaire which solicits their views on such topics as management and control, relations to immediate superiors, to peers, to the job, and training effectiveness. The anonymity of the respondents and their commanding officers is preserved. The analyzed results permit comparisons with the average results for similar units and with one's own unit in previous years. The system has been well received by the Danish armed forces.[19]

---

[17] Neil W. Chamberlain and Donald E. Cullen, *The Labor Sector* (2nd ed. New York: McGraw-Hill, 1971), pp. 259–64.

[18] Sumner H. Slichter, James J. Healy, and E. Robert Livernash, *The Impact of Collective Bargaining on Management* (Washington, D.C.: The Brookings Institution, 1960), pp. 951–52.

[19] James W. Miller, "The 12th International Symposium on Applied Military Psychology," (Office of Naval Research Conference Report C-26-76, London, 22 November 1976), pp. 9–10.

Personal Development, Participation and Professionalism

To the extent that professional attitudes can flourish in an organization, the occupational model is weakened. Surprisingly, however, this does not mean that the tendency to seek collective action will be similarly weakened. Because management in many cases has estranged itself from its professional employees and thwarted their ambitions, these employees have begun to organize. Two current examples highlight this point. On 6 October 1976 interns and residents at three hospitals in New York City began a short-lived strike for the recognition of their union, the Committee of Interns and Residents (CIR). They were protesting a National Labor Relations Board ruling which held that they were students, not full-fledged employees. Although among the reasons CIR arose was protest against hospital planning which resulted in the house staff working thirty-six to forty-eight consecutive hours, and other bread-and-butter issues; interviews with the young doctors revealed a further set of issues deriving from their self image as professionals. "They spoke of wanting to end the paternalism they said the hospital administrators used in dealing with them. They said they wanted more of a say on their working conditions and on the way patients were treated."[20] Thus the residents and interns were using a union action to support professional goals. In a straightforward statement of the same goals, a new union, with conventional ties to organized labor, has recently emerged. The American Federation of School Administrators, AFSA, was chartered in 1976 as an affiliate of the AFL-CIO. AFSA consists of fifty-four locals representing 10,000 principals and school executives across the nation. The newly elected president of AFSA, Walter J. Degnan, in his report to its convention, said:

> The existing associations to which administrators presently belong have neither the power, the organization, nor in some instances, the inclination to be concerned with the problems of administrators whether they be individual or group. We are committed to the defense of the professional perquisites of each and every professional we represent.[21]

Although professional perquisites can become confounded with bread-and-butter issues and may serve to camouflage such issues, as in disputes between teachers unions and management about class size, the very fact that personnel, who are unquestioned professionals or management, have organized is very significant. It points to top managerial insensitivity to the career models of these personnel and to the distinction

---

[20] David Bird, "Interns and Residents at 3 Hospitals Start Picketing to Gain Recognition," *New York Times*, 6 October 1976.
[21] *Monthly Labor Review* 99 (September 1976): 58–59.

between *operational* membership in management and membership by *title* alone.

A recurring theme among professionals and managers in the United States, among junior officers in the FRG and the Scandinavian countries, and among servicemen and civilians in this country is the desire for some form of either "fate control," participation in the system of which they are a part, or where relevant, a recognition of their professional skills and responsibilities. The implications of this for the United States Armed Forces are enormous. It requires an operational definition of command prerogatives so that the service aspects and the living aspects of military life can be separated. In this manner the *personal* lives of the servicemen can become just *that*. It requires that participation by junior- and middle-level officers be encouraged in an effective manner in as wide a range of decisions as is compatible with the military mission. This means incorporating such procedures into a training and an evaluation procedure for supervisors so that they may be implemented in practice. It means further, that military professionalism among junior career officers must be encouraged by actions, not by high-sounding phrases alone, for to do otherwise risks bestowing responsibility and holding back authority. If a form of military codetermination should evolve, it should be *actual* and not *cosmetic*.

Lord Horatio Nelson presents an honorable and successful precedent for acting in this manner. Nelson's strengths were seamanship, tactics, fervent patriotic zeal, and a talent for developing the support of his subordinates. As a matter of command policy, he departed from the then current autocratic style and involved his subordinates in his decisions, thus converting his captains into a "band of brothers." He shared his plans and thinking with his subordinates thereby changing their responses from automatic reactions to knowledgeable, enthusiastic participation and obedience. In the absolutist context of his times this modest form of participation in the command process by subordinates was as radical a departure as codetermination in the military appears to be today.[22]

Military Management Actions, Union or No Union

The actual or potential emergence of a trade union imposes the responsibility upon management to have a clear understanding of how his enterprise operates—what is critical, what is merely desirable, and what is fossilized tradition and *may* be superfluous. This is analogous to the exercise an office manager should go through prior to automating or computer-

---

[22] *Nelson's Instructions to his Captains before the battle of Trafalgar,* (9 October 1805), in the British Museum.

izing a clerical operation. The reasons are the same in both cases; changes in the procedures will cost. In both cases, however, whether or not a union emerges or a computer is purchased, the greater understanding of the existing organization should enable the manager to improve it. In the case of the armed services, it is important to examine all rules, regulations and procedures, because, should a collective agreement ever come into being, there will emerge, from both the negotiated agreement and the "case law" deriving from grievance procedures, a "web of work rules" which define the limits and restrict the actions of management. These work rules start with the base conditions which obtained when the first collective bargaining agreement was negotiated, and they may be left unchanged, elaborated on, or modified in subsequent agreements. Oftentimes work rules, which at present are featherbedding, arose because a procedure which once had economic value for management was incorporated into an early collective bargaining agreement, and was not negotiated out of subsequent contracts either because of management's reluctance to pay the negotiated price, or management's inadvertence. Such work rules, if not mitigated by a clearly perceived common interest by personnel in the various bargaining units with management in the joint enterprise, can have a paralyzing effect on the introduction of new technologies or procedures.

It would require a very large effort to examine the operating rules of the services in the light of the variety of units which comprise the armed forces. Carrying out such an exercise, concurrent with defining command prerogative in a more restricted fashion, will increase the likelihood that the suggestions in the preceding sections can be implemented and, hopefully, that the performance of the services can be improved as a result.

Congress and Military Compensation and Retirement Plans

In the preceding the emphasis has been on actions, however challenging and difficult, which could be carried out by the management of the armed forces acting on their own authority. With regard to compensation, on the other hand, the Department of Defense proposes but Congress disposes. Servicemen, by and large, have an inadequate understanding of the financial rewards of military service. These rewards comprise regular military compensation (RMC) which is a combination of basic pay; allowances for housing and food and tax advantages on the allowances to which is added benefits such as medical and dental care, commissary, and PX privileges; and a lavish pension. A Department of Defense survey of 70,000 servicemen revealed that 40 percent of the enlisted men and 25 percent of the officers placed numerical values on the RMC and benefits which were less than the RMC alone! Overall, 61 percent of the officers and 65 percent of the enlisted men underestimated their RMC and benefits when asked to name an equivalent civilian salary.[23] These benefits are currently under attack. Representative Les Aspin has pointed his finger at the pension system whose cost of 8.23 billion dollars in fiscal year 1977 exceeded the pay, allowances, and travel costs for all army personnel in that year. By the year 2000 an annual military pension bill of 34 billion dollars is anticipated. The average enlisted man is forty-one when he begins to collect a pension which in aggregate is 132 percent of his lifetime RMC or military salary; comparable figures for officers are forty-six and 144 percent. For comparison, the lifetime pension as a percentage of lifetime salary for the federal civil service and for congressmen is 49 percent. Federal civil service pensions vest in five years, military pensions after twenty years.[24]

The Defense Manpower Commission has recommended a large number of changes in benefits and in particular in nondisability retirement. These suggestions are directed toward shaping service careers, maintaining equity for the servicemen, and saving money. One result would be to limit immediate pension payments on retirement to those with either thirty years of noncombat service or twenty years of combat service.[25] It is clear that before very long some form of rationalized federal pension system will evolve to coordinate military pensions, social security, and federal civil service pensions. The fiscal problems of our cities, which New York City has brought so forcefully to public attention, can be attributed in part to the heavy burden of maintaining politically expedient but fiscally irresponsible pensions for large numbers of municipal employees. The necessity of avoiding a similar problem on a national scale by bringing all national retirement plans in line with resources is clear. Military retirement plans are an early candidate because of their magnitude and suggested changes are certain to generate or to accelerate a movement to military unions. Such a union or unions may become an effective force before Congress is able to review and rationalize the retirement plans for federal civilian and military employees. The risk exists that such unions will be able to incorporate the existing retirement and benefits plans together with the many rules, regulations, and procedures which characterize the armed forces into what will, in effect, become a collective bargaining agreement. Should this come to pass, subsequent modifications will be difficult and costly. Thus there is a time pressure on the Congress to act, just as there is on the management of the armed forces.

---

[23] U.S. General Accounting Office, "Need to Improve Military Members' Perceptions of Their Compensation," (FPCD-75-172, Washington, D.C.: 1975), p. 9.

[24] Les Aspin (U.S. Representative from Wisconsin), "Guns or Pensions: A Study of the Military Retired Pay System," (Washington, D.C.: November 1976), pp. 1–40.

[25] Defense Manpower Commission, *Defense Manpower*, pp. 341–83.

Personal Summation

The basic fear which the idea of military unions arouses is that of a strike or other actions such as sick-outs. Obviously, should military unions emerge, the national interest would require that they and the management of the services accept binding arbitration, with an appeal mechanism to a presidential commission or similar body. As Chapter 5 has shown, there is a well-developed analogous procedure in the federal civil service. Should the AFGE, for example, succeed in organizing units in the armed forces, the experience of the federal civil service (rather than that of municipalities in dealing with striking police and fire-fighter unions) would be the dominant precedent. This experience is one of a management hobbled by work rules rather than of a strike-prone work force. My strong misgivings about military unions are based on this precedent. This is not to say that federal employees have not struck, but that the event is very rare. Postal employees struck in 1970, and in 1968 air-traffic controllers rigidly followed operating regulations in a job action which reduced civil aviation flight schedules to chaos. Armed forces union job actions, in the extremely unlikely and presumably unlawful instance of the rejection of binding arbitration, would probably approximate the actions of the air traffic controllers. The multiplicity of bargaining units which would emerge in a unionized military might make it feasible to use "soldiering on the job" as a weapon in negotiations without posing an immediate threat to national security. This scenario of the breakdown of orderly negotiations is so unlikely that its inherent threats are a misleading diversion from the real danger, as I see it.

Another major fear which military unions induce is that the unity of the chain of command would be violated. This has occurred, as is well-known, without the benefit of a union presence, in the benign instances of interventions by Congressmen and in such malign cases as the riots and near mutinies on the U.S.S. *Kitty Hawk,* and the U.S.S. *Constellation* in 1972.[26] Unions do not foster or encourage disregard of line authority or infractions of discipline. The wildcat strike is as much a revolt against union leadership as it is a rebuff to management. Apprehension about weakening the chain of command is misleading because it, too, diverts attention from the main problem which military unions can create, which is in the *management* of the armed forces, not in their *command*. It is here that the experience of management in the federal civil service is particularly germane, and the implications so disquieting.

---

[26] "Hearings by Special Subcommittee on Disciplinary Problems in the U.S. Navy of the House Armed Services Committee," 92nd Congress 2nd sess., October 1973.

The global challenges against which our armed forces must protect us are such that American manpower will be outnumbered in any major confrontation of superpowers. Our response has been to apply technology to warfare so as to both compensate in a cost effective manner for our numerical inferiority and to keep abreast of the advances of our potential adversaries. The impact upon military deployment and organization of technology is seen in such examples as: nuclear weaponry and delivery systems, surveillance from space, remote piloted vehicles, augmented individual fire power, greater mobility, and in such activities as the use of sensors in the Sinai to enable a few hundred men to do what would have required thousands just a few decades earlier. (That these observers, because of political considerations, are civilian contract personnel does not detract from the significant precedent of using civilians to carry out a high technology military mission.) In this fast changing environment the management of the United States armed forces must be able to exploit technological and organizational innovations and to deploy manpower resources as required, easily and rapidly. Without this managerial flexibility the risk exists that our armed forces will become rigid in their response to new situations and therefore less capable of performing their critical mission.

The traditions of military service have tended to strengthen doctrinaire and rigid thinking in command and management. The Maginot line was the creation of military management responding to their perception of national values, needs and resources. In an ultimate example of rigid behavior, this management set its doctrine in concrete and it crumbled in war. It would be unfortunate if the apprehension that the possibility of collective bargaining arouses among the leaders of the United States armed forces, were to lead to a Maginot-line mentality with regard to traditional command prerogatives and authority. It is critical that military management recognize, early on, the conditions which foster the emergence of collective bargaining in the armed forces, treat them as a challenge, and respond with creative, structured, and informed opinions. Several of these options have been discussed in this chapter. The management of our armed forces, as well as our society as a whole, should view collective bargaining as a positive, evolutionary process, which, either of itself or by stimulating constructive organizational responses by management, can lead to stronger and more effective armed forces.

Appendix A

S. 3079   94 Cong. 2 Sess.
S. 274   95 Cong. 1 Sess.
H.R. 51   95 Cong. 1 Sess.

S. 3079

IN THE SENATE OF THE UNITED STATES

MARCH 4, 1976

Mr. THURMOND (for himself, Mr. ALLEN, Mr. BARTLETT, Mr. BROCK, Mr. CHILES, Mr. CURTIS, Mr. DOMENICI, Mr. EASTLAND, Mr. FANNIN, Mr. GARN, Mr. GOLDWATER, Mr. HANSEN, Mr. HELMS, Mr. HRUSKA, Mr. LAXALT, Mr. McCLELLAN, Mr. McCLURE, Mr. MORGAN, Mr. MOSS, Mr. NUNN, Mr. WILLIAM L. SCOTT, Mr. TAFT, Mr. TALMADGE, Mr. TOWER, and Mr. YOUNG) introduced the following bill; which was read twice and referred to the Committee on Armed Services

A BILL

To amend chapter 49 of title 10, United States Code, to prohibit union organization in the armed forces, and for other purposes.

1   *Be it enacted by the Senate and House of Representa-*

2   *tives of the United States of America in Congress assembled,*

3   That (a) chapter 49 of title 10, United States Code, is

4   amended by adding at the end thereof a new section as

5   follows:

6   "§ 975. **Union organizing and membership prohibited**

7   "(a) As used in this section—

8   "(1) 'Member of the armed forces' means a mem-

VII—O

2

1   ber of the armed forces who is (A) serving on active

2   duty, (B) a member of a Reserve component, or (C) in

3   a retired status.

4   "(2) 'Labor organization' means any organization

5   of any kind, or any agency or employee (including any

6   member of the armed forces) representation committee

7   or plan, in which employees (including members of the

8   armed forces) participate and which exists for the pur-

9   pose, in whole or in part, of dealing with employers con-

10   cerning grievances, labor disputes, wages, rates of pay,

11   hours of employment, or conditions of work.

12   "(3) 'Employer' includes the United States Gov-

13   ernment.

14   "(b) It shall be unlawful for any individual, group, as-

15   sociation, organization, or other entity to enroll any member

16   of the armed forces in, or to solicit or otherwise encourage

17   any member of the armed forces to join, any labor organiza-

18   tion.

19   "(c) It shall be unlawful for any member of the armed

20   forces to join or to solicit or otherwise encourage any other

21   member of the armed forces to join any labor organization.

22   "(d) The provisions of subsections (b) and (c) shall

23   not apply in any case in which any individual, group, asso-

24   ciation, organization, or other entity enrolls any member

25   of the armed forces in, or solicits or otherwise encourages

3

1 any member of the armed forces to join, any labor organiza-

2 tion, or in any case in which a member of the armed forces

3 joins a labor organization or solicits or otherwise encourages

4 another member of the armed forces to join a labor organiza-

5 tion if the activity, purpose, or function of the labor organi-

6 zation with which the member is concerned is unrelated to

7 his membership in the armed forces.

8 "(e) (1) Any individual violating subsection (b) or

9 (c) shall be punished by imprisonment of not more than

10 five years.

11 "(2) Any labor organization guilty of violating subsec-

12 tion (b) shall be punished by a fine of not less than $25,000

13 or more than $50,000.".

14 (b) The table of sections at the beginning of chapter 49

15 of title 10, United States Code, is amended by adding at the

16 end thereof the following:

"975. Union organizing and membership prohibited.".

95TH CONGRESS
1ST SESSION   **S. 274**

IN THE SENATE OF THE UNITED STATES

JANUARY 18, 1977

Mr. THURMOND (for himself, Mr. ALLEN, Mr. BAKER, Mr. BARTLETT, Mr. BELL-
MON, Mr. BENTSEN. Mr. HARRY F. BYRD, JR., Mr. CHILES, Mr. CURTIS,
Mr. DANFORTH, Mr. DOLE. Mr. DOMENICI, Mr. EASTLAND, Mr. GARN, Mr.
GOLDWATER, Mr. HANSEN, Mr. HATCH. Mr. HAYAKAWA, Mr. HELMS, Mr.
HOLLINGS, Mr. LAXALT. Mr. LUGAR. Mr. McCLELLAN, Mr. McCLURE, Mr.
MORGAN, Mr. NUNN, Mr. SCHMITT. Mr. SCOTT. Mr. STEVENS, Mr. STONE,
Mr. TALMADGE, Mr. TOWER, Mr. WALLOP, Mr. YOUNG, and Mr. ZORINSKY)
introduced the following bill; which was read twice and referred to the
Committee on Armed Services

A BILL

To amend chapter 49 of title 10, United States Code, to prohibit
union organization in the armed forces, and for other
purposes.

1   *Be it enacted by the Senate and House of Representa-*

2   *tives of the United States of America in Congress assembled,*

3   That (a) chapter 49 of title 10, United States Code, is

4   amended by adding at the end thereof a new section as

5   follows:

6   **"§ 975. Union organizing and membership prohibited**

7   "(a) As used in this section—

II

2

1   "(1) 'Member of the armed forces' means a mem-

2   ber of the armed forces who is (A) serving on active

3   duty, (B) a member of a Reserve component, or (C)

4   in a retired status.

5   "(2) 'Labor organization' means any organization

6   of any kind in which employees (including members

7   of the armed forces) participate and which exists for

8   the purpose, in whole or in part, of dealing with em-

9   ployers concerning conditions of work. Such term does

10 not include any fraternal or professional organization

11 unless such organization supports, advocates, or asserts

12 the right of employees of the Government of the United

13 States or members of the armed forces to strike against

14 the Government of the United States.

15   "(3) 'Employer' includes the United States

16 Government.

17   "(b) It shall be unlawful for any individual, group,

18 association, organization, or other entity to enroll any mem-

19 ber of the armed forces in, or to solicit or otherwise en-

20 courage any member of the armed forces to join, any labor

21 organization.

22   "(c) (1) It shall be unlawful for any member of the

23 armed forces to be a member of or to solicit or to otherwise

24 encourage any other member of the armed forces to join

25 any labor organization.

26   "(2) It shall be unlawful for any member of the armed

3

1   forces to actively support any activity of any labor organiza-

2   tion if such activity (1) is a protest against, is intended to

3   focus public attention on, or is for the purpose of bringing

4   about changes in, the working conditions of members of the

5   armed forces, or (2) supports, advocates, or asserts the

6   right of members of the armed forces to join or be repre-

7   sented by labor organizations.

8   "(d) The provisions of subsections (b) and (c) shall

9   not apply in any case in which any individual, group, associ-

10 ation, organization, or other entity enrolls any member of

11 the armed forces in, or solicits or otherwise encourages any

12 member of the armed forces to join, any labor organization,

13 or in any case in which a member of the armed forces joins

14 a labor organization or solicits or otherwise encourages an-

15 other member of the armed forces to join a labor organiza-

16 tion if the labor organization concerned does not represent,

17 or purport or attempt to represent, the interests of members

18 of the armed forces in any dealings or negotiations, or in

19 any attempt to deal or negotiate, with the Government of

20 the United States and does not advocate or assert the right

21 of members of the armed forces to strike against the Govern-

22 ment of the United States.

23   "(e) (1) Any individual violating subsection (b) or

24 (c) shall be punished by imprisonment of not more than

25 five years.

4

1   "(2) Any labor organization guilty of violating sub-

2 section (b) shall be punished by a fine of not less than

3 $25,000 or more than $50,000.".

4   (b) The table of sections at the beginning of chapter

5 49 of title 10, United States Code, is amended by adding

6 at the end thereof the following:

"975. Union organizing and membership prohibited.".

95TH CONGRESS
1ST SESSION   **S. 274**

A BILL

To amend chapter 49 of title 10, United States
Code, to prohibit union organization in the
armed forces, and for other purposes.

By Mr. THURMOND, Mr. ALLEN, Mr. BAKER, Mr.
BARTLETT, Mr. BELLMON, Mr. BENTSEN, Mr.
HARRY F. BYRD, JR., Mr. CHILES, Mr.
CURTIS, Mr. DANFORTH, Mr. DOLE, Mr.
DOMENICI, Mr. EASTLAND, Mr. GARN, Mr.
GOLDWATER, Mr. HANSEN, Mr. HATCH, Mr.
HAYAKAWA, Mr. HELMS, Mr. HOLLINGS, Mr.
LAXALT, Mr. LUGAR, Mr. McCLELLAN, Mr.
McCLURE, Mr. MORGAN, Mr. NUNN, Mr.
SCHMITT, Mr. SCOTT, Mr. STEVENS, Mr.
STONE, Mr. TALMADGE, Mr. TOWER, Mr.
WALLOP, Mr. YOUNG, and Mr. ZORINSKY

JANUARY 18, 1977
Read twice and referred to the Committee on Armed
Services

95TH CONGRESS
1ST SESSION

H. R. 51

IN THE HOUSE OF REPRESENTATIVES

JANUARY 4, 1977

Mr. ICHORD introduced the following bill; which was referred to the Committee on Armed Services

A BILL

To amend title 10, United States Code, to prohibit collective bargaining with the Armed Forces, and for other purposes.

1   *Be it enacted by the Senate and House of Representa-*

2   *tives of the United States of America in Congress assembled,*

3   That (a) chapter 49 of title 10, United States Code, is

4   amended by adding after section 974 the following new

5   section:

6   **"§ 975. Collective bargaining with armed forces prohibited**

7   " (a) It shall be unlawful for any individual not subject

8   to section 892a of this title or for any organization to enroll

9   any member of the armed forces (other than a member in

10   a retired status) in, or to solicit or otherwise encourage

11   any member of the armed forces (other than a member

I

2

1   in a retired status) to join, any organization which has as

2   its purpose, in whole or in part, engaging in collective bar-

3   gaining with any civilian officer or employee of the Depart-

4   ment of Defense or, in the case of the Coast Guard when it

5   is not operating as a service in the Navy, the Department

6   of Transportation or with any member of the armed forces,

7   concerning grievances or other terms and conditions of serv-

8   ice in the armed forces.

9   "(b) (1) Any organization violating subsection (a)

10 shall be fined not more than $50,000.

11   "(2) Any individual violating subsection (a) shall

12 be fined not more than $1,000 or imprisoned not more than

13 one year, or both.".

14   (b) The table of sections for chapter 49 of title 10,

15 United States Code, is amended by adding at the end the

16 following new item:

"975. Collective bargaining with armed forces prohibited.".

17   SEC. 2. (a) Chapter 47 of title 10, United States Code

18 (the Uniform Code of Military Justice), is amended by in-

19 serting after section 892 (article 92) the following new

20 section (article) :

21 "§ 892a. Art. 92a. Union organizing and membership

22   "Any member of the armed forces (other than a mem-

23 ber of the armed forces in a retired status) who forms,

24 joins, or belongs to any organization, or who solicits or

3

1 otherwise encourages any other member of the armed forces

2 (other than a member of the armed forces in a retired

3 status) to form, join, or belong to any organization which

4 has as its purpose, in whole or in part, engaging in collec-

5 tive bargaining with any civilian officer or employee of the

6 Department of Defense or, in the case of a member of the

7 Coast Guard when the Coast Guard is not operating as a

8 service in the Navy, the Department of Transportation or

9 with any member of the armed forces, concerning grievances

10 or other terms and conditions of service in the armed forces

11 shall be punished as a court-martial may direct.".

12 (b) The table of sections for subchapter X of chapter

13 47 of title 10, United States Code, is amended by inserting

14 after the item relating to section 892 (article 892) the

15 following new item:

"892a. 92a. Union organizing and membership.".

Appendix B

AFGE constitutional amendment allowing the recruitment
of military personnel
Adopted 23 September 1976

RESOLUTION

WHEREAS, military personnel of the United States armed forces have the right under the U.S. Constitution to become members of labor unions, and WHEREAS, the AFGE is the only appropriate general U.S. government employee union affiliated with the AFL-CIO available for such military personnel to join, and

WHEREAS, numerous such personnel have recognized the need for collective representation of their interests and have sought membership in, and representation by, the AFGE in recent years, and

WHEREAS, AFGE is competent to provide effective legislative, legal, professional, and certain other representation to such military personnel on many comparable matters affecting conditions of work, and on comparable basis, except in a period of general war or national emergency, as now provided by AFGE to civilian and military technician personnel of the military services, and

WHEREAS, such membership and representation would substantially benefit both civilian and military personnel in meeting common problems, effective labor-management relations in the U.S. Government, efficient and responsive management of government operations, the career attractiveness of voluntary military service to able young Americans, and military discipline and the national security of the United States, and

WHEREAS, military members may voluntarily accept the standards of union conduct prescribed by Federal law, and

WHEREAS, the membership dues and fees paid by military members can be used to provide proportionally greater legal and other permitted representation to compensate for any lesser union representation provided in other areas, such as negotiation of collective bargaining agreements, resolution of individual employee complaints, and in any other areas where union representation is not permitted by Federal law, or is determined not to be feasible or desirable from a practical or policy standpoint by a majority of the military members of AFGE themselves, and

WHEREAS, the development of new means by which the U.S. Government indirectly employs manpower resources outside the regular civil service system may create a gap in the ability of labor unions to represent adequately such employees,

THEREFORE, be it *RESOLVED*

That Article III, Sec. 1 and Sec. 1(a), of the Constitution of the American Federation of Government Employees be amended to read as follows:

> Section 1. All persons of the following classes, without regard to race, creed, color, national origin, sex, *age,* or *political affiliation,* excepting those over whom jurisdiction has been granted to other national or international unions by the American Federation of Labor and Congress of Industrial Organizations, shall be eligible for full membership of this Federation.
>
> Section 1(a). All employees of the United States Government, and any of its instrumentalities of whatever nature, *including military personnel of the armed forces,* and of the District of Columbia; *and all other persons providing their personal services indirectly to the United States government,* are eligible for membership in this Federation.

Appendix C

Department of Defense Directive no. 1325.6, 12 September 1969

September 12, 1969
NUMBER 1325.67
ASD(M&RA)

DEPARTMENT OF DEFENSE DIRECTIVE

SUBJECT   Guidelines for Handling Dissident and Protest Activities Among Members of the Armed Forces

References: (a) U. S. Constitution, First Amendment
(b) Title 50, U. S. Code Appendix, Section 462
(c) Title 18, U. S. Code, Sections 1381, 2387, 2385, 2388
(d) Title 10, U. S. Code, Chapter 47 (Uniform Code of Military Justice)
(e) DoD Directive 1334.1, "Wearing of the Uniform," August 11, 1969

I PURPOSE AND APPLICABILITY

This Directive provides general guidance governing the handling of dissident activities by members on active duty of the Army, Navy, Air Force, and Marine Corps. Specific problems can, of course, be resolved only on the basis of the particular facts of the situation and in accordance with the provisions of applicable Department regulations and the Uniform Code of Military Justice.

191

II POLICY

It is the mission of the Department of Defense to safeguard the security of the United States. The service member's right of expression should be preserved to the maximum extent possible, consistent with good order and discipline and the national security. On the other hand, no Commander should be indifferent to conduct which, if allowed to proceed unchecked, would destroy the effectiveness of his unit. The proper balancing of these interests will depend largely upon the calm and prudent judgment of the responsible Commander.

III SPECIFIC GUIDELINES

The following guidelines relate to principal activities in this area which the Armed Forces have encountered:

A. *Possession and Distribution of Printed Materials*

1. A Commander is not authorized to prohibit the distribution of a specific issue of a publication distributed through official outlets such as post exchanges and military libraries. In the case of distribution of publications through other than official outlets, a Commander may require that prior approval be obtained for any distribution on a military installation in order that he may determine whether there is a clear danger to the loyalty, discipline, or morale of military personnel, or if the distribution of the publication would materially interfere with the accomplishment of a military mission. When he makes such a determination, the distribution will be prohibited.

2. While the mere possession of unauthorized printed material may not be prohibited, printed material which is prohibited from distribution shall be impounded if the Commander determines that an attempt will be made to distribute.

3. The fact that a publication is critical of Government policies or officials is not, in itself, a ground upon which distribution may be prohibited.

B. *Off-Post Gathering Places.* Commanders have the authority to place establishments "off-limits," in accordance with established procedures, when, for example, the activities taking place there, including counselling members to refuse to perform duty or to desert, involve acts with a significant adverse effect on members' health, morale, or welfare.

C. *Servicemen's Organizations.* Commanders are not authorized to recognize or to bargain with a so-called "servicemen's union."

D. *Publication of "Underground Newspapers."* Personal writing for publication may not be pursued during duty hours, or accomplished by the use of Government or non-appropriated fund property. While publication of "underground newspapers" by military personnel off-post, on their own time and with their own money and equipment, is not prohibited, if such a publication contains language the utterance of which is punishable under Federal law, those involved in the printing, publication, or distribution may be disciplined for such infractions.

E. *On-Post Demonstrations and Similar Activities.* The Commander of a military installation shall prohibit any demonstration or activity on the installation which could result in interference with or prevention of orderly accomplishment of the mission of the installation, or present a clear danger to loyalty, discipline, or morale of the troops. It is a crime for any person to enter a military reservation for any purpose prohibited by law or lawful regulations, or for any person to enter or re-enter an installation after having been barred by order of the Commander (18 U.S.C. 1382).

F. *Off-Post Demonstrations by Members.* Members of the Armed Forces are prohibited from participating in off-post demonstrations when they are on duty, or in a foreign country, or when their activities constitute a breach of law and order, or when violence is likely to result, or when they are in uniform in violation of DoD Directive 1334.1 (reference (e)).

G. *Grievances.* The right of members to complain and request redress of grievances against actions of their commanders is protected by Article 138 of the Uniform Code of Military Justice. In addition, a member may petition or present any grievance to any member of Congress (10 U.S.C. 1034). An open door policy for complaints is a basic principle of good leadership, and Commanders should personally assure themselves that adequate procedures exist for identifying valid complaints and taking corrective action.

IV EFFECTIVE DATE AND IMPLEMENTATION

This Directive is effective immediately. Two (2) copies of implementing regulations shall be forwarded to the Assistant Secretary of Defense (Manpower and Reserve Affairs) within ninety (90) days.

Melvin R. Laird (signature)
Secretary of Defense

Enclosure–1
Constitutional and Statutory Provisions

Sept 12, 69
1325.6 (Encl 1)

CONSTITUTIONAL AND STATUTORY PROVISIONS RELEVANT TO HANDLING OF DISSIDENT AND PROTEST ACTIVITIES IN THE ARMED FORCES

A. *Constitution:* The First Amendment, U.S. Constitution, provides as follows:

"Congress shall make no law . . . abridging the freedom of speech, or of the press; or the right of the people peaceably to assemble, and to petition the Government for a redress of grievances."

B. *Statutory Provisions:*

1. *Applicable to All Persons*
    a. 18 U.S.C. §1381—Enticing desertion.
    b. 18 U.S.C. §2385—Advocating overthrow of the Government.
    c. 18 U.S.C. §2387—Counselling insubordination, disloyalty, mutiny, or refusal of duty.
    d. 18 U.S.C. §2388—Causing or attempting to cause insubordination.
    e. 50 U.S.C. App. §462—Counselling evasion of the drafe.

2. *Applicable to Members of the Armed Forces*
    a. 10 U.S.C. §917 (Article 117, UCMJ)—Provoking speech or gestures.
    b. 10 U.S.C. §882 (Article 82, UCMJ)—Soliciting desertion, mutiny, sedition, or misbehavior before the enemy.

   c. 10 U.S.C. §904 (Article 104, UCMJ)—Communication or corresponding with the enemy.
   d. 10 U.S.C. §901 (Article 101, UCMJ)—Betraying a countersign.
   e. 10 U.S.C. §888 (Article 88, UCMJ)—Contemptuous words by commissioned officers against certain officials.
   f . 10 U.S.C. §889 (Article 89, UCMJ)—Disrespect toward his superior commissioned officer.
   g. 10 U.S.C. §891 (Article 91, UCMJ)—Disrespect toward a warrant officer or noncommissioned officer in the execution of his office.
   h. 10 U.S.C. §892 (Article 92, UCMJ)—Failure to obey a lawful order or regulation.
   i . 10 U.S.C. §934 (Article 134, UCMJ)—Uttering disloyal statement, criminal libel, communicating a threat, and soliciting another to commit an offense.

Contributors

EZRA S. KRENDEL, Professor of Operations Research in the Wharton School of the University of Pennsylvania, is known for his pioneering research in the mathematical description of human control behavior. Over the past twenty-five years he has participated in and been consulted on a variety of planning and cost/effectiveness studies for the United States Departments of Defense, Commerce, Transportation, and Justice as well as for industries and municipal government. He is a member of the National Labor Panel of the American Arbitration Association. Currently he is active in a variety of studies of the effectiveness of the criminal justice system. Professor Krendel is responsible for approximately 50 publications in a variety of scholarly journals.

BERNARD L. SAMOFF is Adjunct Professor and Associate Chairman, Department of management at the Wharton School. Professor Samoff joined the faculty of the University in 1974 after a 32-year career with the National Labor Relations Board, and the last eleven years as Regional Director, NLRB, Philadelphia. He is the author and co-author of some thirty-five articles and book reviews in the area of industrial relations law and policy, and was a part-time lecturer at various colleges and universities.

WILLIAM GOMBERG is Professor of Management and Industrial Relations at the Wharton School, University of Pennsylvania. Professor Gomberg has spent his entire adult life in collective bargaining associated activities, and has written over 100 articles and books on the subject. At present, he is heavily involved in public sector arbitrations, both for grievances as well as for the establishment of production standards. These activities involve police and fire union/municipalities; teachers' unions/school districts, and the letter carriers' union/United States Postal Service.

CHARLES R. PERRY is Associate Professor of Management and Industrial Relations in the Wharton School of the University of Pennsylvania. Dr. Perry's primary research and consulting activities have been in the field of collective bargaining with special emphasis on the public sector. In addition, Dr. Perry has been active in research into the impact of government policies and programs in the civil rights and manpower training areas and is currently engaged on a study of the impact of the Occupational Safety and Health Act. Dr. Perry has been on the faculty of the Wharton School since 1966 with the exception of two years spent on leave to serve as Executive Assistant to the Director of the Office of Management and Budget.

MICHAEL E. SPARROUGH, the recipient of an MBA degree from the Wharton School of the University of Pennsylvania, is Director of Research for the Air Line Pilots Association. He has been employed by the United States Department of Labor as an economist, and has specialized in analyzing trends in collective bargaining and assessing the economic impact of settlements reached in key bargaining situations. Mr. Sparrough has written several articles for the *Monthly Labor Review* and has conducted research on the impact of manpower programs and on labor relations in the federal sector.

ROGER FRADIN received his MBA degree from the Wharton School of the University of Pennsylvania, and is Assistant to the President of Ademco, the major operating division of the Pittway Corporation. He is also at work on a Juris Doctor degree from the University of Pennsylvania Law School. While at the Wharton School, Mr. Fradin was a research associate at the Industrial Research Unit and directed a number of research efforts in industrial relations. He is an author of a study on industrial upgrading systems, published by the Industrial Research Unit in November 1976.